FIRESIDE

Your Battle for

[formerly *The Battle for
Stock Market Profits*]

BY GERALD M. LOEB

The Battle for Stock Market Profits
The Battle for Investment Survival
Checklist for Buying Stocks

Stock Market Profits

How to Make Money and
Keep It in Today's Market

by Gerald M. Loeb

A Fireside Book
Published by Simon and Schuster

Copyright © 1971 by Gerald M. Loeb
A Fireside Book
Published by Simon and Schuster
A Division of Gulf & Western Corporation
Simon & Schuster Building
Rockefeller Center, 1230 Avenue of the Americas
New York, New York 10020
ISBN 0-671-20751-2
ISBN 0-671-21760-7 Pbk.
Library of Congress Catalog Card Number 70-130483
Designed by Irving Perkins
Manufactured in the United States of America

4   5   6   7   8   9   10   11   12   13

To Rose
without whose understanding, inspiration,
and encouragement this book would not exist

Thanks to Clarence E. Watson, Director of Program Planning and Management Research at the City University of New York, who edited the original material and selected and arranged it for this book.

My sincere thanks also to Sam Meyerson, my editor at Simon and Schuster. An author who works with Sam is a happy author.

Contents

Contents

Contents

Foreword

The first part of this book concerns the use of my Checklist to give you the essential facts needed for making an investment decision. This is followed by a practical discussion of my concepts for successful investing and recommended courses of action based on the facts developed in the Checklist. It is the kind of action and investment philosophy that is *not* based, as I once facetiously remarked, on the way it's taught at Harvard Business School.

Every investor has the problem of how to get the most out of his investments. Many read books on the subject and study in other ways, but in the end are confronted with the practical problem of what to do.

Years ago, in the early Twenties, I was initiated into writing down my reasons pro and con before making a purchase or a sale. This was suggested to me by an investor who had amassed many millions. More recently I have seen the increased need for a written analysis.

There is no doubt that in the stock market man cannot live by theory alone. He needs hard, cold facts to help him make decisions. The problem has always been how to marshal these facts easily and line them up for quick inspection.

The help investors could receive from a Checklist has been brought home to me again and again in my daily work. Many readers of *The Battle for Investment Survival* and other books on investing have written letters to me that brought out this need.

During my fifty years of investing in stocks, my major successes invariably have been preceded by a type of written analysis and follow-up. Such records can keep an investor out of trouble. They can bring him peace of mind after he has made his stock purchase. I have been convinced that with so much uninformed buying by new investors in the various security markets in this country, a Checklist is the working tool for building profits.

The necessity has grown so urgent that finally I have prepared a Checklist. The present work sheets are the result; here they are for you to use. The accompanying text is brief. As in the work sheets themselves, the endeavor is to keep to fundamentals—to include everything that is essential and concentrate on it—and to exclude everything else. Years of trial and error have condensed what is needed to the essential and the minimum. This has the dual effect of spotlighting study where it accomplishes something and saving time.

Space is provided for writing down the cogent reasons for making transactions—before you risk your savings. It can also help you later to evaluate your successes and failures.

The battle for people's time is as sharp as the "battle for investment survival." You need time and attention to succeed in Wall Street, and it will take time to fill out the work sheets in this book. But I think it will be the most profitable time you ever spend.

The tables are only for those who are serious about the investment of their money—those who frequently will spend an extra hour in order to gain above-average investment results.

I hope you can make the Checklist an integral part of your investment thinking and a more profitable approach to the stock market. I have tried to sit in an armchair before the fire and tell you what counts most in planning your investments. I have found that most successful security transactions are sparked by what I call the "ruling reason." How to find this correctly and efficiently is the first purpose of this book.*

—G. M. Loeb

* Readers who may wish to refer to parts of the text that merit further rereading and study will find pages at the back of the book where they can jot down the subjects and their page numbers for later review.

1 *The Ruling Reason*

Writing things down is the best way of all to find the "ruling reason" to buy or sell a stock. When all is said and done, there is invariably one single reason why a particular security transaction can be expected to show a profit or why a holding should be eliminated. All too often many relatively unimportant statistics are allowed to obscure this single important point.

Any one of a dozen factors may be the point of a particular purchase or sale. It could be a technical reason—a coming increase in earnings or dividends not yet discounted in the market price; a change of management; a promising new product; an expected improvement in the market's valuation of earnings—or many others. But in any given case, one of these factors will almost certainly be more important than all the rest put together.

2 *Closing a Commitment*

Recognizing this ruling reason, and singling it out is important in deciding when to close a commitment. In other words, the paramount factor which you recognized when you bought a security will either work out or not. Once you can say definitely that it has worked (that is, reached your objective) or not worked, the security should be sold. One of the greatest causes of loss in security transactions is to open a commitment for a particular reason and then fail to close it when the reason proves to be invalid. Only too often we make irrelevant excuses to ourselves for holding a security long after it should have been sold. Perhaps it was bought in the first place because "it acts well on the tape." Then, when it acts badly on the tape, we fail to do as we should—that is, sell it—and we deceive ourselves with some meaningless consideration (*e.g.,* "earnings ought to go up this year") which would never have persuaded us to buy it in the first place.

When you open a commitment, whether it is a purchase or a short sale, you are, so to speak, on your home ground. Unless everything suits you, you don't play. But when you are called upon to close a commitment, you have to make decisions, whether you see the answer clearly or not. The latter situation is like being stuck in a car on a railway crossing with the train approaching. You don't know what to do, but you have to do something: go backward, go forward—or jump out.

When it comes to selling a stock already owned, psychological factors have caused losses to a tremendous number of investors. Psychologically we are naturally and rightfully bullish. It goes against the grain to be pessimistic, and that is the way it should be or there would be no progress. But at times it pays in the pocketbook to take a bearish point of view temporarily. Even if this is recognized, it is difficult for most people to do, and doubly difficult to advise someone else to do.

Investors will forgive their advisors a great deal in the way of telling them about good stocks that go down instead of up, but it seems to be an unforgivable sin to get a client out of a stock and then have it advance instead of decline.

3 *Uncovering and Interpreting Vital Information*

The Checklist is a supplementary tool to my earlier book *The Battle for Investment Survival.** It should be useful not only to the first investor but also to the experienced and seasoned professional. Obviously each will use it differently. There are headings that the first investor at first won't understand—and many that the professional will find missing. In order to keep within space limits, there are necessarily headings which are general and have to be liberally interpreted. For example, the figures needed for industrial, railroad and utility analysis vary. It is expected that the user will do a certain amount of adding some of his own captions.

What I have tried to do is to include mainly those categories that over the years have seemed to me the key guideposts to profitable analysis. With my concept of the "ruling reason" in mind, it will be obvious that at times all thought will be concentrated in as little as a single category, but even this may require far more space for putting ideas on paper than I can give here. The less important categories will be useful only for a quick checking to be sure no weighty unfavorable factor exists as an offset, or to find the key in the first place.

The sheer size of analytical reports means little in reaching a conclusion that pays. I recall back in 1929 reading a private report on a railroad that was reputed to have cost thousands. It took many weeks, if not months, to prepare, and involved much traveling. It even reported how many ties were used in the line. The report, elegantly bound in

* *The Battle for Investment Survival,* Simon and Schuster, N.Y. $6.95.

limp leather, concluded that this railroad was a sound purchase. The company later went into bankruptcy. What was wrong here? Failure to appraise the ruling reason—in this case the coming depression and the swing to autos and air travel.

On the other hand I have seen correct decisions reached in a very short time by simply scanning the basic factors and correctly sensing the ruling reason.

Perhaps this is another way of saying that it demands a lot of "genius" and "flair" to succeed. It is true that no amount of study, research or practice can make one successful in the handling of capital, if one really is not cut out for it. But to find out one's capacity one must try—and trying has no chance without intelligently and usefully directed knowledge. This means uncovering the vital information and having the ability to interpret it profitably.

4 *Objective: Capital Gain*

I think it is likely that the great majority of investors will have capital gains as their principal objective. The work sheets of the Checklist can be used by the investor who looks first at dividend income and price stability, but they are primarily devised for those that look for profit. In the postscript to *The Battle for Investment Survival,* I wrote two brief commentaries entitled, "Why Buy Quiz" and "When Sell Quiz." The introduction to the first states: "If you want double dividends, double profits and half losses, try filling out a quiz sheet on every issue you are considering buying." (The Checklist is your "quiz sheet.")

(1) How much am I investing in this company?
(2) How much do I think I can make?
(3) How much do I have to risk?
(4) How long do I expect to take to reach my goal?

The "When Sell Quiz" includes the following pointers:

If you have a loss in your stocks, then I think the solution is automatic provided you decide what to do at the time you buy. . . . [Otherwise] the question divides itself into two parts. The first is, Are we in a bull or a bear market? Few of us really know until it is too late. For example, if you think it is a bear market, just consider selling your stocks regardless of almost any other consideration.

If you think it is a bull market, or at least a market where some stocks move up, some mark time and only a few decline, do not sell unless:

(1) You see a bear market ahead.
(2) You see trouble for a particular company in which you own shares.
(3) Time and circumstances have turned up a new and seemingly far better buy than the issue you like least in your list.
(4) Your shares stop going up and start going down.

A subsidiary question is, Which stock to sell first? Two further observations may help here:

(5) Do not sell solely because you think a stock is overvalued.
(6) If you want to sell some of your stocks and not all, invariably go against your emotional inclinations and sell first the issues with losses, small profits or none at all, the weakest, the most disappointing actors, etc. Always keep your best issues for the last.

Not since perhaps 1920 have I been investing in the stock market without knowing that two rules and fifty words will never tell anyone when to sell.

This book should make these ideas come alive and complete and make it possible to put them to practical and profitable use.

5 *Using the Checklist*

It must be assumed that the user of this Checklist has at least read *The Battle for Investment Survival* and probably other stock market books as well. It is also assumed that as part of the process of considering or making investments he will have contact with at least one broker, banker or investment counselor, and probably with other investors.

Remember the concept of the ruling reason. If you know what this is, you may only need to fill in some of the data. If you don't, filling in all the vital data may help you to find out. Or, after filling them all in, you may find that there is no real ruling reason, then perhaps the security had best be left alone. In one case the emphasis may be all on one set of factors, and in the next case an entirely different set may come to the fore.

6 *Sources for Your Work Sheet*

The outlines and checks suggested call in the main for historical material, which is a matter of record and exceedingly simple to procure. Much of it is in the leading financial daily and weekly publications. Individual company statistics are available in most cases on very inexpensive summary sheets, which can usually be had from your broker. Annual reports, interim reports, post-meeting reports and proxy material are ordinarily furnished on request by leading publicly owned corporations. In addition, as I have said before, it will rarely be necessary to fill out everything.

Unfortunately the most important categories are the intangibles, and for that very reason the hardest to evaluate. For example, a fundamental investment principle is "buy good management." It has always been a source of wonder to me how the average investor can know. I have had the advantage of being able to meet and visit with management. Sometimes I am convinced. Sometimes I am not. Sometimes I am on the fence. Sometimes I am right. Sometimes I am wrong.

Yet the question of management is all-important, and some conclusion has to be reached—occasionally directly but more often on the judgment of a second party.

One of the most successful investors of all time—a man credited with being worth $80 million—was quoted in the press as saying about one of his purchases: "They asked me if I didn't want to see the balance sheets of the company. I said no, I've met their people, and that is good enough for me. Everyone I met seemed to know his business, what the company objectives were, and how they proposed to get there. Why look at the books? In growth companies, you need people with vision and organization."

This is not to say that seeing the balance sheets and earnings statements is not essential. Only very occasionally can a sound investment decision be made without them.

I recall that many years ago—1940 I think it might have been—I took a position for clients totaling almost a quarter of a million shares of stock on the basis of just three factors. It was selling at a bankruptcy price; I absolutely knew it was not going into bankruptcy; I absolutely knew the turn in earnings was a few months ahead. Knowing these things, I did not have to look at any of the other statistics of the company.

Another all-important category is the estimating of future earnings, dividends, growth trends. Here again is an item of overwhelming significance, but usually very difficult to pin down. There are of course mechanical methods of projecting the past into the future, but these are at best makeshift. Some reliable contact, either direct or through a second party, is usually necessary. The fact should be faced that even management itself goes on assumptions that might be realized; might be exceeded; might be completely mistaken.

The very unpredictability of these things is what gives us the profits and the losses in business, which in turn are reflected in the security markets and finally in our own bankbooks. If everything were cut and dried, completely predictable, there would be no profit and no loss, no opportunities, no failures.

The riddle of the future is basic to life. In so many of our activities it is not fully recognized. To me, one of the attractions of security investment is that by its very nature we come to grips with this problem head-on. That is also a reason why I think there is no such thing as a good or safe investment which is not at the same time a good speculation.

In discussing the Loeb Checklist, I put myself in the shoes of people who are hungry for help in the struggle between emotion, impulse, and reason in the buying and selling of stocks. Let's take a look at the typical problems investors face and examine the reasoning processes one must go through to answer pertinent questions such as "What do you say to yourself when a stock which has been performing well stops growing in price and heads downhill?"

To get meaningful answers, one needs an analytical checklist of reasons pro and con for making a purchase or a sale. This is the first order of business in keeping emotion and impulse under control and allowing the ruling reason to emerge.

Here are some pointers to the most effective use of various categories in the Checklist, selected to highlight an investment consideration or for purposes of clarification. Later on, all the sections will be pulled together under the heading, G. M. LOEB CHECKLIST.

7 *Checklist Quiz on Capitalization*

Capitalization

(a) Bonds and Preferreds at Par ....————————

(b) Bonds and Preferreds at Market Value ....————————

(c) Capital Stock at Market Value ....————————

(d) Total Market Value of All Outstanding Securities ————————

(e) Other Pertinent Notes re Capitalization—
Long-term Bank Loans, Leasebacks, Tax Carry-
back or Forward, Accounting Reserves or Credits————————

Notes on Balance Sheet and Working Capital

Book Value

8 *Financial Statements*

Capitalization: This refers to the total liabilities of a business including both ownership capital and borrowed capital. It consists of bonds, preferred stock, and common stock. Bank loans are not usually shown as part of the capital structure but may be a signicant consideration. No matter how much I try to reduce the business of evaluating a stock for purchase, one must review the capitalization. Check the number of outstanding shares. It tells you how big the company is to begin with—whether it is so small that its survival is doubtful or so big that further high percentage growth requires enormous total dollar gains. Too large capitalization is a market "drag."

The second important factor is to relate the amount of common stock outstanding to the amount of fixed obligations such as bonds, preferred stock, and loans which have prior claims on a company's earnings. This gives you the leverage. A company with *all* common stock has no leverage. One with many prior claims and very little stock has large leverage. Leverage is good when you are sure the stock is otherwise a good buy. It magnifies common stock earnings and market values. By the same token, if a stock is trending down, high leverage is unfavorable I have always felt if the market is going down it is better to have *no* stocks rather than those you think may go down the least.

Acceptable leverage varies with the type of business, so it is not practical to suggest any ratios here. Broadly speaking, you are not going to buy any stock unless you think it is going up, so that to a degree high leverage is desirable. It is another way of using "other people's money." The creditor—the bondholder, mortgage holder, bank, institution, who lends your company money—lends at a much lower rate of interest than the profit you expect to make using that money. Therefore, if you are right in selecting the right stock at the right price and the right time, you will make money much quicker with a high-leverage issue.

While it is really a side issue here, it may be of interest to point out that the highest total market value that can be realized by a corporation from its securities outstanding is always a balanced capitalization. A company with all common stock is, in most cases, "too safe." One with too many prior obligations and not enough common equity is "unbalanced" and "too risky."

If balance-sheet items seem important to a particular proposed purchase, look for "hidden" senior securities like bank loans, which are not usually shown as part of the capital structure. There can also be "hidden" fixed charges—for example, when a food-chain company leases all its stores instead of owning them, the rentals are just as much a fixed charge as bond interest.

Working capital is "current assets" minus "current liabilities," which you will find in the balance sheet. It is a fair indication of whether the company has enough liquid assets to carry on its business readily. Current assets include inventories, which may be hard to turn into cash quickly; if working capital includes a high proportion of inventory there may be a cash problem. This varies from company to company; some turn over inventory in a matter of days, and others in many months, so compare the inventory to the annual sales figure. Analysts like to check the "current ratio." Are current assets 1¼ times, or twice, or five times as big as current liabilities? The higher the ratio, generally, speaking, the better the liquid position.

This section can give you other useful ideas. Total capitalization may be compared with gross sales, and this figure in turn can be checked against other companies in the same industry. An old rule of thumb has been that a total market value of $1 per $1 of annual sales was about right as a starting point. Fashions change and conditions in industries vary. This kind of figure should be carefully checked. Another good question is, What percentage is added to total market valuation by a one-point rise in the stock? If the percentage is very high, the stock can't be expected to move very far unless there is a dramatic improvement in prospect for the company.

One other thing you should bear in mind when looking at the capital structure and balance sheet is the possibility of new financing. Particularly if working capital is very low, financing may be required. Is there room for more debt? Or would it have to be equity? Make a cross-check to the price/earnings ratio, if equity financing seems indicated; the higher the ratio, the more money a company can raise against a given percentage increase in its common stock.

I rarely find "book value" a controlling figure. Some stocks with very low asset values compared with market price have done the very best. Amateur analysts are often deceived and intrigued by high book values, feeling, in most cases incorrectly, that they are somehow buying a "bargain."

The fact is that high book values, if real, are of importance mainly if a company is actually being liquidated or its assets distributed. They are sometimes important as reflecting a need for large amounts of capital to run a business, useful in times of excess-profits taxes as favorable tax bases. Theoretically a realistically high book value can mean that it would be costly for new competition to enter the field.

Above all, check the footnotes. They often reveal more than the statement.

9 *More Comments on Leverage*

The effect of what professionals call "leverage" is the factor that can make per-share earnings comparisons as unlike as oil and water. Suppose you are considering the purchase or sale of a "growth" stock. The Checklist Quiz on Capitalization (see page 23) will help you to determine:

(1) If there is real growth in property, sales and profits, and
(2) If the growth, when expressed in final per-share earnings, is partly derived from differences or changes in capitalizations.

For example, let us consider a company with only common stock outstanding. In this case, the total net and final net per share will change in the same percentage relationship. If such a company has 10 million shares outstanding and earns $10 million, it reports $1 a share. If the total earnings are cut in half to $5 million, per-share net is cut proportionately to 50 cents. If the total net is doubled to $20 million, then per-share net will also double to $2.

However, if the company is capitalized a little differently, the differences between percentage changes of total net earnings and per-share net earnings becomes marked and significant. Let us suppose that this same company is capitalized at about 60 percent in bonds and 40 percent in common stock and shows the same $1 per share earnings. Now if total earnings should be cut in half to $5 million, the per-share earnings would drop to something near 30 cents a share. On the other hand, should total net double, the increase per share would be nearly $2.50.

The changes can be magnified even more by imagining a

capitalization of bonds and preferred stock with a thin equity amounting to only 15 percent. If we adjust this to show the same $1 per share on the common at the $10 million net earnings level, then a drop in the total net earnings to $5 million, or one half, would throw the common into a net deficit. The preferred dividend under these circumstances would be only about half earned.

The rewards, in the event that total earnings doubled, would be very great. This would result in a jump to about $5 a share on the small amount of common outstanding in this over-leveraged company.

Per-share net can be further distorted if the bonds or preferred stocks are convertible, or if there are warrants to buy stock in the capitalization.

Conservative capitalizations vary with the nature of the business. The more stable the year-to-year earnings, the higher the fixed obligations (such as interest charges) to the common may be. The less stable the earnings the lower they should properly be.

The danger is to overlook the risks and incorrectly appraise the reported per-share figures in lopsided and top-heavy capitalizations. Unfortunately, overleverage capitalizations are becoming as popular as credit cards. Increasing per-share "earnings" by reducing equity and increasing charges ahead of the common is usually something akin to achieving growth through the use of mirrors. "Instant" growth in earnings per share often happens when one company acquires another by issuing fixed obligations in payment.

Leverage is a favorable factor in bull markets and when used by management that knows what it is doing. It is fatal in down markets, or when employed by the less skilled or simply the overambitious, or worse.

Get your broker or financial advisor to explain the capitalization of companies in which you expect to invest. There are times, and there are stocks, where excessive leverage can be a temporary advantage. It has its place, just as does buying on credit or margin.

The hazard from both is when they are employed by people who fail to understand the magnified risks which the enhanced profit potentialities entail. The major point I want to make here is that if you do not feel capable of making a judgment, consult with someone who is.

10 *Importance of the Balance Sheet*

It used to be that the first thing a competent investor examined when considering the purchase of a stock was the balance sheet. Too many of today's "analysts" look first at an "earnings projection" for several years in the future and tend to place undeserved confidence in their findings. The trouble is that realization of these projections is often improbable, sometimes impossible, and practically never predictable.

Scarcer and more expensive money puts the spotlight on balance sheets and points up their usefulness as an investment tool. Weak balance sheets may forecast to the alert investor probable cutbacks in capital spending, dividend cuts or omissions, and even bankruptcies. The careful security buyer will want to be sure that a company's balance sheet is strong enough so that working capital needs can be cared for without unfavorably diluting equity.

Balance sheets are used to measure profitability. This is in reality a bookkeeping figure. There are tables available showing the percentage earned on the total capital employed in a business and on the stockholders' equity. This is sometimes figured for the last year and perhaps for an average of three or five or ten years. At this writing, for example, a railroad stock has a book value close to $125 per share. It sells in the market under $45. On the other hand, a well-known growth stock has a book value of near $7 per share and sells above $150. The realistic appraisal of a stock's value as an investment takes in many factors. A Rolls-Royce at $10,000 might be a lot cheaper than a Volkswagen at $4,000.

Annual reports and other company information for stockholders are improving, but far too many could use even more improvement. Don't let anyone ever tell you these official reports are not worthy of study. They most certainly are. Only at the time of a new issue of securities does a company disclose more information. It is advisable to study back annual reports of your company that are of interest and those of competing ones in the same industry, since a comparison with the competition is essential. Annual reports are important in shedding light on whether management tends to overstate or understate things. If management spoke but once, realistic appraisal and interpretation would be difficult. After a few years of examining reports, it is another story. Management quickly becomes recognized for its degree of trustworthiness, frankness, and clarity. For example, IBM management has consistently enjoyed the confidence of investors over the years because of its conservative estimates of earnings, by publicly anticipating when possible any unfavorable development well in advance of its happening, and by playing down spurts in earnings growth due to unusual circumstances not likely to be sustained over a long period of time. One learns to put an optimistic interpretation on IBM management's appraisals and to allow for this in sizing up the company's stock for investment. When the "confidence quotient" is high, the price of the stock reflects this fact, since it is not so likely to be jarred by unfavorable surprises.

On the other hand, one learns to suspect the overly optimistic predictions of some managements whose track records in the past have not lived up to their eloquent pronouncements. The doubt and uncertainty generated by past overstatements of a company's prospects will have a negative influence on the price of its stock until confidence is restored.

11 *Checklist Quiz on Profit & Loss Statement*

Profit and Loss Statement (Last Reported Full Year)

(a) Gross Sales .... PER SHARE_____

(b) Operating Earnings .... _____

(c) Fixed Charges .... _____

(d) Extraordinary Gain or Loss .... _____

(e) Income Taxes .... _____

(f) Net Income .... PER SHARE_____

(g) Profit Margin .... _____

(h) Comment on Earnings Trend .... _____

Cash Flow

    (a) Cash Flow .... PER SHARE_____

    (b) Comment .... _____

Average Earnings

    (a) Average per Share: Last Five Reported Years .. _____

    (b) Last Reported Year .... _____

    (c) Estimated for Current Year .... _____

    (d) Estimated for Next Year .... _____

Dividends

    (a) Average per Share: Last Five Years .... _____

    (b) Last Reported Year .... _____

    (c) Estimated for Current Year .... _____

    (d) Estimated for Next Year

PROFIT AND LOSS STATEMENT

This is of course the heart of almost any study. Are profits going up? If profit margins are high, are they vulnerable and temporary? If low, can they be improved? Or do they reflect a permanently unsatisfactory situation? Occasionally, and on a temporary basis, profit margins will be deliberately and intelligently sacrificed to gain volume. The best textbook I know on security analysis devotes over

150 pages to explain a single financial statement in detail. I mention this to be sure my readers realize how briefly I am touching high spots here. This is by design, as the theme of the above Checklist is to come to grips with the essentials and not waste time on frills.

A few more P & L statement pointers:

You almost need an accountant to explain the full significance of the income taxes a company pays, but one point is easy to remember. The rate of federal corporate income tax is fixed—currently at 52 percent, so that taxes should be just a little larger than net income after taxes. If this figure doesn't hold good for your company, there must be a reason. If taxes look high, perhaps management is taking less depreciation than the normal permitted amount (see below under *Cash Flow*). If taxes look low there may be more than normal depreciation taken. Or perhaps there is a "carry-forward" of losses from previous years so that income is only partly taxable, or not subject to taxes at all.

Fixed interest charges give you another angle on leverage. Incidentally, it is worth checking back to the balance sheet to see how much debt matures in the current year. Debt maturities have to be met out of cash flow, and sometimes they can throw out your calculations about the amount of money available for dividends and capital expenditures.

Cash Flow: Cash flow is the sum of reported net income and non-cash charges such as depreciation, depletion and amortization. This represents the amount of money that a company has available out of earnings for capital expenditures and dividend payments. In recent years the cash flow of a corporation has received increasing attention from sophisticated investors as a measurement to be considered in determining whether the earnings of a company are over-stated or understated. It is on the one hand a valuable figure, and on the other it can be subject to misuse. It is a mistake to try to justify a high price/earnings ratio by substituting cash-flow figures for normally reported earnings. It should be realized that sooner or later different methods of calculating earnings from cash flow end up in the same place. Companies with high cash flow are generally (but not always) more interesting. The use to which the money is put must be analyzed carefully or a misleading impression may result.

There is a reverse side to this coin. This is where management feels that allowable tax deductions for depreciation and obsolescence are inadequate. Some managements do nothing about it, in which case their earnings are currently overstated. A very few set up a tax-paid depreciation reserve, deducted from profits, which would more likely reflect the correct situation.

Average Earnings and Dividends: Some per-share figures on current earnings and dividends, with comparisons with the past, and what you hope for the future, will later be the key figures in much of your final valuation, appraisal and conclusion. I have suggested here the most convenient categories. There is nothing hard and fast about these. In some cases 10-year averages can be used as well as 5-year, if they happen to be handy, though I prefer the shorter, more up-to-date figures. In setting out these figures, you will naturally see the per-share earnings for each year on the guide card or annual report you use. These may tell you more than the average figure.

Incidentally, reported "earnings" are in no sense uniform. There are many different, absolutely legal methods of arriving at them. That is why "cash flow"—a comparison of reported earnings with taxes paid—and a glance at a "source and disposition of funds" table in annual reports where supplied—are all useful guides to making correct comparisons.

"Earnings" mean one thing to the Government for tax purposes, another to the stockholders, often a third to the management, and too often a fourth to public-relations counsel!

As an example, the accounting required of railroads by the Interstate Commerce Commission makes no allowance for accelerated amortization. To cite an extreme case, a few years back a large Eastern carrier reported earnings, under ICC accounting rules, of $8.03 per share. If rapid amortization had been deducted according to normal accounting practice, earnings would have been $3.81 per share.

There are many ways of handling the reporting of windfalls or nonrecurring profits (or losses).

Where the final decisions focus on earnings it is important to look at total as well as per-share figures, and especially on an overall basis, as well as after charges—otherwise the effects of leverage will be misleading. Earnings of $1 a share from an all-capital-stock company are worth far more than the same $1 a share from an over-leveraged concern.

While as a practical matter the net judgment of the marketplace manages somehow to take varying reporting methods into account, the average investor tends to take reported figures at face value. Extraordinary and nonrecurring gains or losses must be isolated. The same should be done with those due to tax or accounting adjustments of previous years. The footnotes usually reveal such differences best.

12 *Checklist Quiz for General Information*

General Information

  (a) Where Traded . . . . _____

  (b) Monthly Volume of Shares Traded . . . . _____

  (c) Price Range: Last Five Years . . . . _____

  (d) Price Range: Current Year . . . . _____

  (e) Short Interest . . . . _____

  (f) Relative Action . . . . _____

  (g) Insider and Institutional Transactions . . . . . . _____

  (h) Pattern of Movement . . . . _____

  (i) Important Dates (Dividend Meetings, etc.) . . . _____

GENERAL INFORMATION

The trick here is to skim and scan everything and stop only at the key points.

Where Traded: If a stock is actively traded on the New York Stock Exchange, this is a plus value. It has the best market, the most information promptly and reliably issued about it. But this does not rule out less active stocks, those traded on regional or foreign exchanges, or over-the-counter. The point is to recognize that if you accept some lesser standards here, you should at least expect to gain more by that sacrifice.

Volume of Shares Traded: Another point about volume

of trading is to compare it with total shares outstanding. When the turnover percentage is high, a change in the price of the stock, good or bad, is likely. And profits or losses come from change. For example, monthly turnover in American Motors before the success of the Rambler car averaged less than a million shares. As its success came to be known the turnover rose to a high point of 7 million shares—more than 40 percent of shares outstanding—in October 1958. This record volume coincided with a price breakthrough after 4½ years of stagnation. The stock then rose from under 9 to over 30 in 22 months.

Price Range: Price ranges are usually the first thing anybody looks at in deciding whether to buy or not. They are rarely used correctly. Generally one group of persons, psychologically oriented toward what they think are "bargains," try to buy near "lows." The "lows" often reflect bad value, not bargain value. And often they neglect a downtrend. Surely a succession of daily new lows is a reason to avoid a stock—not to purchase it.

Others, differently oriented, will buy high or on a repetition of daily new highs. This often (but not always) works out to better advantage, if done with understanding and discretion.

I like to compare annual highs and lows with reported per-share earnings for the same years. This will reveal graphically the tendency of stocks to question the continuance of high earnings in very good years or poor earnings in very bad years, and sell in relation to the more normal ones. Amateurs often feel that if a company is in the red for a time the stock is worth "nothing," which is always ridiculous, but doubly so in these days of tax-loss carry-overs. Nor will the earnings of a big flush boom year necessarily advance a stock to average price-earnings ratios.

The market will correctly wait and see whether they are "flash in the pan" earnings or a real and continuing new plateau.

Short Interest: On an overall basis, the daily short-sale figures as supplied by the odd-lot houses are at times very valuable. They should be studied as a percentage of total odd-lot sales. If low, say under 1 percent, they may well have a bearish significance, but of course are then only one of many factors that might be offset by other figures. When consistently high, these figures can be very bullish and are in such cases rarely offset by other factors. When odd-lot short sales are more than 2 percent of total odd-lot sales for any period of time, they are important and should be watched. The all-time high was 10.7 percent on June 24, 1970. The figures showing the short interest of individual companies are reported once a month in the financial pages of your daily newspaper. These short-interest figures are more useful in pointing up a trend than as absolute indicators. A rising trend is bullish—a declining trend bearish. However, great caution has to be used to weigh these odd-lot figures, as with everything else, against other factors that might reinforce or negate them. It is also important to be sure the figures in any particular case reflect a real short interest and not a special situation such as an arbitrage, etc.

Relative Action: Figures on the relative action of a group of stocks in a given industry as against individual stocks in the group are now available in figure or chart form weekly from *Barron's* or from various financial services. They are calculated on computers and purchasable from various services. They are most useful. A stock could advance and yet, relatively, might be doing quite poorly compared with others in its group or in the market generally.

These figures have various uses. Sharp deviations from

the norm are helpful signals for checking. Relatively strong stocks are often the best buys when the market is coming out of a reaction and starting up.

Insider and Institutional Transactions: Insider transactions, like the short position, are a most interesting set of figures. They are slow in being reported. I always look at them, although I cannot say they normally exert much influence on me. Too often they represent transactions, especially sales, for reasons other than the insider market opinion. Also the opinions of insiders, curiously or not, as you choose to look at it, are not as consistently "right" as their access to what's going on would lead you to expect.

Institutional transactions are receiving wider publicity all the time. We read about the "Favorite Fifty," the "Pick of the Pros" and other published lists, of what the investment trusts and mutual funds buy. These are valuable if understood and used properly.

The most popular issue, the one that stands at the top of the list at any given time, is not always there solely because of fashion. Often it is there because its price has risen sharply. It may be a good buy on its first appearance at the top. As it stays there it inevitably becomes a very poor buy. The ideal purchases are new issues that appear in the lists for the first time. They should be checked for the possibility of becoming more popular and rising toward the top of the lists.

A relatively new, obscure, or untried issue, possibly traded over-the-counter, on a regional exchange, or abroad, that appears in a well-managed fund for the first time is worthy of a special check. Many new investment ideas can be unearthed in this way. There is a degree of safety in an issue of this kind when you know that experts have included it in at least a small part of a broad portfolio.

Pattern of Movement: By "pattern of movement" I mean so-called "chart action." I feel this is of vital importance, though I fear that the art of effective chart reading is growing more difficult day by day. The narrower markets stemming from actions of the Securities and Exchange Commission, Federal Reserve restrictions, and New York Stock Exchange rules, many Washington-inspired, have made market movements less likely to be trustworthy and more likely to be misleading. For example, filling a big order to buy or sell may give a stock a false appearance of strength or weakness. True, the order itself has been revealed on the tape, and its impact is important. But filling it may attract a following of traders who will desert as soon as the move stops. This can cause much costly whipsawing. Trades made on the N.Y.S.E., especially in big blocks, distort volume figures.

Then, too, I suspect that the number of self-styled tape and chart readers has been increasing by leaps and bounds. So have the "services" based on charts. The result is that widely understood chart signals are more and more losing their significance.

Successful chart reading today not only calls for the standard and primary knowledge of the art, but beyond that allowance must be made for the expected general reaction to orthodox chart indications. Thus one needs, so to speak, double confirmation.

It reminds me of two very smart men in a deal. One wants to find out what the other is thinking. The second wants to keep it from him. But each knows that the other is aware of his intentions. The resultant reasoning goes something like this: The first thinks, "If I am truthful, I will give myself away." So his first thought is to say the opposite of the truth. But then he reflects that his opponent has reasoning power to allow for this. So maybe if he is truthful it won't be taken at face value. And so on, ad infinitum.

So with today's chart indications. Are they trustworthy? Or do they reflect only a transient and unimportant group of hangers-on? It is always well to remember that what a majority knows is not worth knowing.

Charts showing the movement of a stock over a period of years have value in quickly showing its pattern: whether it is a growth stock, cyclical, defensive, static, etc. Of course, this explains the stock's past. Consideration must be given to new factors which may alter the future pattern. But even here I find charts still valuable. If nothing more, they will tell you whether you are getting aboard on the ground floor or on the 40th.

13 *Checklist Quiz on Valuation and Trends*

Price/Earnings Ratio

    (a) Five-Year Average . . . . ———————

    (b) Last Year . . . . ———————

    (c) Estimated for Current Year . . . . ———————

Dividend Yield

    (a) Five-Year Average . . . . ———————

    (b) Last Year . . . . ———————

    (c) Current Year . . . . ———————

Historical Growth

    (a) How Many Years for Earnings
    to Double in Past . . . . _____

    (b) How Many Years for Market
    Price to Double in Past . . . . _____

    (c) Comment on Future . . . . _____

VALUATIONS AND TRENDS

Now we come to the keynote and most important part of the checklist. Back in the very early twenties when I began to invest in the stock market professionals were called "statisticians." Nowadays they are "analysts." No longer do they work in the "statistical department." Today it is "investment research." Let me coin a new one: "valuationist"—because our end product is not related to statistics or research but to valuation. What is the stock worth? What is it going to be worth? True, it is a great company, but is it selling too high? The news ahead is wonderful but is it discounted? Perhaps it is too high but is it going higher? These are the questions to which we must find the best possible answers. And they call for valuation.

Price/Earnings Ratio: Valuation starts with simple things. Of these, the price/earnings ratio is the most widely used. So we want to look it up. Write it down. Consider it from every angle—not just the a, b, c of my checklist.

Let's take a good look at the year-by-year annual ratio. From this you have to make your all-important estimate of the future. Is it going to improve? If so, is it one of the ways you can make a profit?

Don't be arbitrary. A very high price/earnings ratio can

at times go higher. If you don't believe this, look it up. There was a day long ago when "ten times earnings" was the standard statistician's yardstick. No "ten times" man ever got aboard IBM.

But there comes a day too when "the bell rings," and a high price/earnings ratio becomes a danger signal. How do you tell? I guess we all wish we knew.

The price/earnings ratio is of fundamental importance. It can fluctuate as much as or even more than earnings. It is also subject to planned influence. A book could be written on the P/E ratio alone.

Dividend Yield: Dividend yield is related to the P/E ratio and almost the same reasoning applies, in most cases with less force. It has some value at times. There may be a stock of investment quality that becomes a good buy at a given income-yield level. An expected higher dividend may be the ruling reason for an advance in a stock if it is not generally known and discounted.

Historical Growth: Many will wonder, I know, what this caption means—if anything. It is just a little gadget of my own. If it is growth we are talking about, I like to look back and see how long it took for earnings to double in the past. It is easier than looking at varying percentage-growth figures. If you can say simply that earnings doubled in five years, and then again in three more—or whatever it may be —you have a clear grasp of how "growthy" the company really is.

And then compare the growth in price. More often than not, in recent years, this growth has been a great deal faster than the growth in earnings. The point is, will it keep happening?

14 *Checklist Quiz for Objectives and Risks*

Ruling Reason for Commitment

Anticipated Profit

(a) Price Objective . . . . _____

(b) Estimated Time to Achieve It . . . . _____

Risks Assumed

(a) Points per Share . . . . _____

(b) Total Dollars at Possible Close-out Price . . . . _____

Personal Commitment

OBJECTIVES AND RISKS

These are really your personal evaluation of the factual and statistical data you have compiled. I have found it logical to fill in this section after the rest of the work sheets are completed.

Risks Assumed: There are times when these can be closely estimated and times when they cannot. For example, a short-term trade made on tape action should properly be closed out on an equally short-term reversal or disappointment. A commitment made on fundamental grounds should not be undertaken without recognizing that it may take months to work out—or to fail. It must be given more leeway, which means allowing for a greater risk both dollar-wise and percentagewise. The risk is also much harder to estimate. Perhaps the best thing to do is to stipulate arbitrarily that after a certain lapse of time, or a certain paper loss, the situation must be realistically reappraised.

It should be realized that risks are also related to the size of the market in any given issue. They are smallest where the security is active and has a close bid-and-asked price and the turnover is large. Allowance must be made for a thin market on regional exchanges and over-the-counter, or inactive issues generally, regardless of where they are traded.

Personal Commitment: The great value of fixing these estimated figures in your mind is that it will help you to decide whether a commitment is worthwhile, when or at what price to consider closing it out, and above all, how big it should be. I have the feeling that if a proposed investment is on the borderline, it is better to pass it up than to take a small position.

As between investment considerations and tax considerations, the former should always rule. However, it is worth remembering that the payment of a tax obviously reduces the capital available for reinvestment by the amount of the tax paid. For example, you have stock which cost you $60,000, and is now worth $100,000. If you sell it to switch into another stock, you will have a possible tax liability of $10,000 (varying with your personal tax return and with each year). You will have $90,000 available for the new investment. So, to make the switch worthwhile, the new commitment must be one where $90,000 will do more work for you than $100,000 left in the old situation.

As a general rule, where you have a very large capital gain, it is a good idea to plan a sale of your stock by installments, almost regardless of the outlook for it. This approach prevents you from feeling "locked in," as many people do if they have to take the tax bite all at once. It is also a measure of protection against possible unforeseen increases in the tax rate—or against a decline in the value of the stock.

15 *Comparison with the Dow-Jones Industrial Average*

Industrials: The course of the Dow-Jones averages and also earnings and P/E ratios combined for comparative purposes are published in several places and easy to secure. While many analysts consider them superfluous, I do not. I want them as a yardstick to see whether the company under analysis is just going with the tide or making faster progress or actually rowing upstream as it were.

Thus if Dow average earnings per share doubles and the company reviewed doubles, it can be said to be in step. Without looking at the Dow figures the doubling may have at quick glance seemed more of an achievement than is now revealed.

The objective of the Checklist is to help investors do much better than the Dow-Jones industrial average. The professional investor aims to make more percentage gain in a rising market and to lose less in a declining one.

The Dow should be used as a major tool for evaluation, not simply as a handy way of measuring the level of the market.

For example, suppose the Dow is standing at 500 and you want to buy a certain stock selling at 50, or 10 percent of the Dow. You are bearish on the general market and expect the Dow to decline to, say, 400 in six months. Yet you believe that six months hence your pet stock will be at 60, or 15 percent of the Dow. Why? It requires great buoyancy in earnings, an increase in the price/earnings ratio, or other favorable factors to carry a stock up in this fashion while the market and the economy are slipping. You should be very sure of your facts before venturing on such dangerous ground.

The Dow stocks, incidentally, have been chosen by Dow-Jones & Company as representative of industrial stocks in general. Very occasionally changes and substitutions are made. At any given time it is likely that some of the Dow stocks are going up, some are doing nothing, and some are going down. The percentage difference in performance between the best- and the worst-acting stocks in the average is often very great. I think the inquiring investor will find it profitable to tabulate the Dow stocks along the lines of the comparative group analysis briefly discussed further on in the Checklist. Buying the half-dozen Dow stocks that check out most favorably is a relatively safe way of testing your investment skill and can be very profitable.

For example, in a typical period, with the Dow average declining a shade over 10 percent, the leading stock at that time gained almost 50 percent and the poorest performer lost almost 40 percent. Shifts can be rapid. In another period, with the Dow gaining about 10 percent, the very same issue that had lost almost 40 percent gained over 25 percent.

The differences between the Dow stocks and the Favorite Fifty stocks should be realized. The Dow issues are intended to be a typical cross section and are changed only at great intervals. Stocks making up the Dow may include some with average valuations and outlooks, some with high valuations and the best kind of outlook, some with low valuations and prospects, and some in between.

The Favorite Fifty, on the other hand, are currently selected issues already thought by majority institutional opinion to possess above-average attractiveness. Therefore at least one of the avenues of possible profit—the change from unpopularity and a low valuation to popularity and an increased valuation—has already occurred at least in varying degrees.

There are many other averages and indexes given attention nowadays in addition to the Dow. The New York Stock Exchange has constructed its own index. The Standard and Poor's 500 Stocks is getting to be very well known. There is an American Stock Exchange index and an over-the-counter index.

The "performance" cult has spawned various fund indexes and averages, the most widely known being those published by the magazine *FundScope* and Arthur Lipper and Company.

The Dow averages correctly reflect the trend of selected blue chips. If your fund is managed more conservatively or more speculatively you can consider this when comparing your results with the Dow. You could also, for purposes of measurement, select one of the other averages that more closely resemble your own portfolio with regard to risks and volatility.

CHECKLISTS AND VARIOUS EXAMPLE FORMS

The various checklists, charts, and checkcharts which follow will enable you to record vital data and to review it regularly. Fill them in to the best of your ability and it will make your security investment policy a more scientific approach to good investment results. Many a loss can be worthwhile if the reasons are understood and future mistakes of the same kind reduced.

It seems useful to illustrate several kinds of forms in order to give investors ideas for record keeping and more complete checking. These include the "Record of Purchases and Sales," the "Investment Inventory," the "Portfolio Balance Check," and the "Group Analysis" form. Of course, it is not always necessary to fill out every form. As you get into your record-keeping, it will be obvious to you which categories are essential for various types of companies.

CHECKCHART STOCK ACTION

This is a very important record. Don't fail to keep it.

CHECKCHART CASH/EQUITY RATIO

This is another important record. The term "cash" as used here means available buying power. This might in fact be either cash or short-term highly liquid treasury bills or other salable paper.

The term "equity" is simply the total current market value of your portfolio. Obviously, if you are uncertain or pessimistic the percentage of cash should be higher. If you are bullish or optimistic you will want less cash and more stock. A great many investors neglect to give sufficient consideration to this aspect.

Following is the complete Checklist. Permission is granted to Xerox additional copies for your use.

16 *G. M. Loeb Checklist*

1. Name of Security . . . . _____

2. Price . . . . _____

FINANCIAL STATEMENTS

3. Capitalization

    (a) Bonds and Preferreds at Par . . . . _____

    (b) Bonds and Preferreds at Market Value . . . . _____

    (c) Capital Stock at Market Value . . . . _____

    (d) Total Market Value of All
         Outstanding Securities . . . . _____

    (e) Other Pertinent Notes re Capitalization—
         Long-term Bank Loans—Leasebacks, etc. . . . _____

4. Notes on Balance Sheet and Working Capital . . . . _____

5. Book Value . . . . _____

6. Profit and Loss Statement (Last Reported Full Year) _____

    (a) Gross Sales . . . . (PER SHARE) . _____

    (b) Operating Earnings . . . . _____

    (c) Fixed Charges . . . . _____

    (d) Taxes . . . . _____

    (e) Net Income . . . . (PER SHARE) _____

    (f) Profit Margin . . . . _____

    (g) Comment on Earnings Trend . . . . _____

7. Cash Flow

    (a) Cash Flow . . . . (PER SHARE) _____

    (b) Comment . . . . _____

8. Average Earnings

    (a) Average per Share: Last Five Reported Years . _____

    (b) Last Reported Year . . . . _____

    (c) Estimated for Current Year . . . . _____

    (d) Estimated for Next Year . . . . _____

9. Dividends

    (a) Average per Share: Last Five Years . . . . . . _____

    (b) Last Reported Year . . . . _____

    (c) Estimated for Current Year . . . . _____

    (d) Estimated for Next Year . . . . _____

10. General Information

    (a) Where Traded . . . . _____

    (b) Monthly Volume of Shares Traded . . . . . . _____

    (c) Price Range: Last Five Years . . . . _____

    (d) Price Range: Current Year . . . . _____

    (e) Short Interest . . . . _____

    (f) Relative Action . . . . _____

    (g) Insider and Institutional Transactions . . . . . _____

    (h) Pattern of Movement . . . . _____

    (i) Important Dates (Dividend Meetings,
        Stockholders' Meetings, Dividend Dates,
        Impending Announcements, etc.) . . . . _____

VALUATIONS AND TRENDS

11. Price/Earnings Ratio

    (a) Five-Year Average . . . . _____

    (b) Last Year . . . . _____

    (c) Estimated for Current Year . . . . _____

12. Dividend Yield

    (a) Five-Year Average . . . . _____

    (b) Last Year . . . . _____

    (c) Current Year . . . . _____

13. Historical Growth

    (a) How Many Years for Earnings to Double
        in Past . . . . _____

    (b) How Many Years for Market Price to
        Double in Past . . . . _____

    (c) Comment on Future . . . . _____

OBJECTIVES AND RISKS

14. Ruling Reason for Commitment . . . . _____

15. Anticipated Profit . . . . _____

    (a) Price Objective . . . . _____

    (b) Estimated Time to Achieve It . . . . _____

16. Risks Assumed

    (a) Points per Share . . . . ———————————

    (b) Total Dollars at Possible Close-out Price . . . . ———————————

17. Personal Commitment

    (a) I will commit $————————

    (b) This will be————————% of my security capital

    (c) I will risk ————————points, which would be $————————

    (d) My price objective is———————— in————————months. If I realize
         this price, I should have a capital gain of $———————— gross.
         From this must be deducted my tax at estimated short-term
         or long-term capital gain rates, leaving a theoretical net profit
         of $————————, or a gain of about ————————% on my equity in
         an estimated ————————months.

18. Recap

    (a) Date Original Purchase . . . . ———————————

         Price Paid . . . . ———————————

         Dow Average on Date of Purchase . . . . ———————————

    (b) First Revaluation

         Date . . . . ———————————

         Price . . . . ———————————

         Dow Average . . . . ———————————

53

Comment . . . . _____

Action Taken . . . . _____

(c) Second Revaluation

Date . . . . _____

Price . . . . _____

Dow Average . . . . _____

Comment . . . . _____

Action Taken . . . . _____

(d) Final Closing

Date . . . . _____

Price . . . . _____

Dow Average . . . . _____

Profit or Loss . . . . _____

Tax   Net . . . . _____

Comment . . . . _____

G. M. LOEB CHECKCHART STOCK ACTION

Supervision of stocks you own, or which are on your list as possible purchases, is vitally important. A simple way to alert yourself to possible favorable or unfavorable developments is to jot down weekly closing prices. The result will not be scientific or conclusive, but it will flash a red or green flag for further investigation.

CASH/EQUITY RATIO It is many times more difficult to judge the trend of the market than to select individual stocks.

Nevertheless it pays to make an effort to have more stock and less buying power when you think risks are low, stocks are under accumulation, or rising. Likewise you should aim at having more cash or equivalent and still less stock when risks seem high, stocks under distribution, or the trend down. This table will help you judge your position. Writing in your figures monthly should be sufficient.

Date	Amount in Cash	Amount in Stock	Total Amount	% Invested in Stock
August 10, 1970	$10,000	$5,000	$15,000	33%
Sept. 10, 1970	12,000	3,000	15,000	20%
January 1, 1971	5,000	10,000	15,000	66%
March 10, 1971	7,500	7,500	15,000	50%
July 1, 1971	9,000	6,000	15,000	40%

(In the example shown above, the "total amount" continues the same over the five periods written in. Actually, as your holdings move up or down, the value of the account will change with each calculation.)

Date	Amount in Cash	Amount in Stock	Total Amount	% Invested in Stock

Date	Amount in Cash	Amount in Stock	Total Amount	% Invested in Stock

STOCK ACTION CHART OF
MONTHLY CLOSING PRICES

Stock	January Closing	February Closing	March Closing	April Closing	May Closing	June Closing
IBM	335	344	332	296	266	256
Standard Oil of N.J.	56	54	57	53	53	55

Stock	July Closing	August Closing	September Closing	October Closing	November Closing	December Closing
IBM	250					
Standard Oil of N.J.	61					

(Many investors have found it advantageous to write down the closing prices of their stock holdings each month, or weekly if you prefer it. This can be easily done using ruled worksheets.)

BALANCING YOUR PORTFOLIO

I have often been misquoted on the merits and demerits of diversification. I did say something to the effect that nobody ever became rich or beat the averages with a broadly diversified list of securities. This is true. But not all of us are equipped to become rich.

To state it practically, the less expert we are investment-wise the greater the need for diversification. While this keeps one from great successes, it also saves one from dire calamity.

One can tabulate diversification in several ways. The table below classifies securities for investment according to the risk involved. Investors frequently diversify according to industry. Or company. This is the popular method of setting up investment-trust and mutual-fund portfolios.

There is another way to diversify. This is according to time. If you invest all your funds at once, you must be very expert to select just the right time. If you hold funds back and invest a fraction, say 10 percent, or 20 percent when available, and a second fraction a month or two or three later or on some seemingly favorable market juncture, you reduce risk. Of course you reduce potential profit sometimes also, but safety costs money just as insurance does.

PORTFOLIO BALANCE CHECK

	% of Total Funds	Maximum $ Commitment to Any Single Situation
Cash and Equivalent		
Long-Term Bonds		
(a) Investment		
(b) Speculative		
Short-Term Trading		
Dividend-Paying Commons— Investment Grade		
Dividend-Paying Commons— Speculative Grade		
Non-Dividend-Paying Commons— Good Markets		
Non-Dividend-Paying Commons— Thin Markets		

RECORD OF PURCHASES AND SALES This form is used to keep a record of realized profits and losses, short- and long-term, for tax purposes on closed transactions.

Date		No. of Shares	Name of Security	Purchases	
Bought	Sold			Price per Share	Total Paid
3/25/70	5/27/70	100	American Tel. & Tel.	53	$5,360
10/15/66	7/10/70	100	IBM	150	$15,069
5/21/70		100	Standard Oil of N.J.	52	$5,259

(The examples shown are approximations for illustrative purposes.)

Sales		Total Profit		Total Loss	
Price per Share	Total Received	Long Term	Short Term	Long Term	Short Term
44	$ 4,345				$1,015
250	$24,915	$9,846			

| Date | | No. of | Name of | Purchases | |
Bought	Sold	Shares	Security	Price per Share	Total Paid

Sales		Total Profit		Total Loss	
Price per Share	Total Received	Long Term	Short Term	Long Term	Short Term

| Date | | No. of | Name of | Purchases | |
Bought	Sold	Shares	Security	Price per Share	Total Paid

Sales		Total Profit		Total Loss	
Price per Share	Total Received	Long Term	Short Term	Long Term	Short Term

The Battle for Stock Market Profits

INVESTMENT INVENTORY This type of form is more or less standard and used for tabulating your holdings. Some investors do this in alphabetical order; some find it best to do it by industry groups; others by quality; and others by placing the largest positions first. It is also used to keep check of results by comparing current prices with cost prices and prices at the close of the previous year, in a different way from the "How Am I Doing" valuation chart that follows.

| No. of Shares | Description of Issue | Acquired | | Total Cost |
		Date	Price per share	

COMPARATIVE GROUP ANALYSIS

There are some very successful investors who think in terms of individual companies and some equally successful investors who think in terms of groups. Among the wide number of stocks one can pick from nowadays, there are many special situations that for all practical purposes stand alone. However, there are others like business machines, airlines, electronics, etc., that clearly are part of a group. Where an issue of this sort is picked or where you make a decision to favor a particular group, it is important to jot down some of the comparative figures to conclude which is the best. "The best" in this case means the best for you— it might be the most volatile, or the safest, or the issue with the greatest profit potentiality. I am only suggesting some typical categories. There will be many times when an individual investor will find need to use a substitute category.

The headings shown below ate enough for a thumbnail comparison of different stocks in the same industry group. The last price and the price range (for the current year) give you a quick pointer to volatility. The space for earnings can be used either for the last reported year's figures or for a current estimate. You might add a P/E ratio. Under "Growth" you can make an entry if the group you are studying does in fact have a growth trend. Something like "earnings doubled in four years" should be sufficient. Where growth is not a consideration, the column may be used to indicate cyclical trends; *e.g.,* "deficit in 1958" or "net off 45% in 1960." The balance sheet position can be indicated in a word—"strong," "weak," "leveraged," etc. You will have a ruling reason (see page 15) only on two

The Battle for Stock Market Profits

GROUP ANALYSIS FORM—DIFFERENT STOCKS IN
SAME INDUSTRY

Name of Stock	Last Price	Price Range	Earnings	P/E Ratio

Growth	Relative Action	Balance Sheet	Ruling Reason

or three issues—the ones you favor most—and in the end, probably on a single issue only.

INVESTMENT À LA CARTE

It is obviously impossible to draw up a checklist which is custom-made for every investor, from the beginner to the seasoned professional.

It is likewise impossible to tabulate all the question-and-answer categories that are needed to cover all the hundreds of different kinds of investment securities and situations.

The working tools here offered to the investor are those which, in my experience, he will need most frequently. In any given case he will use some and discard others. Sometimes he will need to work out additional tools and write them in for himself.

The work sheets are best adapted for use on the largest, best-known securities of investment grade. They will be of little service on the small, new growth companies.

Their main purpose is to help you find, or confirm, the ruling reason why a particular purchase may be expected to show a profit. Probably you have such a reason in mind when you start to fill out the checklist. By the time you are through you should have a lot more evidence, one way or the other.

Here are some of the ruling reasons that have produced profits in the past:

Favorable change in management.

Undiscounted increase in earnings.

Increase in investor regard (higher price/earnings ratio).

Undiscounted increase in dividend.

Liquidation or sale at figure above current market.

Impact of new product on earnings.
Favorable merger or acquisition.
Purchase at start of new up cycle.
Fight for control.
Whatever the reasons, writing them down will tend to separate the wheat from the chaff, the sheep from the goats.

HOW AM I DOING?

Here is a way to figure. Too many investors disregard taxes which must be paid sooner or later unless stocks are kept for one's heirs and never sold during the investor's lifetime. So too do many disregard "unrealized losses."

NET VALUE AT START OF PERIOD

Valuation Date   Dow Industrial Average

Gross Value of Security Account at Market

(cash awaiting investment plus
securities owned)

Deduct Tax Reserve

Deduct loans if not fully paid

NET VALUE AT CLOSE OF PERIOD
Percent change

Revaluation Date   Dow Industrial Average Percent Change

Cash or Securities Added During Desired Period

(or deduct if taken from account)

Credit Dividends Received Less Taxes

Debit Taxes Due on Closed Profitable Transactions (or credit tax loss carry forward on losses)

Gross Value of Security Account at Market

Deduct Tax Reserve

   (or credit tax-loss carry forward)

Deduct loans

If no cash or securities were added or subtracted, the final figure shows the net investment performance for the period. It is assumed dividends are left in the account. This can be compared with the index or average that comes nearest to your aims. It can also be figured as a percentage increase or decrease in the time period.

SHARE ACCOUNTING

If you add or deduct any appreciable amount of cash or securities during the accounting period it will be difficult using the method above to arrive at precise results. In such cases it will be more realistic to consider your assets just as if it were a "fund" and calculate a per-share book value. This can be simply done by valuing all your assets at the start and using an arbitrary figure to use as a divider for your book value. Thus if your assets are valued at $100,000 and you use 5,000 as an initial "capitalization" and divider your book value would be $20. Each time you wish to add or subtract securities or cash you do it on a per-share basis. For example, if the account appreciated to a total value of $120,000 and you withdrew $10,000 you would calculate that you withdrew 500 shares at $12 a share leaving 9,500 shares outstanding. This would then become your divider until you made further changes.

The disadvantages of using total figures are that your account would show a percentage loss that was not due to investment changes. Using unit figures your account would show no change which would be correct from an investment standpoint.

RESISTANCE AND RALLY LEVELS

One of my partners, many years ago, introduced me to a simple numerical record system to help spot good and bad action. He used it successfully instead of charts. In his day IBM was named "Computing-Tabulating-Recording Inc.," and no one had started thinking of "relative actions" or working it out. These figures are a guide to relative action as well as to reaction bottoms and rally tops.

Obviously stocks that can register higher bottoms and tops are among the strongest and those showing lower bottoms and tops are among the weakest. Use a red ballpoint pen to circle the bearish figures and a green one for the bullish indications.

RESISTANCE AND RALLY LEVELS

Name of stock	Low	Hi	Low	Hi
Dow Indus				
Date				
ABC Company				
Date				
XYZ Company				
Date				

17 *A Fresh Point of View on Some Investment Philosophies, Old and New*

Now that the Checklist has given us the essential facts needed to make an investment decision, one is still confronted with the practical problem of what to do. To turn my original premise around, there is no doubt that where the stock market is concerned, man cannot live by hard, cold facts alone. He needs experience, philosophy, and flair.

The remaining chapters will attempt to provide some philosophical but hardheaded concepts and courses of action to use with the facts developed in the Checklist. I shall go on the assumption that the reader can and will approach these concepts for successful investing with an open mind and that he is willing and able to profit from my experience and lessons learned over many market ups and downs. Most of all, let us hope that it will not be necessary for the reader to experience disaster in order to be able to understand how it can happen and how to be on guard to avoid it.

18 *Stock Market Discipline*

The safest investments of all are more often than not in stocks that have gone up, are going up, seem high, but continue to go up. The favorable market actions and premium prices in such cases mirror expanding futures. The really good stocks almost always seem overpriced. It requires discipline to make yourself pass up the low-priced "bargain" and buy seemingly high-priced growth.

The Battle for Stock Market Profits

Investing is not an exact science. Rather, it is an art—often baffling and unpredictable. If investing were an exact science, accountants would be experts in the market. This is rarely the case. The dyed-in-the-wool accountant tends to imagine that the values he finds in his better-than-average grasp of corporate figures should find exact reflection in market prices. This hardly ever happens. The best psychologists are usually the best investors. Successful investing requires a special kind of judgment and flair in analyzing market behavior which is associated more with psychology than with pure fact or formula.

Regardless of our basic convictions about a stock, if it goes in one direction it encourages us to believe it will continue moving the same way. Trend is a powerful influence on buyers and sellers of stock. If you are building a long position in a stock, there is a great deal to be said about following the trend in its earlier and middle stages. The same is true if you are attempting to cash in on a profit or liquidate a loss in a seemingly down movement. My experience indicates that, by and large, quality is of secondary importance to trend in making money in the stock market.

The difficulty with these principles is that they cannot be applied by automation, but must be consciously ordered by humans who experience various conflicting states of mind, greed, and inertia. Theory is one thing; practice is another. Most of us dislike to take a loss and also dislike to pay more for stocks that we missed lower down. It is not my purpose here to discuss the pros and cons of following trends, but rather what to do if you believe in them.

My suggestion is to act by steps. The "step system" simply means doing things by degrees—step by step—if you are not certain enough to take action all at once. The idea is that when things go against you in a market and you are not sure of yourself, correct the situation a step at a time. The same logic would apply if things went your way. In this case, increase your position by steps as your judgment is confirmed in the marketplace.

It is surprising how this policy will get people out of a declining market who would stay in otherwise. It works just as well in getting people into a rising market that they might otherwise easily miss. It is like taking more of a particular kind of medicine if it agrees with you, and cutting it out if it doesn't. When weakness begins to appear in a stock, particularly if it seems that funds are disposing of large blocks, it is probably prudent to trim your holdings. Doing it in steps might leave you with some stock if the unfavorable indications prove misleading.

Discipline yourself against inertia when obvious trends are taking place. "Don't just stand there; sell something." There is no law against buying it back if the situation changes. Taking action will keep you sharp and should insure you against having a stock precipitously "fall out of bed." You will have sold it before a decline reaches disaster proportions. If it turns out that the decline was temporary, you may wish to buy it back. If it costs you more than what you sold it for, regard the difference as an insurance premium.

19 *Decisions, Decisions*

The *decision to buy* a stock with dynamic potential in an uptrend may be more important in the final analysis than when you buy it. If the only thing you have against such a purchase is that "you missed it" when the price was "right," usually you haven't missed it at all. Really good opportunities usually appear overpriced but continue to go up. The fact that a trend has been well established at the time of your purchase is worth money to you. The seller of the stock at this stage, who took a position in the stock when it was "cheap," may take a relatively small profit compared to the buyer at this higher price who hangs on as long as prospects are exceptional and the general market is rising.

I wonder how many stock market fortunes have been lost, after a promising growth stock had been decided upon, by "waiting to buy it cheaper"—and missing it completely. If you are confident that a stock will produce a high-percentage, long-term gain, don't play around—buy it. Today's high may be tomorrow's low, and you'll never make the scene with surging stocks you didn't buy. Even an investor who was unlucky enough to pay the year's high for Polaroid, IBM, or Xerox each year for several years back would have done very well over any reasonable period of time.

Conversely, *making the decision to sell* a stock in a declining market, or because its prospects are declining, is the important thing. If you feel that a stock is no longer an attractive holding, again, don't play around in the hope of selling it at a higher price. If your appraisal is correct, today's low may be tomorrow's high, and once a downtrend has developed in a stock, its price in the marketplace can erode at an alarming rate. It is in the selling of stocks already owned that, as the saying goes, the men are separated from the boys. This is because a decision must be made every market day, consciously or unconsciously: whether to hold or sell each stock in one's portfolio. If you hold a stock you would not now consider buying, why not sell it and invest the proceeds in a more promising situation? There are always winners around, so why go with the losers?

20 *Do Something About Selling*

I think most stockholders are generally overinvested. They seem to feel that the maximum return from their capital only comes from being fully invested, often to the point of borrowing. I do not think this is correct. I feel investors should have a cash or equivalent reserve such as Treasury Bonds, in order to have buying power when a real opportunity appears. I held this view even when Treasury bills paid less than 1 percent.

A second reason why it is not wise to be fully invested is that you should consider using your funds only when the risk-reward ratio is right. Nobody, professional or otherwise, can select a long list of stocks that are all much more likely to go up than down except at major bottoms. These only occur at intervals. When they do occur most of us cannot recognize them for what they are. They generally happen when investors are short of cash and do not want to accept losses in their stocks to buy better opportunities. It follows that investors have too many stocks.

In a well-managed corporation close tab is kept on the return on capital invested in various divisions. If some fail to come up to the management's objectives, they are closed down or sold. The same policy is effective in the stock market. Only own the stocks that promise the most at the least risk. Own more of each. Keep the remainder of your capital liquid, awaiting opportunities that meet your standards. Cut your losses and do not let your profits evaporate or, worse yet, turn from black to red. Failing to sell quickly in a declining market is without doubt the major reason for poor investment results. I have been buying and selling stocks since 1920 so I know from long experience it is easier said than done. I know such a policy can increase taxes. I know it occasionally causes investors to lose good positions. Now and then you are whipsawed. I think the benefits in the long run very much outweigh the costs. It is the only investment policy that secures its direction from judgment. Just "sittin', starin', and rockin'" works when you are in luck. It can occasionally be catastrophic. Much of the time it does not pay—certainly not on a properly annualized basis.

No single rule or formula will answer the important question of when to sell. Each circumstance must be judged on its own. It is usually better to err in selling too soon than not to sell at all. One of the considerations in determining a selling spot is to sell on great strength and not wait for trouble to spur you to liquidate. Watching "relative strength" often can give investors good clues to a reversal ahead. Breaking support levels and trendlines may get you out. Perhaps it will be quite late and at large price concessions, as this is the most popular "stop-loss" procedure. My advice is to consider selling any stock which reacts 10 to 15 percent from its top.

In my book *The Battle for Investment Survival* I list quite a few suggestions on when to sell. John Magee, in his book *Technical Aspects of Stock Trends,* devotes about 100 pages to important technical stock-reversal patterns. The real trick is sell early, and before weakness is obvious to everybody. I think there is much to be said for gradually selling some stock on strength if you have a substantial profit. This is particularly true if the market has been going up a long while, or quite sharply, or on extraordinary volume. The important thing is to do something about selling. It is better to do it inefficiently than not at all.

I am not of the school that makes a "V" gesture if I lose

less than the other fellow. I think one should aim to profit. If the climate seems bad, come in out of the cold!

The usual discussion about stocks and bonds centers around the term "investment": What the investor also needs to be aware of is the word "dis-investment" and the term "money management."

21 *Contrary Opinion as a Tool in Stock Selection*

The really successful in the stock market, as in all lines of endeavor, are very much in the minority. It is obvious that they do something differently than the majority. Shakespeare wrote, "To be contrary brings bliss," though he did not relate the thought to the stock market. A sizable number of investors believe profits can best be secured from a policy of contrariness. If you know when to be contrary and what viewpoint to oppose, it can be a helpful ploy. If you take the opposite view at the wrong time or against the wrong opponent, you can just as easily be a loser.

Anyone who buys or sells stock is acting "contrary" to the one on the other side of the transaction. There is no such thing as being generally contrary. When there is no one to take the other side, trading simply ceases. There is "no bid" or "no offer." You can be contrary in specific ways. It is a fact that written and vocal opinion is frequently very biased toward the bearish or bullish side. No matter how silent or invisible, there are always other investors taking the opposite view. The unlucky investor who bought at the top of a popular wave bought from some seller who held the opposite view.

What is usually meant by being contrary is to go against the publicized majority. There was a time when the little man or odd-lotter was supposedly mostly wrong and the big operator more often right. There are both fact and fallacy in this view. The majority of investors who embrace this theory and go contrary to the small man hardly know how to successfully apply it. Acting contrary by selling short when stocks advance and the published short-interest figures begin to climb can be very costly. Like the rest of us, short sellers are sometimes right and sometimes wrong. Years ago I saw them make a pocketful of money selling St. Paul short before it went into receivership. I saw others lose even more going short another carrier that was being accumulated for takeover.

If you desire to be contrary, be sure words and action match. There is a time to go with the crowd and a time to go against it. If investors are scared in a decline, it means nothing until they are frightened enough to actually panic and liquidate.

No one measure should ever be considered to be standing alone. A stock can be inactive, depressed, unpopular and generally neglected and not be a buy. It might stay that way for much longer than any investor would wish. Or it might start a new cycle of decline and start going lower again. It would not pay in such circumstances to go contrary to the popular apathy. Another stock might be in the same liquidated position, with the vital difference that there is an improvement in its fundamental position ahead. At the start this would not likely be visible or generally believed. At this stage some shrewd buyers do see the better prospects. Their buying increases the volume of transactions. This causes the stock action to improve. Slowly investors and analysts begin to evaluate its strength and the reasons for it. The wise investor at this point will go with the crowd. He needs to wait until he feels the stock's popularity is at a peak before going contrary. This is a difficult thing to know. It can happen in a few months, and occasionally the stock takes two or three years to shoot its bolt. Its price action always varies. It can skyrocket straight up as well as plummet. More likely it will establish a new trading range near its highs. From that stage, it can either move into a new period of advance or, having exhausted its potential, start back down. It might decline part way, all the way, or lower than where it all began. You can find examples of every conceivable type of movement. Nobody knows in advance. I repeat, nobody.

What then is the secret of the successful "contrarian"? It is not supposedly just "going against the crowd." I like to buy stocks when few purchase opinions are around—provided I think more are coming. I like to buy when professionals have begun to take a position with more buying likely to follow. I know my chances are better than if I wait until a great many buy suggestions are around and the funds are heavily aboard. Then it becomes time to be contrary and consider selling! I would rather follow big buyers and act contrary to small buyers, but only at early stages in a possible move. The record shows that the largest buyers make mistakes too. If the specialists on the New York Stock Exchange are reported increasing their purchases of stocks in general and the odd-lot shorts are reported as increasing their sales, if other factors satisfy, I may go contrary to the odd lots. There is no formula. To be a successful "contrarian" you must be able to outjudge your adversary. You need to size up your opponents and the extent of their buying or selling power. You must try to anticipate future news and whether it will tend to help your position. Above all, I think being contrary successfully is being late. The man who fishes for the bottom or who reaches for the top is never the winner. Keep your contrariness under wraps until you think you sense the exhaustion of the trend. When you finally take a position, whoever is on the other side will be acting "quite contrary" at least as far as you are concerned. Remember that it takes crowds to make major rises and falls. The art is to judge correctly when the momentum is really there and when its strength is spent. When the crowd takes the bit in its teeth, price movements always go to excess. There is an old stock exchange proverb: "No price is too low for a bear or too high for a bull."

The growing use of computers is fostering an excess of market "togetherness." There is currently a preponderance of important portfolio managers who believe in very similar principles of stock selection. These methods get programmed into a number of computers that tend to turn bullish or bearish at about the same time. The effect is to increase the intensity of the signals and alert a constantly widening participation.

It seems that the more one studies and examines the many techniques of security and market forecasting, the more the true answer seems to be a combination of experience, contacts and flair.

22 *What Does the Market Tell Us About Investor Attitudes?*

Investor attitudes have been changing a great deal. Investors are looking more and more for an annualized net profit after taxes and after adjusting for dollar depreciation. They are disenchanted with big companies operated for any purpose other than maximum profits now. Using adjusted prices, the investor who bought American Telephone in 1960 at 50 and found it under 50 in 1970 is not very happy. He averaged a 4 percent pretax dividend income. There are many prominent companies in the same position. I am not singling out any particular issues, but just mentioning a few at random that quickly come to mind. Del Monte Corporation sold in 1969 at the same price as it did at one time in 1961. I think you could have bought Crown Zellerbach at some time during 1955 or 1956 at something close to its price in 1969. Pacific Gas has been in a narrow price range for many years. Standard of California sold in 1969 about where it sold during 1963. The investor who bought American Telephone at around 30 in 1958 and sold it at over twice that price in 1961 was happy. Some of those that have been big gainers in one period have been big losers in another. The point I am trying to make is that investors want more for their money. They need more in inflationary times. To try and get more they are willing to turn their capital over more frequently. They are also delegating the management of money. We see this in the decrease in the percentage of odd-lot trades and the increase in transactions in big blocks. We see it in the continued rapid growth of funds. There has been a turnover in individual account managers and advisers in banks, in-

vestment counselors, and brokers. Younger, more aggressive men with less experience are taking over. The investor
is tired of hearing of the supposed merits of high-grade,
long-term bonds and public-utility stocks. They are less
interested in blue chips that have arrived. What they want
are the blue chips of tomorrow. These current attitudes
mean that markets will be more volatile than in the past.
The range between the high and low will be greater. The
moves will be sharper. Price/earnings ratios will also have
a wider spread. The stick-in-the-mud corporation will command lower and lower P/E ratios. The companies investors
think are going somewhere will enjoy premium ratios. Undoubtedly both will be carried to unsupportable extremes.

The increased number of full-time professionals watching
market influences will make for changes being discounted
further in advance. Some investors will make more and
others will lose more. This whole phase of the situation
started with the publicity given to some sensationally high
percentage gains achieved in a single year by a few mutual
funds. Very few investors stopped to figure why, nor did
they evaluate the risks involved. There has been some disillusionment but not enough to really change the situation.
So much for investor attitudes.

As to my point of view—I am in the investment business,
yet I find that whoever applied the use of the word
"security" as descriptive of stocks and bonds certainly either
had his tongue in cheek or was a master salesman. I find
Franz Pick's definition of a bond as a "certificate of confiscation" much more accurate. Those who buy long-term
debt and lock it up must sooner or later inevitably lose in
more directions than one. This does not refer to the activities of the speculator who buys various kinds of bonds at
key spots to resell. His profit comes from trading. The fact

that he trades in bonds is no endorsement of their investment position. Anything an expert trader buys and sells can be profitable without reference to its investment value if bought and locked up. Obviously I am not referring to very short-term, highly liquid paper, which I classify as interest-paying currency. As to stocks, years ago I heard a statement of unknown origin that "stocks were made to sell." It is true that a great mass of promotional shares are printed to sell. The original Federal Securities law, passed in 1933, is known as the "Truth in Securities" law. Despite disclaimers by the Securities and Exchange Commission, the man on the street does not always realize that the SEC is not authorized to pass on the merits of securities or decide which ones may be offered to the public. As long as the offering circular tells the truth, promoters can sell anything. The paper they offer can be overpriced, the promotional fees can be exorbitant, the water in the offering can be high, the management poor, and the prospects dubious. As long as these facts appear in the prospectus, there is no further protection to the investor. It is also true that the major efforts even of ethical security salesmen and brokers is directed at getting their clients to buy. Despite this perhaps overfrank and downbeat viewpoint, I still say that good stocks selected right, bought at the right times and prices, and sold with the same degree of expertise are, in my opinion, the best medium for attempting to preserve or increase one's wealth. They have many advantages over real estate, diamonds, antiques, stamps, art, commodities, and gold. Stocks have superior liquidity and collateral value. They can be bought and sold at lower cost. Their individual values are less difficult to ascertain than other mediums of investment or speculation.

Our savings are always under attack from many directions. Cash or equivalent, except for brief periods during a bear market, is the worst haven of safety. The record over the years of the stock markets around the world versus the currencies around the world prove this. You may lose in stocks, but if they are intelligently handled, you will lose less than in hoarded money.

The keys to successful investment are the cash-equity ratio and the list of individual stocks you own. When there are many uncertainties in the situation, I advise keeping the stock ratio low. It is impossible to put a standard figure on it because there are so many variables in the size and directions of varying accounts. I have known speculators in days gone by who at times had no stock and were short, while at other times they had more stocks than they could pay for.

As to individual stocks, I believe in owning very few. I do not want to buy stock unless I buy enough to show me a worthwhile profit if I am right and potentially hurt me if I am wrong. In practice, if things go my way I would tend to buy more. If things go against me, I would aim to sell out and minimize the damage. I only want to select an individual stock to buy with a unique extra reason that suggests it is the best buy. This is the opposite of building a "portfolio" of "core stocks," that is, a long list of popular leaders in popular groups. From the standpoint of corporation management, I suggest that the primary aim is to run the company for the benefit of today's stockholders. This is the best way to avoid being taken over by another company and to avoid a low market price.

23 *History and Cycles*

49,397 shares. This figure is not a "block of stock." It is the total volume of transactions on the New York Stock Exchange on December 30, 1914. I do not think that history will give you the keys to the future, but I do find that many things which are thought of as "new" today are not new at all. Recalling the past should give an investor a more rounded view of the probable future.

My recollection of the stock market goes back to 1920. I thought then that it was helpful to read books about what happened in the past. It is just as essential to the modern investor, particularly one who has only been in the market for a few years. A book that covers market history from 1812 to 1965 is *The Big Board* by Robert Sobel. Another interesting book is *The Great Crash* (of 1929) by John Kenneth Galbraith. A very useful annual chart combining pertinent news items and the Dow averages is compiled and published by X. W. Loeffler (Box 399, Westwood, New Jersey—price $3.) This covers the period since 1922, and the current edition is four feet long! The first interesting item was the election of Calvin Coolidge in 1924. The Dow industrials were then 110. They took off for their 386 top in September of 1929.

It is interesting to note that many of today's developments occurred in those days. The New York Federal Reserve Bank discount rate was 3 percent in 1924. It was increased several times until it finally reached 6 percent in 1929. The Federal Reserve issued warnings on speculation. Call money advanced to 20 percent. The decline in the market started in October with the 1929 low established on November 13 at 195. I remember the day because I returned from Europe on the White Star liner *Olympic*. We had a famous passenger on board in the person of Mr. J. P. Morgan.

The market rallied strongly in early 1930 with many investors believing the decline was over. It topped off in April, up about 100 points at 297. Then the long agonizing decline resumed with the final low in the Dow at 41 in July. England went off the gold standard in 1931. The chances are that the business recession in the United States might have ended if this British action had not put renewed pressure on us. In February 1932, U.S. Steel omitted its dividend. I never put much faith in supposedly high income yields or low price/earnings ratios. One never knows when the dividend will be reduced or passed, or when the earnings will decline. All through this period, money eased. By 1942 the discount rate was less than 1 percent. The yield on Treasury bills between 1938 and 1940 was practically zero.

In 1932 Roosevelt was elected. In 1933 came the bank holiday, and the United States went off gold. Silver started to advance. The two Securities and Exchange Acts were passed in 1933 and 1934. The market advanced into the spring of 1937 to a high of 195. Stocks then went into a sharp decline and by March of 1938 were down to 97. These swings must be thought of in terms of percentage. A 100-point move in the Dow when it was in the neighborhood of 100 is one thing, and a 100-point move when it is in the neighborhood of 1,000 is quite another.

World War II began in 1939. The inflation we now talk so much about began in 1940. Today's dollar buys about 35 percent of what the 1940 dollar did. Roosevelt was asking for price controls in 1941, the year of Pearl Harbor. The market made its low at 92 in 1942 after the battle at Midway and the favorable turn in the war against Japan.

Average volume of trading on the New York Stock Exchange was at its lowest in 1942, at about 455,000 shares a day, which was below the average volume of trading when prices made their bottom in 1932. This was about a tenth of the average volume of trading in 1929. The market advanced to its May 1946 high of 213. V-E day and V-J day both occurred in 1945. Margins were increased as the market advanced. 1946 marked the start of the decline in the bond market. High-grade long-term triple-A corporate bonds sold at that time to yield under 3 percent. The stock market fell to an October low of 160. 1947 saw the enactment of the Taft-Hartley Law. Truman was elected in 1948. June of 1949 saw the start of the bull market.

The first major interruption of the rise that began in 1949 came in 1957. News items of the period included the start of the Korean war in 1950. Money became more expensive, with savings-bank interest increased to 2½ percent. Margins were further increased. Eisenhower was elected and reelected. In 1956 the market high was 524. Stocks fluctuated in a trading range, and then in 1957 fell from a July high of 523 to an October low of 416. 1957 was the year of Sputnik. The recovery lasted until January 1960, with the Dow at 688. It then dropped to the year's low of 564 in late October. Following this, stocks rallied again to 741 toward the end of 1961, then dipped again in 1962. A high of 1,001 was reached one day in February 1966 although the closing Dow average was under 1,000. During this period Kennedy was assassinated and Johnson was elected. The Securities and Exchange Commission took action against Texas Gulf Sulphur. The prime rate, which was 4½ percent, began its series of increases. By October 1966 the market was down to 735. The decline was partly due to a money crunch and partly due to market excesses, especially in new issues. It rallied to 994 in 1968. During this time Great Britain devalued the pound. In 1969 the Dow declined to 788. In May of 1970 it dropped to 631.16.

A study of business and financial history suggests that while stock prices and money rates move in cycles, they can keep going up or down to a greater extent and take much longer to do so than any anticipate. It is always difficult to stop and turn the trend, as inflation fighters know only too well. Sidney Homer's great 600-page *History of Interest Rates* highlights this with the fact that the Berlin Stock Exchange once quoted a market rate of interest in excess of 10,000 percent per annum. The 8 percent interest on a U.S. Treasury 19½-month note issued in 1969 doesn't seem so high against this background. Interest rates inevitably must reflect the rate of dollar depreciation and taxation.

There have been many periods of general and specific sharp decline in consumer and wholesale prices. There have even been declines in average hourly earnings of labor. The one statistic that never seems to fail is that eventually the value of money decreases and the cost of living increases.

24 *The Importance of Liquidity*

What is the most important attribute of a really safe investment? I think it may very well be liquidity. Liquidity is the ability to buy or sell at low cost and with minimum delay. In the stock market this means shares with large bids and offers and a narrow spread between the two.

Liquidity is a relative term. If you own a hundred shares of a stock, it can be very liquid from your point of view. A fund owning 100,000 shares might find the same issue difficult to buy or sell. Liquidity has been decreasing. What is liquid now might be less so in the future. A brilliant financier said, years ago, "Capital is like a rabbit. It flees at the slightest hint of danger." It is important that your investments are such that you can flee if need be or change their nature both quickly and cheaply should the occasion arise.

U.S. Treasury 91-day bills are exceedingly liquid. An ordinary non-interest-paying checking account in a commercial bank is extremely liquid. There are many forms of savings that are liquid in normal times, but withdrawal might be delayed in times of stress. For example, passbook savings-bank deposits and S&L deposits may not be withdrawn without advance notice, should the rule be invoked. Mutual funds may have the option of paying in kind (which means distributing their assets pro rata) rather than in cash.

Securities with the best markets also make the best collateral for a loan. It is a principle among brokers in Wall Street never to include stocks "in the bottom of their box" in making up their bank loans. Pledging low-quality securities is a reflection on their credit. Investors should not own such securities unless the prospect of a very large gain makes the odds worthwhile.

In the stock market the turnover in large blocks of stock has been increasing. The trading in odd lots has been declining. There are fewer decision-makers as investors delegate authority to professionals. The result is a decrease in the overall liquidity of the market. Another result is limitation of growth in the number of corporate stockholders.

Robert W. Haack, president of the New York Stock Exchange, emphasized the importance of the small individual investor in the following statement: "The central market depends for its existence on a combination of large and small orders. Specifically, it is the flow of small orders that creates liquidity and provides the basis for continuous action. Direct ownership of shares is good for the economy. It is in the interest of companies to have a widespread base of public ownership." *The Institutional Investor,* a controlled-circulation monthly journal for professionals, used as its cover story one month an article titled "Where Has Liquidity Gone?" This reveals the importance of this development to investment officers and portfolio managers.

The investor running his own investments should be cognizant of the current liquidity loss. It is evident in the increasing number of times that trading is temporarily suspended in individual issues. It is shown by the large percentage declines that develop more frequently as blocks of stock come into the market for liquidation. The private investor can keep himself liquid. It is another matter when an institution or investment manager needs to acquire or liquidate a large block of stock. As an illustration, some time ago trading in the shares of Revenue Properties, Ltd., a Canadian company, was stopped in the U.S. The individual investor could have sold his shares in Canada that same day at about $19. If you had the same number of shares in charge of an investment manager he could probably not sell your shares until something was worked up for the total holdings of all his clients and perhaps a house fund as well. This stock, as it happened, later sold under $1 and for a time was not traded anywhere.

A type of stock with practically no liquidity is unregistered stock, or "letter stock," as it is known in the street. Letter shares are bought at varying discounts, often exceeding 50 percent of the market value of registered shares of the same company. They are strictly for the experienced professional who knows his way around. Yet these, too, may get badly burned.

The relation of liquidity to risk was brought home to me by one of the leading London dealers in "Yankee" shares. He rated the risk in a stock by what it would cost him to "turn," *i.e.*, buy and resell. Thus, if he could buy 10,000 shares of a very liquid stock and turn around and resell it at a concession of ⅛ of a point, he felt there was less risk than in buying 1,000 shares where it might cost 5 points to turn around. The best professional investors consider liquidity an important factor in valuing stocks. If two securities existed of precisely the same nature, except in liquidity, the highly salable issue would command a higher market price. The lay investor should likewise take this factor into consideration in appraising his own stock purchases.

25 *Owning the Right Stocks*

The stock market says different things to different people. It all depends on where you look and what securities you own. Even in a bear market there is more opportunity to profit from owning the right stocks than is generally realized. Picking the right stocks is an important key to success. It is all well and good to talk about the "average," but it is the individual shares you own that will determine your net gain or loss for the year ahead. Here are some points to bear in mind.

When the market is highly volatile, much of the trading is done by full-time professional managers. Many show large losses in a bear market year. Bad as this is, it is nowhere near as bad as a market recovery without being fully aboard. Some strength may come from premature buying by such managers who are afraid to be left behind. They can be just as afraid to be wrong on the downside. One stock lost 27 points, about 20 percent of its market value, in one week when professional managers had a change of heart.

Rosser Reeves, in his book *Reality in Advertising,* writes of what he calls the essential "U.S.P." These three letters stand for Unique Selling Proposition. He points out that from the dawn of history mankind has been interested in leverage. "Give me a lever long enough," said Archimedes, "and I will move the world." "What's the leverage?" asks modern man, and, from the stock market to diplomacy, the question is at once a dream, a bandied phrase, and a glint in the eye. I interpret Mr. Reeves's leverage not in the ordinary market sense of high volatility. I use it here to mean selecting a stock to buy with a unique extra reason that suggests it is the best buy. This is the opposite of building a portfolio of core stocks, *i.e.,* a long list of popular leaders in popular groups. Such "U.S.P." shares exist. You might only find one a year, but if you do it will pay you generously. You might pick several and find only one which is the real winner later. As this happens, you cut out your mistakes and increase your ownership in your successful stock.

I think the best long-term candidates will be located among issues that have not been popular for several years and are in a low trading range or just breaking out of it. You should seek shares with a "secret ingredient." By this I mean some merit not now fully discounted in the price. What everybody knows is rarely worth knowing. The big profits come from buying pre-glamour and pre-growth.

A friend of mine is an expert on fund management. He is in a position to evaluate the "whys" of fund performance or the lack of it. He told me the two things that impressed him most from his studies. First, if the fund managers had automatically sold out every position that ran to a loss of 20 percent (I would tend to cut my loss before it went that far), their overall performance would have been much improved. Next, he found that the big profits (and the big uncut losses) came from a very limited number of stocks. The main body of the portfolio canceled itself out with some up and some down.

For the best possible chance at doing well in the market I buy these points of view. They are old hat with me. They are so fundamental that they need constant repetition.

The risks in the so-called "best actors" that have been rising and popular for several years are high. This is true even if they have held well recently, and perhaps are strong or at new highs. This type of stock is mainly suitable for the rare, very nimble short-term trader. Many stocks can lose their glamour fast, even in a single week.

With 91-day Treasury bills paying a good return, there is little reason to worry about so-called "unproductive" capital awaiting common stock investment. I would feel the same if bills paid 1 percent or less, as they have in the past. It will profit you more to buy only the very few issues at the time and prices when they have real "U.S.P." and keep your capital safer and more productive in bills until you find what you really feel has the ingredients you are seeking.

26 *Selling Short: Bear Is Rarely Successful*

Most investors buy stocks and hope they will advance so that they can sell them at a profit. The other side of the coin is the increasing number of stock traders who sell stock first and hope it will go down so they can buy it back cheaper. Every month the total amount sold short, as this procedure is called, is made public.

It is natural to assume that you can make a profit in buying when the market advances; conversely, why not sell short and try to profit when the market declines? The truth of the matter is that the bear is rarely successful. The greatest growth in shorting seems to come from the increasing number of "hedge funds." The hedge funds attempt to be short of stocks they hope will decline and at the same time be "long" (which means to own) stocks they hope will advance. Most of these funds are private but the few that are publicly owned have had volatile ups and downs. Declines in asset value in the first eight months of 1969 ran as high as almost 40 percent compared with a 12 to 13 percent drop in the Dow, despite the funds' right to sell short.

One reason short sellers find it hard to succeed is that bear markets have been shorter and sharper than the major bull market advances. They never begin until the market has advanced considerably beyond reasonable expectations. It is very difficult to judge the degree of excess. It can be very costly trying to find the top. On the other hand, if you wait until you think the trend is definitely down, you may be unable to sell in a sharply falling market. (Short-selling orders cannot be executed except at an advance from the last sale. Potential short sellers also must check first with their brokers to be sure the latter can borrow the stock required.) Another reason is that impending unfavorable corporate news is very difficult to procure in advance. A third reason for failure in selling short is the psychological difficulty of adjusting our personal thinking. It was Daniel Drew, the financier, who said, "He who sells what isn't his'n, must buy it back or go to prison." A stock can only decline to zero, but no one knows to what astronomical heights an occasional issue might climb. The classic example was the bear panic in the spring of 1901 when in a few days Northern Pacific advanced from under 150 to 1,000. Time, and just sitting on an investment in the shares of an established and listed company, can often pull an investor out of an initial mistake. He may even collect some dividends while he is waiting. Sitting on short sales can be expensive. The short seller has to pay the dividends rather than receive them and there are other possible costs and difficulties. Emotionally it is disconcerting to most people if the market is going against them.

A principal reason for lack of success in selling short is that it is human nature to sell short the stocks that have advanced the most. They almost always advance still further. The short seller tends to sell too soon. Later, and at higher prices, he often takes his loss.

Once a month, the short interest in individual issues is released by the New York and American stock exchanges and is printed in many newspapers. Those monthly tables list all stocks on the two exchanges in which a short position of at least 20,000 shares existed on the 15th of the month previous or where there was a short position change of at least 10,000 shares in the two months previous. Many traders calculate the percentage which the total sold short bears to the total shares outstanding in a given company. Every short seller inevitably at some time has to become a buyer to cover his sales. The more shares outstanding, the better his chances. Some of the largest short positions are usually found in stocks that are very strong or even establishing new highs for the year in a lower general market. On the other hand, if you examine stocks near the year's lows you will find very few shorts outstanding.

If you desire to test your flair at short selling here are some suggestions:

Limit your loss—this is essential. No one can tell the excesses to which a market can rise. Totally unpredictable news can change a picture from unfavorable to favorable. You don't have to be caught in a corner to lose a great deal of money. National Video was $9 in 1965. Even though the company only enjoyed a brief earnings spurt, the stock nevertheless advanced to 120 the following year. By 1968 it was back under $9. Ordinarily I would not sell short unless I felt that the trend of the averages and the majority of stocks was downward. I think you will have more chances of success if you avoid the temptation to sell the widest swingers on the theory that what goes up the most will necessarily drop the farthest and the fastest. There are times you might get a smaller profit but with less risk by selling investment-type issues. For example, stocks like Du-Pont, Texaco, FMC, etc., are among the best in the country. In a recent year, DuPont dropped from 165 to about 100, Texaco from 39 to 30, and FMC from 38 to around 20. Compare this with a popular short such as Xerox, with a price range during this period of 86–109 and selling at the high when this reading was made. Another place to look for possible shorts is in groups that are starting down from being overexploited. This happened in the bowling group, airlines, publishing and others at various times in recent years. Unless you are one of the very few who can foretell a dividend cut or sharp drop in earnings before it shows up in the market, you will do better to leave short selling to the professionals.

Two helpful statistics are the percentage of odd-lot short selling and percentage of Stock Exchange member short selling. Normally these two are doing the opposite. I would go with the members rather than the small traders. One should be careful about selling short if the odd lots sell short over 2 percent of total odd-lot sales. On one day in the summer of 1970 it exceeded 10 percent. On the basis of past history, even the professional would often have done better by putting his funds out at interest until ready to buy rather than trying to beat the downs as well as the ups.

The only practical possibility of profiting from taking a short position is to sell a trend and hope for its extension. It can even be disastrous to short the stock of a company that is badly managed or has an indifferent record. Sometimes stronger corporations will acquire these weak sisters in the belief that they can improve their positions or to buy their tax losses. This may run up the price of the stock you have shorted.

The hazards of short selling can be seen from examining what has happened in the past. One might consider the airlines. They enjoyed enormous market advances from 1962 into the summer of 1966. They then declined with the general market and, despite the difficulties which were brewing, went up sharply with the overall recovery of prices then under way. It was only after the spring of 1967 that these stocks began declining, both absolutely and relatively. There were plenty of traps for the premature short seller who, on the way up, felt that airline price/earnings ratios were getting overgenerous or that profit margins were threatened. He lost money even though his premises later proved correct.

Color TV gives us another example. Few analysts had any illusions that the upturn in Admiral earnings could be sustained, yet the stock advanced from an adjusted value of about 7 in 1965 to over 60 the following year. By the middle of 1967, Admiral was in the red and the stock declined into the low 20s. Only the trader who shrewdly let the advance run its full course and the stock turn down is likely to have profited. Admiral was a good short sale at about 40 on the way down toward 20. It was a poor sale at 40 or 50 on the way up to above 60.

There are times when fundamentally weak stocks advance and times when the very best blue chips decline. The primary objective when you sell short is to secure a profit for yourself out of a bear trend. Wait until you think the backbone of an advance is broken and the trend seems clearly down. You have a chance of profiting from selling stocks making new lows, but relatively little chance among those making new highs.

In most walks of life the early bird undoubtedly gets the worm, but in selling short it is mostly the tardy sellers who succeed.

27 *Trends Are Difficult to Change*

It has been a long time since October 1929. Each anniversary of the decline in stock market prices seems to stimulate comment, mostly of the "Can it happen again?" type. It may be useful to recollect what happened then in other sections of the economy. The following personal reminiscences are chronicled as a matter of interest—they are not a forecast of things to come.

New hotels are going up everywhere these days. The rates they charge are necessarily very high. They are based on current building, operating, and financing costs. I lived in New York City in 1929. Hotels of all kinds were then going up on every side. They were in deep financial trouble almost overnight. I paid $12,000 a year rental for my two-bedroom-and-living-room suite in the Savoy Plaza. A year later I paid $4,000 a year, and this rate prevailed for about ten years. When the Savoy was wrecked to build the General Motors Building a few years ago, the final rent for that apartment was in excess of $20,000 a year. During the 30s, occupancy rates in many cases dropped to under 50 percent. Hotel equities were wiped out. Hotel mortgage bonds declined to very low figures. Commercial rentals also dropped severely. I know of cases where landlords practically waived the rent entirely just to keep the space occupied. The hope was that when times improved the building owner would have a rent-paying tenant again.

Wages and salaries decreased until about 1933. In 1931 my mother was in an accident and in a New Orleans hospital. I paid the going rate for a 24-hour registered nurse—$8 a day. Today you would need three nurses at up to $129 for a 24-hour period.

Everything, including labor, was negotiable in those days. List prices were meaningless. During the 1933 bank holiday I paid $8 a day for a $40-a-day suite in an Atlantic City luxury hotel. Today's prices in many luxury resorts run closer to $85 per day.

Cash was king. If you had cash you could buy tremendous bargains. There were equities in co-op luxury apartments that sold for six figures in 1929 going for just $1 in the 1930s. The owners could not pay their taxes, mortgage interest, and maintenance. (Like everything else, co-op apartments are inflated again.)

The contraction of trading volume on the New York Stock Exchange was severe. 1929 had seen a 16,000,000-share day and average trading of over 4,000,000 shares daily. It was 1942, thirteen years later, before Exchange volume reached its final annual low of about 10 percent of the boom total or just over 400,000 shares daily.

We had to cut everything in the security business to keep solvent. Employees who were kept on the payroll were put on "Scotch" weeks, *i.e.*, they reported and were paid only every other week. Partners earned next to nothing or lost large amounts.

Of course the stock market went down. Shares of stock represent property values, earning power, dividend-paying ability and future prospects. These all decreased. Stocks were also liquid when most property was not. What seems forgotten is that practically everything went down with the principal exception of the purchasing power of the dollar.

United States Steel was a typical blue chip of the 20s. In 1929 it earned in excess of $21 a share, paid an $8 dividend, and at one time sold above 260. In 1932 it lost $11 a share, and in 1933 it passed its dividend. In both years it sold under $25. Any investor who, during this period, confined his appraisal of U.S. Steel market values to price/earnings ratios based on 1929 earnings, or on those of the previous five years, would have found his calculations completely misleading.

Prices of homes declined sharply. There was a mortgage moratorium.

A friend of mine who bought a diamond for "security" in 1929 paid $10,000. When he attempted to sell it in 1932 for the purpose of raising margin he could not get even $2,500.

The point of recalling these scattered incidents is that there is never any such thing as a one-way street when it comes to economic trends. Another point to realize is that trends are difficult to change. Evidence abounds as to the difficulty of halting and then reversing an inflationary trend. Once headed down, it is equally difficult to level off.

The New York Federal Reserve Bank rediscount rate dropped from 6 percent in 1929 to under 3 percent a year later without stopping the decline in business. There were other factors that kept things sliding.

In a broad overall way these things are highly unlikely to happen again. It is well known that there have been basic changes both economically and socially that make general collapse unlikely. In fact, if a panic began, the chances are that Government attempts to check the catastrophy would eventually take an inflationary course. Losses from inflation are less visible to the average man and more palatable to politicians.

Specifically, however, in various industries and securities 1929 *can* happen again. In fact, it has been happening right along. Some of the declines in individual stocks in 1962 and 1966 were tremendous. The number of "scheduled items" (bad loans) in the S&L field grew so large a few years ago that reporting the figures was dropped in some cases.

Human nature being what it is, inflation will always be with us. An enterprising printing company reproduces the "12-cent course dinner" which made Delmonico's famous in 1834. This was when six dollars a week was a good wage and a man could keep a country and town house staffed with seven servants (and save money besides) on $3,000 a year.

The important point to keep in mind is that there were many ups and downs on the way to today's $12 dinner. Webb and Knapp, Bill Zeckendorf's great real-estate firm, went under in 1965. If recent rents and real-estate values had been reached without delay, Webb and Knapp would now be on top of the world.

It is essential for investors to look at the current tides as they affect varying investments and not blindly think that the long-term depreciation of the dollar will pull them out of any mistake they make.

28 *Bonds—Possible Profits or Guaranteed Confiscation?*

For many years the income on fixed investments was so low that institutions were almost the entire bond market.

My experience in the bond and money markets goes back to 1921. There is a current value in recalling the recurring fashions in bond investment. In 1921 investors bought bonds for income. I worked in an office on the ground floor of the world-renowned Palace Hotel in San Francisco. When a new bond issue was floated we had a sign painted and placed in the window. People came in off the street and bought the bonds as if stopping in at a cigar store for a purchase. I recall selling such issues as Goodyear Tire and Rubber, First Mortgage 8 percent bonds, at prices under 100, all due at 120. Long-term, partially tax-exempt U.S. Governments paid almost 6 percent. Over the years income returns dropped and bond prices increased until 1946. Various fully taxable U.S. Government bonds then returned only from about ½ of one percent to a shade over 2 percent.

In 1929, before the depression, investors bought bonds for imagined safety. A great many made the mistake of failing to realize the importance of quality and short maturity. By 1932 the sheep were divided from the goats. Many low-quality issues declined like stocks. I remember the Alleghany 5 percent bonds, which had sold at over 100 in 1929 dropping below 10. In 1932 and for some years after smart investors bought bonds for capital gains. There were many issues that could be bought very cheap, especially rails, in default and reorganization. In many cases the chances for future profits were substantial.

The income tax began in 1913. Rates increased with the years. Sometime after 1940, Government bonds began to be taxable. Income-tax rates rose more steeply. Many investors then turned to tax-exempt bonds. Calculations began to appear everywhere detailing the advantage of nontaxable income. Nothing was said about the greater costs of buying and selling and the often considerably lower marketability of many tax-exempts. Nor was anything said about the possibility of decline in price. Losses in long-term bonds, taxable and tax-exempt, have been substantial in recent years. The losses in the 1930 period were mostly due to bad credit. The losses in more recent years have been due to rising interest rates and thus affect even the issues with the very highest credit.

The next fashion was the convertible bond, or the bond with warrants to buy common stock. This developed as inflation began to be more widely discussed and as the stock markets advanced. The convertible bond (or the bond with warrants) is, in fact, a package. The investor is not just buying a bond. He is purchasing a bond plus an option to convert or buy stock. The price of a convertible bond should be broken down by the investor into its component parts. Every bond has an estimated current straight bond value, as if it had no special privileges at all. The market price, with rare exceptions, will be considerably over the

109

straight bond value. The option to buy common will also have a value, sometimes called the market premium over the conversion privileges. The market price of the package will go up or down depending upon the changes in value of its components. Thus, if interest rates increase, the straight bond value will decrease. If the stock of the corporation in question goes down, then the value of the conversion rights will decline. Of course, ideally, everything will work in the other direction.

A convertible bond will almost always return less income than a straight bond because only a portion of the package price is actually represented in the debt itself. You might buy a convertible bond, paying 4 percent. It would not be much different from buying a straight 8 percent bond and investing some capital in a nondividend-paying stock warrant on the side. It might just happen to return the same 4 percent that the convertible paid.

I have often said that, to attempt to even approximate what the public really thinks it is getting when it buys a "safe investment," it is necessary to "speculate." This applies as much to bonds as to stocks. Peoples' memories are short. After the decline in the market in 1929 a great many investors avoided stocks for many years, just when they should have been buying them. Recently people who thought various fixed-dollar investments were "safe" suddenly became conscious of the effects of dollar depreciation, taxes, higher interest rates, etc. They incurred losses in their supposedly "safe" investments. These investors run scared and have abandoned the bond market. Others look upon a depressed bond market as a possible source of capital gains. They buy the deeply depressed low-coupon long-term bonds that have the greatest price-recovery potential if interest rates decrease.

A popular word lately is "disintermediation." This means switching money from low-income investments to higher-income investments. The low-income investments are those whose interest rates are not competitive because of Government ceilings. Investors withdraw funds from these securities as well as from savings accounts and S&Ls and invest the proceeds more profitably.

This must be done with considerable expertise. You have to begin with your own conclusion as to the future of interest rates as well as other economic factors. You have to pretty well know the chances of when you will need your capital. The differences between the various ways you can invest your money for income are far more important than the rate itself.

Only an expert can really tell you the vast differences in quality, liquidity, terms, etc. There is an enormous variety in the types of money investments available. Obtainable income has ranged up to over 11 percent in recent years.

Ninety-one-day U.S. Treasury bills, the premier short-term investment, have returned more than 7 percent. These are direct obligations of the U.S. Government. They have maximum liquidity and are constantly bought and sold in tremendous amounts.

Savings accounts, which return less, vary in their safety, liquidity, and insurance protection. They have restrictions that can be invoked in an emergency, giving the banks varying periods of grace to delay payment without default.

Franz Pick's description of a bond as a "certificate of guaranteed confiscation" is especially true in the case of those who buy long-term bonds and hold them. On the other hand, there are possible profits in bonds for informed investors who are shrewd in their buying and selling.

29 *The Market and the News*

During each trading session on the New York Stock Exchange, brokers attempt to fit the fluctuations to the news. After the market is closed, financial writers do it for their market reports.

"The stock market advanced—because of such and such."

"Solar Space Transportation declined—because of this and that."

The investor needs to fit the news to the market and decide the degree and nature of its significance. The right good captain of H.M.S. *Pinafore* said, "Things are seldom what they seem," and this is certainly true in considering the impact of news on the stock market. Practically the only time spot news is really good for stocks, or vice versa, is when it is a complete surprise. The Kennedy assassination in 1963 would be a good example: no one could possibly have had advance information. It was a shock, and the market reflected the shock.

There is an old Wall Street saying, "The baby is born." It refers to the fact that no baby can be born without advance knowledge. If a stock advances over a period of months in anticipation of favorable news, the actual news release often marks the end of the rise. Whether this is true or not depends on how many investors had knowledge or even surmised the coming event in advance or what trend the news would take in the future. The investor has to look ahead. This involves considerable educated guessing.

The "lead time" between developments and their market effects varies enormously. For example, the savings and loan and the building-stock groups made lows during the 1966 money crunch. The stocks advanced sharply since then even though money was still tight and building was still to revive. Even in later market weakness they held relatively well. The "lead time" here is obviously long. Or take the airlines, which were notably weak in recent years on poor earnings. They made their tops during 1967 a few months after their earnings reached the peak. As an example of "lead time" and how you have to make assumptions if you aspire to "buy low" and "sell high," consider Chrysler. Chrysler declined from an adjusted high near 25 in 1955 to about an adjusted low of 9 in 1960. This reflected decreases in sales, percent penetration of market, profits, etc.

It happened that I was in Detroit on Thursday, June 30th, 1960. The day before I had been interviewed by the press and had made the statement that Chrysler had "the greatest potential in the auto industry." The next day William C. Newberg resigned as Chrysler president. The stock sold at about 10 (adjusted). With all the bad news about Chrysler you had to make assumptions to arrive at a correct forecast. (One writer spoke of Chrysler as the ½ of the big 2½ in the auto business.) They were based on a combination of facts, possibilities and potentialities. I was early. It was 1962 before Chrysler took off under the new leadership of George Love as chairman, Lynn Townsend as president, and with a Rockefeller investment in the shares. By 1964 the stock was selling above 60. In 1968, it sold above 70. Earnings advanced to a new record high. Chrysler sold as low as 31⅝ in 1969, or less than half its 1968 peak. In spring of 1970 it was as low as 16⅛. The decline was due to many factors involving the general stock market, the more than average weakness in automobile stocks, and specific factors in the Chrysler situation.

The shrewd buyer of Chrysler in 1960 would have found it much more difficult to have spotted the best time to sell.

113

The stock was split twice on the way up. Dividends were increased. Few thought that Lynn Townsend and Virgil Boyd, whom he brought to the company, could turn Chrysler around so quickly and so completely. 1965 and 1966 were bad market years. 1967 and 1968 were good again. The seller in 1968 now focuses on when and at what price to buy back. Thus, no one could really judge when the momentum in corporate progress slowed. It was more likely that one could judge when the stock market was broadly in a high risk area.

I relate this because statements like "Buy on bad news and sell on good" or "Buy low—sell high" are meaningless in real life. The correct decision to buy or sell involves judging what is really the last bad or good news or how low or how high prices are carried in despair or unreasoning over-optimism.

The largest profits and lowest risks usually come from attempting to judge coming events rather than acting on the culmination of a trend possibly some time in the making and fully discounted in prices.

30 *Investment Clubs*

Should you join an investment club? It could be helpful if you are a new investor and not satisfied with your investment experience. Over 200,000 investors belong to 13,000 clubs registered with the National Association of Investment Clubs (NAIC). There are many more who are not registered. The NAIC emphasizes investor education. I consider it a wise precaution to post yourself with the basic information supplied by the NAIC if you plan to join or form a club. The Association's headquarters are at 1300 Washington Boulevard Building, Detroit, Michigan, 48231.

Forming an investment club involves legal and tax questions as well as investment policy. The 56-page NAIC Manual gives you the pros and cons of such questions as partnership versus incorporation, how stock certificates should be held, the liabilities of members and how to secure a fidelity bond for your protection, etc. It also explains "unit" accounting, which is essential for a club and useful for any investor. The NAIC material also includes a monthly magazine, stock check lists, portfolio management, stock comparison and selection guides and ideas on individual securities attractive for investment.

A recent list of the favorite holdings of registered investment clubs places Occidental Petroleum at the top, followed by IBM, Gulf & Western, Litton, RCA, GAF Corp., and General Telephone. This is an unusual list when compared with the favorites of the institutions or the Monthly Investment Plan of the New York Stock Exchange. Its makeup is very much influenced by the ideas flowing from NAIC, particularly their choice of "stock of the year."

I can see little point to a club made up entirely of newcomers to the stock market. Why they think a dozen beginners can do better as a group than individually is difficult to understand. A club made up of taxi drivers, or doctors, butchers, bakers or candlestick makers needs investment-oriented members to make it click. A somewhat better group can be composed of tyros following the lead of one successful, experienced, competent bellwether investor. There is a possibility here of both types making money and learning while doing. The best club of all is one that is weighted with a good proportion of knowledgeable investors. Here they can pool and exchange information. The junior members can learn from the experienced ones. A well-organized club can often get guest speakers to help inform and educate its members.

There is also the completely informal group that meets once a week at lunch; others meet once a month at night. These are not investment clubs. Each investor does his own investing for his own account. Such groups usually comprise knowledgeable men, leaders in various differing fields. At least half should be investment men, as a knowledge of your own business does not mean a knowledge of what developments will follow in the stock market. I think the more an investor can exchange ideas and learn what others know or are thinking, the more likely he is to make the correct decisions himself.

31 *"Do-It-for-You" Investing*

The mutual-fund performance results in recent periods have given fund investors cause for second thoughts. Many investors bought mutual funds as an "inflation hedge." Instead, the asset value of many funds depreciated at an annualized rate of 25 to 50 percent that year and the majority of mutual-fund investors placed the blame squarely on the doorstep of the professional managers. The truth is that the fault lies on several shoulders.

Investors are just as accountable for the type of individual funds they select, the time of selection, and the price they pay for them as they would be if they were buying an industrial stock. The buyer of American Telephone at 75 in 1964 saw it drop to 50 by 1966, an annualized loss in excess of 15 percent, and in mid-1970 the drop is still in progress. The decision to purchase a fund should be no less the buyers' decision than in the case of A.T.&T.

Some of the blame might be placed on overenthusiastic or improperly trained fund salesmen in cases where investors had funds sold to them instead of doing their own buying, selection, timing and pricing.

Investors have been oversold on buying short-term performance. Much of this "performance" has come from competition among the funds to buy the same stocks. They bid prices up among themselves and temporarily increased their book asset values and "performance." It is surprising that so many investors could be unrealistic enough to accept gigantic percentage gains in a single year as likely average future performance. Tabulations of fund fluctuations during downtrends in 1962, 1966, and 1969–70 should have a sobering influence on the "go-go" funds.

The majority of investors who buy funds expect their money to be "working," *i.e.* long of stocks. This is unwise but nonetheless a fact. This point of view also compounds the difficulties of fund management. Despite declines in the market, the sale of fund shares is still increasing. It will continue to increase over the years.

The experience of the recent past should be helpful in improving the management philosophy of the fund managers and the understanding of the situation by their stockholders. There is a difference between personal investment decision and having others do it for you. Professionals should do better than the average man occupied with his own business, profession or leisure. On the other hand, you must not overrate the skills of professional money managers. There are many musicians; there is only an occasional Stokowski. There are endless architects and builders, but just one Frank Lloyd Wright. Everybody thinks his or her own doctor is

117

the best and only. In reality, medical genius is equally rare. Excellence is the exception. The average of nature's endowments, mental and otherwise, is, unfortunately, low.

32 *Handling Large Sums Costs More*

There is a difference between handling large and small amounts of capital. The manager of other people's money has to deal with large sums. His flexibility is limited as compared to that of the average investor. The small investor can sell 50 shares of stock on the next sale after his order is entered. The portfolio manager controlling a large block of a stock he desires to liquidate is faced with an entirely different problem. Very possibly he also has competition from other block sellers. Another factor is the spread between the bid and offer, which is far wider in large blocks than in average round lots or odd lots. In most of the latter transactions his spread is normally in fractions, but it can be many points in the large blocks. Selling in a declining market invariably involves either taking a discount or depressing prices. The reverse is true when stocks are rising. There are, of course, those on the other side of these transactions who are buying at a discount or at concessions, and vice versa. There are occasions when both the buyer and seller of a block are simultaneously desirous of making the transaction. It is during the periods when the majority of fund managers are on the buying or selling side that the handicaps of handling big blocks are felt the most.

The fact that block transactions have been growing rapidly at the expense of individual transactions is often assumed to mean the market is broadening as a result. On the contrary, it has lost a degree of its liquidity because of the decreased number of decision makers.

A major enemy of sound investing is to allow emotions to dominate investment judgment. The investor must realize that great differences in risk and volatility exist in varying investment-policy approaches. Going up fast and coming down slowly is most exceptional. The investor must also realize that the time span for measuring results must be longer with the lack of flexibility that handling large sums entails. Five or even ten years is a fairer period of appraisal than seven months or a single year. It is unfortunate that the names and the tenure of fund managers are not given the attention they deserve. It takes a little work to see who ran what and when, and to study the record of who supplanted him. I think that many professional money managers—and there are many new, young and relatively inexperienced men at the helm today—will have learned from their 1969–70 experiences. There will be more scaling out on a rise and scaling in on a fall, and less of everyone's thinking they can slip through the same keyhole at the same instant. Less attention will be paid to computer readouts programmed to spot immediate fast moves. Any investor who bought a fund at the top of the market knew he was buying substantially the securities listed in the fund's latest published statement at something like the prices prevailing at that time. He must have felt the market was headed higher. It was unreasonable to imagine that the fund managers could or would liquidate before a fall. In the case of "investment letter" stock, they could not sell nor did they plan to do so.

Judgment on the part of professional managers may be poor for different reasons. For example, buying utility stocks and long-term bonds a few years ago was poor investment judgment. Other men with better judgment were

119

buying groups that advanced while the utilities and bonds declined. It is not in the cards to expect managers of large amounts of capital to greatly vary their equity-cash ratios. The investor must balance his personal handicaps of less knowledge, less time and opportunity against the greater costs and slower pace of the professionally run funds and accounts. He should also realize the safety in the greater diversification offered by the funds. It is true that greater safety pays its price in equally less volatile appreciation. The important factor is the point of view. Banks, savings and loan and insurance companies have substantial overhead costs. These costs have their worth to the saver and insurer. Likewise, fund costs are worth it to the investor who seeks what they offer. It is far wiser to pay these costs, if you yourself do not know what you are about, than to risk losing far more in bad investments or speculation on your own.

33 *How High? How Low?*

How low can a stock go? How high can a stock go? The answer is, there are no limits. Nobody really knows. It is vital to realize this because there are vast sums of capital, much of which is managed by inflexibly bullish professional managers. We also have very large public participation. This public receives almost wholly reassuring advice.

I am not taking the opposite position. I am only pointing out that the advice could be either right or wrong.

The greatest overvaluation, at least in dollars per share, was the Northern Pacific "corner" that occurred in May of 1901. The stock, with a market value of $110 per share, ran up to $1,000 per share against the shorts. After the runup it declined to $300. The facts of Northern Pacific's book value, earnings, dividends, and future counted for nothing at all to the man who sold short.

We have seen great overvaluations recently. People like to talk about 1929, but we can find plenty of examples in 1961, 1966 and 1968.

The lowest figure a stock can reach is just plain zero. Bundles of shares are auctioned off to establish a positive tax loss. Some of the buyers use the shares they purchase for wallpaper.

Let me tell you a true story. In 1940 I took the New York Central to Toledo, Ohio. I sold the largest investor in the city the idea of buying 10,000 Paramount Pictures stock at something over $8 a share. I told him that the company had been reorganized and was in good financial shape. I explained that earnings were rising and so were dividends. The earnings were reported at 63 cents a share for 1939. I estimated them at over $2 a share for the current year of 1940. The price/earnings ratio was just four times estimated earnings. I thought the future was bright. He gave me the order and I filled it. I returned to Manhattan. In a few months the stock had declined to 4¼. If he had wanted or needed to sell he would have lost half his capital!

How low can a stock go? Pretty low, it seems, even if the position of the company behind it is good.

I never lost confidence in Paramount. I telephoned a good friend when it was just under 5 and suggested it was very, very cheap. He gave me an order to buy the stock and I actually bought some at 4¼, starting to fill his order. He panicked and canceled the balance for fear of a further decline. It was selling at twice its estimated earnings for the year. That did not stop him from fearing to buy.

How low can sentiment go? Pretty low!

The story has a happy ending. Paramount started up from its 4¼ low. The earnings I estimated were slightly exceeded. Movies started to enjoy a boom which lasted until television and other factors began to hurt in 1946. By that time Paramount sold as high as 85.

Stocks do not always come back. Earnings estimates are not always fulfilled. This should be kept in mind when you are told that such and such a price/earnings ratio is low. The ratio can go lower if the earnings on which it is based are not achieved.

We have seen price/earnings ratios ranging upward of 50 times in recent years. We have also seen stocks advance to astronomical figures with no figurable price/earnings ratio at all because the companies in question had no earnings!

The way you can insure against costly losses in stocks is to take no facts or opinions as positive. If things don't go right, bend with the breezes. Always be in a position to buy or sell.

34 *Accumulation . . . Markup . . . Distribution*

Two very common words you rarely hear used nowadays by market students and commentators are "accumulation" and "distribution."

The classical idea of stock movements called for an "accumulation" phase in the market. This was theoretically the time that the smart investor was quietly buying. The next phase was the "markup" period with stocks going up and the news improving. Then came "distribution." This was the time when shares were supposed to pass from those that usually profit to those that usually lose. Finally came the market collapse, break, or "bear market." Mr John Magee comments on this in his 486-page book, *Technical Analysis of Stock Trends*. He says in part: "After the panic phase (which usually runs too far relative to the existing business conditions), there may be a fairly long secondary recovery or a sidewise movement and then the third phase begins. This is characterized by discouraged selling on the part of those investors who held on through the panic or, perhaps, bought during it because stocks looked cheap in comparison with prices which had ruled a few months earlier. The business news now begins to deteriorate. As the third phase proceeds, the downward movement is less rapid but is maintained by more and more distress selling from those who have to raise cash for other needs. The 'cats and dogs' may lose practically all their previous bull advance in the first two phases. Better-grade stocks decline more gradually, because their owners cling to them to the last, and the final stage of a bear market in consequence is frequently concentrated in such issues. The bear market ends when everything in the way of possible bad news, the worst to be expected, has been discounted, and it is usually over before all the bad news is out."

I think the accumulation-markup-distribution concept goes back to the time before the passage of the Securities and Exchange Act of 1934. Mr. Magee's book first appeared in 1948 but the quotation is still carried in the 1968 edition. Accumulation and distribution still go on, though the nature of the participants has changed.

The SEC legislation, among other things, was aimed at preventing "manipulation" and "pool" operations in the stock market. In the period ended in 1929–33 stock syndicates and insiders were supposed to buy low and quietly, then propel their stock upward, and finally distribute them at high prices to the unsuspecting public. It did not always work this way. The idea that "they" buy low and sell high is always believable to the man on the street. It was never quite clear even in the pre-SEC days who "they" really were. It is less clear now.

I think we are safe in applying the half-forgotten term "distribution" to what has happened in many stocks between the summer of 1967 and the spring of 1969. Certainly an enormous number of stocks passed from strong hands to weak. It is probably more correct to say that they passed from experienced hands to inexperienced, or from investment holders to speculative buyers. I say this because many buyers were far from being "weak" when it came to money. They had the wherewithal to buy, though their timing, pricing and selection seemingly was turning out to be largely incorrect.

It also used to be thought that the larger the buyer the more likely he was to be right. Thus, the very small buyers or "odd lots" were supposed to be the most likely to be wrong. Things have changed a good deal. The odd-lotters who formerly accounted for over 20 percent of the NYSE listed trading now account for less than 10 percent. One needs to change one's ideas in evaluating their transactions. Nevertheless, I think they still have some predictive value, especially when they go very much in one direction and when the volume of what they do picks up.

Another factor is the great swing toward a delegation of investment management. It makes a difference in judging the quality of buying or selling. None of us can be objective enough to act wholly without sentiment and strictly in accord with our reading of investment probabilities. We can learn more in this ideal direction when making personal decisions than when making them for others. Thinking of the score is another factor that puts most of us off our best performance. At times, some of the professional money managers become just as overwrought as odd-lotters do. This is particularly true of the hedge-fund managers, who attempt to select both stocks to sell short and stocks to buy. The same mentality can rarely be both a successful bull and a successful bear. It takes a different type of thinking.

I think it is just as essential today as it ever was to attempt to judge the position of a stock in its market cycle. Is it being accumulated? Distributed? In between?

The answer as to how to do this embraces the whole subject of how to invest. Looking at a long-term chart is one test. Has the stock in question been in a trading area at low levels for a substantial length of time? Has it been advancing sharply with increasing volume of trading for an extended period? Is it getting nowhere at high prices after a long rise? These are quick clues to the possible point of a stock in its accumulation-markup-distribution pattern.

There are others. Is the stock popular with or neglected by the funds? Is it the subject of few or many brokers' and other advisory letters?

It will pay you to look at these aspects of a stock's position and the age of a move when considering whether to buy or sell. It is important to know whether the (stock) elevator is at the basement or the roof, whether it is headed up or down and how far along the way.

35 *Supervision of Investments*

Proper supervision of your investments is vital, but how can you achieve it? The usual "supervision" is almost worse than worthless, regardless of whether it is bought or accepted as part of your broker's service.

I am writing this at a small ranch in the Sierras. My breakfast served in my room this morning consisted of freshly squeezed orange juice with the foam still on the top of the glass, a truly magnificent omelet, puffy and sweetened with sugar, flavored inside with vanilla and delicately browned outside with butter. Dutch cocoa. Jam. Properly made toast of fine fresh bread and buttered with real sweet butter.

This breakfast was good because it was properly supervised by the owner and the chef and not by a chain computer or a distant, alleged "executive" chef whose job depends on his skill at auditing rather than cooking.

Poor food and high prices get by because the majority of consumers accepts them. In the same way, poor investment supervision gets by because the majority takes it. As things stand these days, the only way to secure the supervision essential to investment success is to do, direct, and demand a little yourself.

I know of no organization that supplies it, regardless of advertising claims. But there are competent and conscientious individuals working in investment-counseling firms, in the investment departments of banks and in brokerage offices, who do accomplish it. You have to seek them out. The "name over the door" means something and I do not mean to unwittingly downgrade its importance. The particular man in the company is sometimes of even greater importance. Whether a firm employs one hundred or ten thousand, there is always a best man and a low man and every grade in between.

The practical approach to profitable supervision by most investors who must give their major attention to their own jobs is to enlist professional help, but to select it carefully and direct advisers to give them the check they require.

Stock market supervision comes first. The most neglected supervision area is your stock-cash ratio. Keep a weekly record. If the market goes up more than you expect, check to see if you own enough stocks. If the market disappoints, consider if you should sell and increase your cash. Neither you nor your advisers will ever know the top or bottom. It is impractical to expect this. It is practical to vary the percentage of your capital invested by steps as developments dictate. Doing this, you will never be caught without stocks in a bull market or without cash when stocks go down.

List all your shares. Write down their weekly closings. Spot those that are stronger or weaker than the rest. Try to check why and whether you should do something. Very often you cannot discover the reason for your stocks' actions. In such cases assume that the strong will tend to get stronger and the weak weaker.

These two checks are kindergarten but very effective.

Theoretically, your advisers or brokers will go far beyond this. They will keep a cross-index of clients by name and by stock. They will make visits to corporation plants and offices. They will program computers to alert them to a wide variety of "indications." They will study your account at regular intervals.

In practice, having a broker or adviser supervise your investments usually fails to work as well as using a checklist on your own and making queries triggered by what it shows.

The reasons are many. One reason is a human one. An adviser is certain to make mistakes and he will be affected by your reactions to them. He will be whipsawed at times. He will lose a good position. He runs the risk of being unjustly accused of ignorance, bad judgment or even bad intentions when he is blameless. This may have a negative influence on his future performance in handling your investments.

A second reason is that for individual accounts the cost is far higher than the fee. It is human to give more time to one's most valuable accounts. However, even the largest accounts cannot get the continuous supervision required unless they can arrange for it to be highly personalized.

Perhaps a third reason is the inflexibility of our thinking. We tend to think that what worked in one phase of the market will work in all phases. We are also all gaited to follow the herd instinct. It is not of great moment if we adopt a clothing style that is unsuited to us as individuals. It can be very costly if we follow the herd's investing fashions once they become too popular.

Look at the dollar and percentage losses of the funds that have led the up parade one year only to falter the next. This is proof of the difficulty of investing other people's money.

When you buy a stock you delegate to corporation management the full-time job of running your company. You must personally assume the small task of monitoring your purchases and sales, the percentage of your funds you keep invested, and the percentage you keep liquid.

Do this and you will improve on what others are supposed to do for you.

36 *Take-Home Pay for the Stockholder*

Organized labor is acutely aware of concepts such as "take-home pay," "portal to portal," "fringe benefits," "coffee-break time," "wash-up time," "paid vacations," "paid sick time," "religious holidays," "birth leave," "funeral leave," etc., etc., etc.

What about the stockholder, the investor who puts up the capital and takes the risks? Years ago his major benefit was his dividend. Bonds, mortgages and bank deposits paid interest. The ownership of income real estate paid rents. It is all summed up in the relatively obsolete word "income."

The first question a prospective stock buyer once asked was "What does it pay?" American Telephone paid $9 annually for thirty-six years and attracted more share owners than any corporation in the world.

Increasing taxation and currency depreciation have eaten into "income." What an investment pays now plays a minor role in investment appraisals. The tightness in money is placing more and more corporations in a position where they need the cash that might in the past have been available for dividends. With some exceptions, an increasing number of our corporations are strapped for cash. Most people cannot buy a home, a car, a TV, or even take a trip, without a loan. The corporations, in many cases, no longer have adequate working capital if they pay out a normal percentage of earnings in dividends.

"Growth" and "capital gain" are the popular aims of the investor today. However, many corporations manage to grow and pay at the same time. Alfred P. Sloan built General Motors into a giant corporation while paying almost 70 percent of reported profits to his stockholders in dividends.

By accepting very low income yields stockholders delegate to the managements of their properties the disposition of the cash flow and most of the corporate earnings. You need only look at the record to see that this money is not always wisely used.

If investors buy such stocks and lock them up, in many cases their net return is very low. Their stocks may go up for a time. If later they decline again the long-term investor has realized no spendable gain other than his dividends.

The investor years ago often could invest and leave the future of his investment in the hands of corporate management. The investor today more often needs to be an astute buyer and seller of stocks. He is not buying into a company. He is buying to resell at a profit. This policy requires very rare skills.

A good example is the action of Sperry Rand between 1956 and 1966. It sold at 20 in both years. The dividend yield for the period 1956–1960 averaged a shade over 3 percent. Between 1961 and 1966 no dividend was paid. The stockholder who sat with his shares for ten years had a very poor investment. The stock trader who bought and sold at intervals had three or four excellent opportunities to make a substantial profit. The range of prices in the ten-year period was 35 high in 1961 and 10½ low in 1962. After 1966 the situation changed, and the holder of Sperry since then has done very well by staying with the stock, even though his dividend return averaged less than 1 percent most of the time.

The difficulty comes because none of us really can forecast in advance the best stocks to own over a ten-year period. For example, the Arthur Wiesenberger Services have a table giving the percentage changes in the Dow-Jones industrial stocks from December 31, 1958, to December 31, 1968. Chrysler leads the list up 400 percent; U.S. Steel turned in the poorest showing at minus 56 percent. There were very unsatisfactory results from such prominent blue chips as Union Carbide, Aluminum Company, and Allied Chemical. Investor favorites such as DuPont, American Telephone, Standard Oil of New Jersey and General Electric were all in the second half of the list, performance-wise.

The situation is constantly changing. The rise in Chrysler, for example, between 1962 and 1964 was meteoric. In 1968 it made a high of 72¾; it backed down below 40 in 1969, and was under 20 in July 1970.

One of the reasons for the great growth in funds and delegation of investment management is the need to put this buying, selling and switching into full-time professional hands.

Experience has shown that this is not always the best solution. Funds start small. If they achieve exceptionally good records they attract large amounts of capital. They lose flexibility and their performance suffers. Other variables include management changes, management aging and, above all, the fixed investment philosophies held by most of us, professionals included. The constant pessimist is right occasionally when the market goes down. Those that believe in growth stocks are right in the periods when growth stocks are popular.

The successful investor will greatly benefit by supplementing meager corporation dividends with regularly realized capital gains.

I favor an annual cashing in of a set percentage of the value of your stocks. Use half of this to supplement your

131

other income and pay your taxes. (Compound interest tables look exciting, especially as none make provisions for any taxes or dollar depreciation. None includes a footnote that the tennis racket you did not buy when your heart was strong will have no value to you when your savings period comes to an end.) Use the other half to provide purchasing power when the next good opportunity comes along. The exact percentage liquidated will vary widely with different conditions. Twenty percent might be a practical figure to use as a starting point in estimating your best amount.

This policy will have many incidental benefits. If taxes increase, you will have cashed in some profits at a lower rate. If prices advance, you will have bought some of the things you wanted at a lower figure. All of us can enjoy many things at one age that we cannot enjoy as we get older or if our health fails. So spend a little.

Investmentwise you should keep your account up to date and improve your investment performance.

37 *How to Take Advice*

Every investor is flooded with ideas for investment. How many depends on how much time he gives each day to reading and listening.

If you read the financial pages, subscribe to financial magazines and investment services, talk to your broker or investment adviser and exchange ideas with your friends, you have a real problem of screening the wheat from the chaff. How well you succeed in doing this is a major factor in determining the success of your entire investment program.

The way to begin is to set up your own investment policy. Write down the total dollar amount you will employ when you are most optimistic. Write down the maximum cash or equivalent you will husband when you are most pessimistic. Write down your current position. This will tell you how much you have to invest in something new, or whether you need to sell and switch if a new idea appeals to you. (If you succeed in cutting your account down to your minimum when you are bearish you will be doing better than most professionals.)

You should also decide on your diversification policy. How many stocks do you want to own? What percentage of your capital should be in each? The range of opinion and policy in these matters is exceedingly wide. You should do much better if you make a plan than if you leave it to chance. One investor I know has about $100,000 for investment in stocks. His policy calls for 90 percent invested in stocks at maximum and 50 percent at minimum. He never really gets optimistic enough to go the whole way or, if he does it is a rare occurrence and not for long. He plans on a 10 percent initial investment in each of eight quality stocks and 5 percent in each of four speculative issues. He never lets the total speculative shares exceed 20 percent of his total capital.

This is how he starts. As times goes on the percentages will vary. A very successful buy will result in making the market value of one of his initial 10 percent investments mount to 20 percent of his total or more. He will have to decide whether to let it alone or cut it back to size. A courageous speculator might increase the position even more if he were the type who believed in enlarging successes and cutting down mistakes.

I am not giving these ideas as a formula, but only as an

example. Each investor must chart his own position limits and policies to best fit his own needs.

You cannot buy every purchase suggestion, even if you limit your selections to just one source. You are forced to pick and choose. It is vital for you to realize this. You should select the occasional idea that strikes you as interesting. Then look it up, check it and make up your mind whether you are sold on the idea of buying.

The next step is to see how it fits into your current market policy. Is your policy to increase your holdings? Can you pay for an additional stock or will you need to switch out of something you already own? How long do you estimate it will take to work out? If it is over six months, what do you think market conditions will look like at that time?

The important thing is never to buy solely on someone else's suggestion. It can pay to listen, analyze, check and consider. The decision must be yours.

I assume you are astute enough to pay no attention to any but the best advice from the best sources. I am taking it for granted that you turn a deaf ear to the self-seeking with an ax to grind and to the uninformed. If you cannot do this or cannot get really honest and able assistance you should not undertake investing for yourself. Better to put half your funds blindly in U.S. Government securities and half in the best-quality investment companies. This way you should have peace of mind and run the minimum risks to your savings.

You must understand how rare it is to be advised if a situation changes for the worse. It is against human nature to admit a mistake. People keep hoping things will turn out all right in the long run. While they wait, most often conditions get worse, and this increases the reluctance of a counselor or broker to advise taking what may now be a substantial loss. Even when properly advised, it is just as hard for an investor to accept the idea of selling at a substantial loss.

An article in a paper or a suggestion in a speech cannot be publicly corrected in any practical way. Take it as being meant when it was given. The situation can change for the better or worse with you none the wiser.

Many years ago one of the most successful investors I ever knew employed a mining engineer to advise him about mining stocks. He had a regular monthly meeting with the engineer and telephone privileges in between. This engineer personally visited many mines. He also lunched at the Engineer's Club where he exchanged views with his fellow engineer friends. His information and opinion was many times more valuable than that of an analyst covering mining securities. At one meeting he gave his client twelve mining stocks to buy. It took my investor friend and myself two full hours to pull this list apart and get down to the one issue that looked best to him and to us. We had to go to Seattle to buy this issue and accumulate a line slowly. It was worth it. It outperformed any other issue on his list and did very much better than the average of the twelve.

None of us can buy everything. The process of elimination is vital to a practical approach.

I look into other people's ideas. I check them out on my own as I suggest here. If they work and I profit, I thank the source if it is an individual. If they fail to work out I never ask any questions. And, of course, there are never any recriminations. If the party who made the suggestion brings it up, I pass it off by saying I forgot, or sold it right out, or did not buy it in the first place. Acting this way will keep the paths open for profitable ideas in the future.

38 *Investment and Speculation**

The investor who thinks the market fluctuations of his investments are not of interest to him because he is buying solely for income can very well be compared with the ostrich burying his head in the ground during danger and feeling himself secure.

The truth of the matter is that everything we do in this world is a speculation, whether we regard it as such or not, and the man who comes out in the open and uses his judgment to forecast the probable course of events, and then acts on it, is the one to reap the returns of his endeavor.

There is a peculiar psychology that makes many investors avoid certain sound stocks or bonds because their broker speaks of "speculative possibilities." These investors judge safety by yield. If a security pays over 6 percent it is classed as "speculative," and is not for them. What security is not speculative? U.S.A. Liberty first 3½'s, as good a bond as was ever issued, declined from 102½ in 1918 to 86 in 1921. A purchaser of ten of these prime bonds at the higher price had a so-called "paper" loss of $1,650 with the bonds at 86. If for any reason he had to liquidate, his "paper" loss became a real one. To this could logically be added a loss in income over higher coupon rate bonds, suffered for a better degree of safety he never secured.

* Written and published November 17th, 1922. This dissertation seemed as new to me when I wrote it as many similar pieces appearing today appear "new." Mine was not "new" in 1922 any more than the thoughts we have today are "new." Investment fashions move in a cycle, as any other fashions do. In time they always come full circle. Today's "growth" cult will in time be supplanted by a "safety and income" cult. This in time will be supplanted by another, and another, and another. The real key to keeping, and hopefully increasing, capital is to attempt to anticipate tomorrow's fashion today.—G.M.L.

What is the solution of the problem of investing primarily for income and yet retaining the very important and useful quality of ready marketability without loss? It is best solved by never making an investment that does not appear, after investigation, to be an equally good speculation.

Of course there is no guarantee that what looks to be both a good speculation and a safe investment may not turn out a disappointment, but it is sound logic that the more thought and investigation given a subject, the greater the probabilities of success.

Another point often raised is, "Can the man of limited means afford to speculate?" The reply to that question depends on what is inferred by the word "speculate." If one means to buy rapidly fluctuating stocks on margin in the hope of getting aboard the right one, the answer is emphatically "No!" But if one's idea of speculation is the right one —that is, to buy sound stocks for cash after a careful study of factors apt to affect their future prices, it is certainly good policy. Indeed, no man ever waxed wealthy without speculating in something. It is always those who already have their pile who are conservative and can well afford to be.

There is no such thing as something for nothing. Those who come to Wall Street with visions of easy money are apt to leave it sadder, if not wiser. We get out of things what we put into them, and brains and money used in an honest effort to secure reasonable income on profits in the stock market generally receive a just reward.

39 *Inflation Fallacies*

The worst way to combat inflation is to buy something as a supposed "hedge" at an inflated price.

Consider equities (common stocks) versus fixed-dollar obligations (cash or near equivalent such as short-term bonds, commercial paper, checking accounts). As a matter of investment policy I have always advised investment for profit and to avoid loss. This means equities for profit and 91-day U.S. Treasury bills to avoid loss. It means relegating consideration of "income" to its proper minor status. This does not mean buying stocks of any kind at any time for any price to avoid dollar depreciation.

It is true that currencies universally lose purchasing power at varying rates and with few general reversals. Franz Pick, publisher of *Pick's World Currency Report,* places the value of the American dollar, as of December 30, 1968, at approximately 39.4 cents based on 1940 equaling 100. This is a depreciation of about 60.6 percent. The dollar is still losing value in 1970. It is Dr. Pick's contention that these figures, which are "official," are not really factual, and that a 35-cent dollar would be nearer to the truth. The figure is lower now.

If you invest in liquid short-term interest-paying dollars, the chances are that you will lose a little net. The interest you receive, minus the tax you pay, and adjusted for the loss in purchasing power of your principal, may show you a small minus yield. The important point is that the loss is small. Depending on your tax bracket, it might be 1 percent or so a year. The loss in the stock market can be very high. It is important to realize that inflation of wages and costs in many cases can mean deflation in profits.

The lesson you can draw from this is to make haste slowly. It is better to slowly lose some purchasing power from holding cash or equivalent than to lose a great deal of capital quickly through careless "hedging." You cannot buy stocks when you think the opportunity is greatest unless you have the funds available.

Years ago my firm hired a leading economist to talk to the partners once a month on the stock market. At his first talk he said he was very bullish and he felt investors should be fully invested. This meant 100 percent to the investor who used only cash, and more to the one who borrowed money as well. A couple of months later, with the market down sharply, he told us his viewpoint had not changed, and he advised investors who followed his views to double up. He did not tell us where we could find the additional funds. It is a mistake to be afraid of having cash. I never believe in being without purchasing power. I always want to be in a position to buy or sell, not just sell or hold. Stock investments must be made on their individual merits and not on any generality that they are supposedly a good hedge against inflation.

40 *Losses*

I am a great believer in cutting losses short and in attempting to keep unrealized profits from turning into losses. This requires constant checking. Professional investors have mechanical ways of going about it. You can prevent heavy losses and prevent your account from getting into a frozen position by doing two things.

First, if the market disappoints you and goes contrary

to your expectations, sell a proportion of your stock. Second, if an individual stock seems weaker than the rest, check it out to your satisfaction or liquidate it. The quick loss and small loss is always the best. Remember, the real reasons for a decline in price are rarely visible when a stock starts to display weakness. They usually do not show up until it is too late.

If you have overstayed your market and find yourself with more stocks and less cash than you would like, the decision to get things in proper shape is considerably more difficult. The same thing is true if you wake up owning the wrong stocks in a big decline.

There is no standard answer to such situations. If I were pushed into a general rule, I would say that I think you will be better off liquidating when in doubt. I might express this another way by saying that if the situation isn't strong enough to suggest a fresh purchase, then you certainly should liquidate. You may be "whipsawed" now and then, but in the long run it should pay off.

Buying more of something that has started badly is known as "averaging." Most times this will prove an unprofitable thing to do.

The important attitude to develop is objectivity. Try to forget you own stock in question. Try to forget you have a loss. Look at it as if it were a stranger and you were thinking of whether it rated an initial purchase. If so, maybe you are justified in holding. If not, take your loss. Get the idea out of your head that you must recover your loss in the same issue that caused it. The surest and quickest way to make a comeback is in the stocks of tomorrow, not those of yesterday. Once an issue has blown its top it usually is a long time dead.

If you are unfortunate enough to lose 50 points in a stock,

don't think you have to try to make 50 points back in another single transaction. You are usually more likely to succeed in attempting a series of trades. Big winners are few and far between and difficult to spot.

Investment considerations should always take precedence over tax considerations. A short-term loss (less than six months) is worth more than a long-term loss and is likely to be smaller. A short-term loss is also more valuable if you can match it with a short-term profit. Do not, however, take the profit just to match your loss. Take it only if it seems good investment strategy to do so. Otherwise you may lose a valuable position in one of your best stocks.

Never wait till December to take tax losses. It is generally the very worst time of year to do it. Watch your list every month. December is sometimes a good month to look for good buys among stocks sold for tax reasons by investors who left it to the last minute.

Investment motives must always govern. There can be no inviolable rule against anything. I just bought a stock for the first time at 34, down from a high above 60. It has been declining for over a year and a half. A new management passed the dividend a few days ago and estimated losses for their current fiscal year of almost $20,000,000. Now if you owned this stock at a loss, and held the same optimistic current view as I hold, here would be the rare case where you would average rather than liquidate. That is why I say, apply the principle of selling if you would not be a current buyer with your cash. If you would be a buyer, then it is the isolated case that is the exception to the rule.

A hasty guide to rallying or turn-around possibilities in stocks in which you have a loss is to measure the degree of loss against that in comparable issues. Those that are down more than the average probably will stay down for a long time to come. Those that are down the least will tend to have the sharpest rebound.

One never can buy to real advantage unless stocks decline. Low prices are of no value unless you have the buying power to take advantage of them. There is another factor here that you are apt to overlook. That is what you plan to do with the proceeds from the sale of an unsatisfactory holding. Sticking with a declining stock can cost you double if it declines further and if it keeps you from buying another share that is advancing.

The important thing to do is to lay out your investment plans as if you owned no stocks at all and only had capital to invest. Make up your mind what percentage of your funds you would commit to equities and how much you would put aside in cash or equivalent reserve. Make up your mind what stocks you would buy under such circumstances. Then, prune and shift your present portfolio to fit your current ideal. Putting the spotlight on your failures is one of the surest ways of achieving overall investment success.

41 *Varied Investment Aims Do Not Always Need Different Stock Investments*

Read these three letters which are so typical of the way many investors look at investment problems.

"Dear Mr. Loeb:
I am a widow, 60 years old, and will never be able to earn any more money. I must protect my money and keep

it safe, and still have enough income to support myself. What can you suggest as an absolutely safe investment with the highest possible income return?"

"Dear Mr. Loeb:
I have several thousand dollars, some inherited and some received as a gift from my parents, and want to increase it as much as I can. I am a young man, and while my present earnings are still small they are enough to care for my needs. I want to speculate for capital gains and profits. Investment income is not important. What can you suggest that will make me the most money? I am willing to chance losing what I have."

"Dear Mr. Loeb:
I want some well-rounded 'businessman's risk investments.' I am in my forties, own my own business, and can afford to take some risk. Can you give me a list of good stocks that pay a moderate income and are likely to advance?"

The widow expects safety and income but no profit. The young man expects profits and is willing to risk his entire capital. The business man wants some profit, some income, and will take some risk.

Investment aims cannot be achieved so easily. Too many feel, incorrectly, that bonds or other interest-paying obligations are safe and suitable for the widow; nondividend-paying stocks would fit the needs of the young man; blue chip dividend-paying stocks for the businessman.

For most purposes and people, safe, profitable and intelligent investments are very much the same, regardless of varying aims. I am talking about those who seek advice

143

from reputable advisers among bankers, investment counselors, lawyers or New York Stock Exchange members. Obviously, this point of view doesn't apply to newly issued stock of a high-risk nature. Neither does it apply to the use of borrowed money or highly leveraged media such as warrants, or putting all your eggs in one basket. These techniques are for those qualified to venture on their own.

42 *Designed for Profit*

Safe investment must be designed to show a profit, whether this aim succeeds or not. Only by trying your best to make more can you hope to succeed in minimizing losses.

To succeed, you must learn two vital things. (1) To correctly define risk; (2) To know the real meaning of that constantly misused word "income."

Risk is ordinarily thought of as the risk in a possible decline in the market price of the security—either stock or bond—that you buy. To select the right type and kind of security, you must check it against the hazards involved. These include unfavorable changes in money and credit conditions, decreases in earning power and interest or dividend-paying ability, unfavorable new taxes, and changes in the purchasing power of the dollar, up or down.

The investor who bought U.S. Treasury 3½% bonds years ago at par (100) and sees them selling under 70 did not properly rate all the risks involved. The U.S. bonds were "safe" inasmuch as their interest was paid. They went down because interest rates, taxes, and the cost of living increased. The buyer enjoyed no "income" at all, but a net loss.

It may appear to be repetitious, but it bears repeating that the net real "income" is the interest or dividends paid by any investment, net, after deduction of taxes, increased or decreased by the gain or loss after tax adjustment in the market value of the security purchased, with the final net figure adjusted to the cost of living. Any other formula is a delusion and a fraud.

An investor in a stock not paying anything at the time the 3½ % bonds sold at 100 might have enjoyed a real net gain over the same period our deluded investor thought he was getting 3½ % "income." "Income" does not need to come from interest or dividends. True income is the excess of what you have overall, above the total of what you put in, adjusted for changes in money value. Thus, what the widow thinks (or is told) is safe may be just the opposite. There are plenty of good speculations involving risk for young men, without risking "all." The businessman is more rational than the others in his request, especially if you change "moderate income" to read "small dividends."

Investment should never be aimed at "income." You make what appears the best possible investments. You draw down what you can afford. This might be dividends or interest. It might be a portion of gains, realized or unrealized. It might be a portion of capital.

The difference in treatment for different needs is more a matter of how much you draw down from the account. The widow supplements her dividends or interest by selling a few shares or bonds each year. The young man reinvests his dividends. The businessman uses his dividends but otherwise leaves the account alone.

An investment should be calculated on a "pocket-to-pocket" basis. You take your money out of your pocket. You get money back in dividends or interest, and the capital gain or loss when you sell out. You pay your taxes. What you have left is what you have made or lost, making proper allowance for changes up or down in the cost of things. This is the real "income" from your investment.

43 *Women Investors*

Women today have a cigarette made just for them, says an ad on TV. When they travel in many cities, a major hotel chain offers them a specially "feminized" room.

For years the ratio of male to female shareowners shows that the female shareowners exceed the male by 51 percent to 49 percent. The latest New York Stock Exchange estimate suggests that there are almost 13,500,000 women stockowners. The only place men come out on top in these statistics is that about three out of four orders are placed by the men. My own experience suggests that almost all orders are entered by men.

Do women who speculate in Wall Street show any difference in attitude or capability than men? Do they worry more? Are they greedier? Are they more prone to hold on to losers? These and other such questions come in to me very often. No scientific study of the subject has ever been made. My own experience dates back to 1921, when I met my first lady investor.

Quite a few books have been published specifically for the woman investor. An old one that I rather liked when it was published in 1956 is entitled *How to Be a Woman of Property,* by Harriet Gardner Palmer (Henry Holt & Company, New York). When I read a book I always mark helpful passages and put the page numbers on the rear cover. In this case I scribbled eighteen references.

Miss Palmer admits that women need to develop some masculine traits for successful investment, but finds women endowed with many natural aptitudes. These include an uncanny flair for appraising human beings, a natural amateur-detective talent of no small prowess, a typical feminine sense of order, and the ability to get to the real root of a problem through mazes of detail. Miss Palmer realizes the elements of style and fashion that govern many security prices, and thinks that women who are alert to style changes can become similarly trained to look for changing fashions in securities.

There are exceptions to any statement, but be that as it may, in this instance I must agree with Professor Higgins: "Why can't a woman be more like a man?"

Fortunately, most women have men do their investing for them. When they do it themselves, their approach to their adviser varies with their individual natures. Almost none comes in and states her problem briefly and frankly. Some feel they must appear "ignorant," others "feminine." There are those who attempt to be "fascinating." But hardly any are simply businesslike.

Rarely have I found them as capable as men when it comes to investing, primarily because their interests lie elsewhere. There are a very limited number who devote a major part of their time to stock market problems. A few of these are very astute. There are female security analysts and even women partners or stockholders in member firms.

Women certainly worry more than men. Perhaps this is because they are more anxious to get the utmost profit and more reluctant to take a loss. Unfortunately, such aims are rarely achieved in stock investing and trading. A top-quality investment fund can often be the best solution for women investors. It requires careful selection, but once this has been correctly done a woman can turn her attention to other interests and have peace of mind. If their capital is of sufficient size, they can employ the investment management department of their bank, or a top-flight investment counselor. The First National City Bank has a regular investment advisory service for accounts as small as $25,000. A really able stockbroker with a New York Stock Exchange member firm can help.

Women love to clip coupons and cash dividend checks. To most women, stocks are "gambling" and bonds or bank accounts are "safe." True, stocks advance and decline much more precipitously than bonds, but over the long run they do better. Losses in "safe" high-grade investment bonds have been substantial in recent years in both purchasing power and price.

Judging from my experience, there are very few women emotionally able to take the objective view needed to speculate successfully. Be that as it may, I hasten to say that any advice heretofore given the men applies equally to women, and more power to them!

44 *The Averages Attempt to Mirror the Movement of Stock Prices*

The Dow-Jones averages are as old and out of date as the 20th Century Limited despite the change of name of the "rail" average to "transportation." Unlike that famous train, now deceased, the Dow-Jones averages still retain their popularity.

Averages are used extensively by investors in an attempt to trace the current course of the market. Averages other than the Dow are growing in importance. Fewer traders follow the "Dow Theory" (which is based on the action of the Dow industrial and transportation averages), in the hope that it will guide them to the future course of the market. Newer forecasting methods using averages are constantly being developed. The most modern use of averages is to measure "performance" and to set management fees.

In addition to the Dow, many other averages and indexes have been calculated in an attempt to mirror the movement of stock prices. With well over 50,000 publicly held and quoted stocks—some going up, some going down, some marking time, and some not traded at all—this really cannot be done. The tops and bottoms for individual issues are reached at different times, often months apart from the highest and lowest average or index figures. The volatility of different issues varies enormously.

Some of the better-known averages other than the Dow include Standard and Poor's 500, the New York Stock Exchange index, the American Stock Exchange averages, and the National Quotation Bureau's over-the-counter index. In addition, there are readily available figures on the movements of high-grade stocks, low-prices shares, glamour stocks and industry groups.

In the mutual-fund field, figures are supplied by the Arthur Lipper Corporation and by *Fundscope* magazine. The latter uses many classifications for ranking funds including categories such as "Performance," "Diversified Growth," "Specialized Growth," "Income," ad infinitum.

A chief objection to the Dow as a measure of what the market is doing at any particular time is its high figure, many times higher than the price of the average stock. This exaggerates market movements. Experienced investors ignore the dramatic price changes of the Dow industrials. They look at the more realistic percentage changes or at averages closer to the price of the average share of stock.

There are a host of different methods that use averages to attempt to forecast future price trends. The prime object of any mechanistic method of forecasting the stock market is that its "signal" shall be consistently correct. It must be given sufficiently in advance so its followers can act profitably and ahead of the other fellow. Some of these methods are modifications of the Dow theory. Others relate to trend lines, divergence, support and supply levels, in almost endless variety.

When averages are used to measure results, either to check performance or to set fees, great care must be taken. The conclusions can be very misleading. There are both funds and investment counselors that use the S.&P. 500 as a yardstick against a portfolio many times as volatile. When the market favors speculative issues, their performance supposedly far exceeds the average used. What the figures do not tell until the market turns down is the higher risk involved. Some even compare a leveraged and possibly hedged fund with the unleveraged and unhedged averages.

Using the popular averages will roughly tell you whether the market climate is bullish or bearish, but little more. Using them as a means of forecasting is another matter. Some methods have merit but only as part of a broad approach to the subject. You must realize that the more popular any particular method becomes, the more it loses its effectiveness. It is vital to match the type of securities in your portfolio with the specific average you select to measure your results.

Where you should focus your attention is on the changing price levels and trends of your own securities. Watching these closely can, in a practical way, improve your investment results. Get yourself into the habit of keeping a written record of weekly prices and trading volume. The figures will very soon begin to give you a meaningful message. Without any "formula," "theory" or "method," you will not fail to see that some stocks act better than others. You will also note unusual changes in activity as well as price. Use these simple "signals" to ask your broker or investment adviser to ferret out the explanation of unusual action, whether good or bad. In some cases, it will lead you to liquidate or increase a position.

The dollars-and-cents value of this checking is high. Leave the averages and the mechanistic theories to someone else, and concentrate on just watching what you own or contemplate owning.

45 *Profit Goals*

"Six percent and safety" used to be a popular goal for investors. It could rarely be achieved. Recently, security buyers were talking of 60 percent returns, and various goals below and above. If such and such a fund can do it, why can't I? Or at least why can't my fund, bank, investment counselor or broker do it for me?

The answer is that these fantastically high percentages are like skyrockets—and we all know that skyrockets come screaming down as well as shooting up.

Investment success must be measured in three dimensions: risk, reward, consistency. The one-year performance figures mean little. Some are due to special conditions. Others are due to windfalls. For example, it is important to note that some of the best-performing funds of 1967 became the worst performers of 1968. Many became still worse performers in 1969–70.

In the same way the largest gainers among stock groups in 1967 dropped considerably down the list of 1968 leaders. Among the funds, those which own bank and insurance issues exclusively did very well in 1968. Savings-and-loan stocks and the fire- and casualty-insurance shares were right at the top of the group performance lists of 1968. The importance of consistency is easily brought out by looking back a few years. These two groups had very poor records then. They were poor performers again in 1969–70. Unless you were smart enough to switch into and out of many leaders at the right time, your average percentage return would be disappointing indeed.

There are also changing fashions in stock categories. Sometimes it is growth stocks. At others, income groups, defensive blue chips, tax-sheltered issues, or counter-trend shares such as golds take the spotlight.

The mania for high performance stimulated the rate of portfolio turnover. Mutual fund turnover was said to be over 40 percent recently. Aggressive speculators look upon this rate as the minimum. Anything less, as they see it, is neglect. They think that more is desirable. It is an open question whether high turnover is profitable. Taxes, brokerage commissions and the spreads between bids and offers take their toll. Human inability to catch all the ups and downs, and switching of interest between issues, hurts even more.

Investment policy has long aimed both at owning the right stocks and varying the amount invested in them and in defensive situations. A very small minority of professionals go further and endeavor to be on the offensive by selling short when stocks go down. Performance goals are stimulating an increasing number of investors to look at the short side.

Professionally, this can be noted by the rapid growth in the number of hedge funds. "Hedge" means, among other things, to offset longs with a percentage of shorts. Expertly done, it works out well. Most investors are not experts. Simply devoting full time as a professional does not, of itself, make an expert. As Jacques Coe says, many hedge funds just give one the chance to be wrong twice.

Investors subscribe to many advisory services. There are possibly 200 to 300 available. Those services that suggest short sales are still few, but their number is growing. The "D.S." stock market forecast, published by Walter Heiby at his Institute of Dynamic Synthesis in Chicago, includes a weekly "market time clock." The clock can swing from 100 percent long to 100 percent short. Should the signals given by the system become exceedingly one-sided, an investor following this system might, for example, keep long 60 percent of his capital in selected common stocks. The 40 percent defensive would not be held in cash or bills, but used to sell short a different list of hopefully weak issues in a declining trend.

We all should desire to secure the best use of our savings. It is almost a must with the rising cost of living. Treading water these days means slow drowning. It is important to weigh carefully the chances of success and not be influenced by the need to achieve it. There are times when it is better to be safe at the cost of losing a little than to risk a lot to attempt the unattainable. I have found over the years that the time to worry is when stocks are at historically high levels, investors are unanimously optimistic, and everything seems wonderful.

153

All of the techniques described here as gaining in use are as old as the hills. Some have real merit when practiced by the right hands at the right times. They can be disastrous otherwise.

High-grade bonds have returned an income in excess of 8 percent. The common stocks of our leading blue chip corporations pay dividends that promise to yield about 4.40 percent. Long-term studies of total returns, income and profit, from common stocks suggest an average over the years of about 9 percent. The point to remember is that in periods where returns have been extraordinarily high, the chances favor rough weather ahead to bring the results over the years back down to the average. This may not sound like a very profound reason to be cautious, but I think it will prove to be a very practical one.

I have long counseled high goals. I have never favored buying for a small return. Any security that does not seem to be a good speculation may turn out a poor investment. Those who bought long-term high-grade bonds over the years have discovered that. The essential point often missed in aiming high is that if the goal does not seem clear—don't shoot. Invest when the opportunities seem large and clear and considerably greater than the apparent risks. Otherwise, keep your ammunition dry.

46 *Planning for Retirement*

Social Security taxes and benefits have been increased many times since the start of the program. The Securities and Exchange Commission registrations of new promotions include many new offerings of stock in nursing home, retirement village, and total-care apartment ventures. The insurance and mutual fund people are on their toes with plans to help the elderly. Retirement today, and that of a decade or more ago, are quite different matters. The retirement age has been dropping, and the span of life increasing.

In past years, when income taxes were low or did not exist at all, people planned and saved for their old age. Income taxes have changed all that and have made pension plans, Medicare and the like popular substitutes.

Government welfare is not "free," though part of its popularity stems from the majority thinking that others are bearing more of their burden. Government administration always costs more than private or personal administration. The more we do things of this nature for ourselves, the less is lost in overhead and red tape. I do not think young people can plan intelligently far ahead for retirement. There is no way of foreseeing how you will feel about many things ten or twenty years from now.

I have seen people save all their lives for "a great big beautiful tomorrow," yet never find themselves in a position to cash in. It might be their health that is the obstacle, or it might be something financial such as depreciation in the value of the dollars they put aside.

I feel it is important to "retire" as you go along, and allot a sensible portion of your time and money to travel, indulgence in hobbies, and relaxation that too many successful people postpone until after sixty-five.

When the official time really approaches, start off by outlining your objectives. Do you really want to take it easy? Or is that not in your nature? If you want to leave all your financial cares behind you, arrange your investments so that the decisions are delegated to others. Under no circumstances should you arrange any retirement investments where the common stock portion falls under 50 percent. Most retirement pay and benefits are in fixed-dollar amounts. Fortunately this is changing rapidly. As time goes on, retirement benefits will be tied increasingly to dollar purchasing power. Failing that, it is better to take the ups and downs of equity investment, to a degree, than to tie yourself completely into fixed-dollar investments. Bear in mind that the risks of a further rise in the cost of living are too great to ignore.

Depending on the amounts involved, your common stock program can be taken care of by mutual funds or by an account of your own run by an investment counselor or bank advisory service. If you need to provide for dependents after death, your stock program can take the form of a personal trust, or if the amount involved is less than six figures it can be a bank discretionary common trust fund. The greatest peace of mind will probably come from participation in a mutual fund or investment trust because here everything is done for you without your involvement.

If you are not the type to take it easy, then you may want to run your own investments or part of them. Here it is important to stop and give yourself a realistic self-appraisal. Is your decision-making ability up to par? How is your courage? Can you afford the risk? Many people interested in investing never find the time required to devote to the market during their active business lives. However, they find both pleasure and profit in the market after retirement, when they are able to give their investments the attention they deserve.

The usual advice to retirees is to upgrade the quality of their stocks as their age increases. They are also sure to be told to lay more stress on income and less on capital gains. I don't feel that advice of this kind should be so general.

You could be the type who derives mental stimulation and satisfaction from the challenge of trying to make a profit. If you need more spendable funds after retirement, they do not necessarily have to come from dividends or interest. Cash can be secured from capital gains or from liquidating by degrees a safe amount of principal.

We all seem to live in the fear that our savings will not prove to be enough to see us through. The cost of illness has increased by leaps and bounds since Government welfare plans have come into being. One advantage of Medicare, although a costly one, is that fears of this kind are reduced.

A safe plan is to check your expectancy of life in a good modern table. If you double the number of years of your theoretical life expectancy, you can safely invade your capital by that amount. Thus, if you have an expectancy of ten years and want to spend more than your income, you are safe in using 1/20 of your capital.

When you are on the brink of retirement, be sure to check your tax situation. You should understand the relationship between the capital-gains tax, the inheritance and the gift tax. If your estate-tax bracket is high, you should estimate the proportion of capital expenditures that will be borne by your heirs and by Uncle Sam.

Don't be overly concerned about your young heirs. Usually more harm than good can be done by leaving funds unearned by the recipient. Above all, think twice before you are talked into making gifts to reduce inheritance taxes. My advice is to keep your capital and your peace of mind! Another pitfall is to try and skip a generation and a tax by leaving capital to a younger generation, and only income to the older.

The need for life insurance varies and, in some cases, is mandatory. However, investigate straight term life. Insur-

157

ance that combines life with investment or endowment is costly and, except for a few very modern policies, provides no inflation protection. Group policies usually cost less than individual policies. Variable annuities are worth investigating.

Private old-age plans involving the purchase of homes or apartments or services, or a combination, are partly insurance plans. The safety and ability to make good are just as important as choosing a top-quality insurance company. If you are not satisfied on that score, it is better to make your investments and pay as you go. Here, your lawyer and banker are musts.

You have a need to hedge against deflation as well as inflation. The safest investments right now are United States Treasury bills. They offer more safety and liquidity than savings banks or savings-and-loan concerns. At this writing, they also offer more income.

The two basic decisions you will have to make are personal and financial. Personally, you should know how you want to spend your time. Financially, you must decide whether your profit-making days are over and your spending days begun, or whether you still want to improve your financial score. Above all, be sure that your emotional, physical and mental capabilities fit the course you plan to pursue.

47 Markets Have Their Phases

Markets have their phases as man has his ages.

In the first or early phase of a market advance, it is natural to find investors cautious. They recall losses in the previous decline.

The second phase occurs when the market has advanced long enough and far enough to change their minds. This is the phase where "everybody" seemingly profits. Stocks go up. Investors are not afraid to buy them. In fact, as they start buying again, and see the shares they buy advance, they are encouraged to buy more. Their friends are also doing well. The financial news is encouraging.

The third phase is when the market seems "high" and some profit taking develops. After this, the trouble starts. Now stocks keep advancing. Many investors find themselves "sold-out bulls."

As the market goes higher and higher they tend to buy back in. The current financial news on earnings or dividends is good and seems to justify the higher price levels. In each bull market, varying ideas gain popular acceptance. Recently these included a belief in "inflation" and the merits of compounded, far-above-average growth.

A few issues advance in a sensational way and attract some of the growing traders who at these times may go short.

When the first phase of the decline begins, it is obscure and only in a few issues. It takes time to affect a majority of stocks. The volatile shares with overlarge short interests keep going up and obscure the attrition in the main body of the market.

Finally the declines gain enough breadth and momentum to make front-page news. Now investors' losses are already substantial. The news still looks good. Investors may buy more to "average" and look for what they think are bargains. The troubles that are fundamentally the cause of the decline are beginning to get publicity.

The question then is how distant is the bottom and at what price level? No one really knows. It depends on such things as the future of taxes and profits and the availability and cost of money. It can be at current levels or higher or lower. Furthermore, the shape of the next important recovery and the issues that will lead it cannot be foretold. In 1930 it took years before the picture improved. In 1962 the turn came very quickly. The odds in favor of correct market policy are higher with decisions made at the time of the upturn than with attempted forecasts before the conditions on which they are based are known.

I write here of "investors' " actions and psychology. What about the investors who took the opposite view from the majority opinion or prevailing viewpoint? For every investor who buys or sells there must be another doing the opposite in order to consummate the transaction. The only answer I have been able to supply is that the "investor" who is talked and written about is the one who is taking the initiative.

What it all comes down to is that successful investing requires a flair, based on complete objectivity toward the task at hand and coupled with an understanding of human psychology. It presupposes a David Harum brand of horse sense, a natural quickness, and an originality of thinking that always remains logical. Among the most baffling problems that security owners must understand and cope with is the ever-changing variation between the time something happens and the time that this happening is reflected in the price of a company's stock. A price adustment sometimes happens ahead of time in anticipation of the news, sometimes afterwards, but practically never at the time of occurrence. These time and price factors form an ever-shifting combination which must be mastered if successful investment is to be achieved.

48 *Does Your Investment Hit Your Target?*

Inflation appears to be a compelling reason for investing more money in equities these days. But you should never lose sight of some basic guideposts to good investing. Why do you make an investment? Obviously to get back more than you put in.

If you think of yourself as an "investor" you probably count most on the "income" you expect to receive from, let's say, bonds. I have a short formula for determining how such investments turn out.

At the end of each year, add the income received. Then subtract your taxes and take off (or add) a percentage for a rise (or fall) in the cost of living. Thus, if you receive $45 on a $1,000 investment, and you are in the 50 percent tax bracket, then that leaves $22.50. If the cost of living has increased 3 percent—and at present it is running much in excess of that—then you deduct $30 more, leaving you with no real "income" and out $7.50.

Finally, add or subtract the change in the market value of your bond with proper tax consideration, and you will have the final result of your investment. This rarely turns out well except in times of deflation and falling interest rates.

The investor who looks at things more realistically is often labeled a "speculator." If you are of that type, you will want to at least try to get more back in purchasing power than you gave up when you made the investment. Therefore you should look for an advance in price that will give you a gain sufficient to cover expenses, taxes, a decrease in the value of the dollar, and yet leave you with a profit besides. This may seem a little elementary, but if you

161

are like most of us, unless you figure out these factors in writing you will not really know where you stand.

An investment well made is far more than half the battle. So, in deciding what to buy and what to pay for it, you must try to look ahead at the market conditions and determine why someone else will be willing to pay you even more.

Large sums of money have been lost since 1933 by investors who have bought blindly with the thought that they are hedging against inflation.

We have had a steady and continuous rise in the cost of living since the election of Franklin D. Roosevelt. Despite the ups and downs of the stock averages, their price path has generally been up while the price path of individual issues has been every which way.

It is easy now to look back and calculate how much you might have made had you concentrated on and supervised a diversified list of blue-chip equities.

In actual practice, few of us do this. We get discouraged at times and sell when we should be buying. We get enthusiastic and buy when we should be selling. We hold individual stocks that look good but go lower. We sell good stocks that look high but go higher still.

The practical and profitable way to attempt to offset the ravages of inflation is not to buy stocks on the broad inflation premise alone, but make each purchase stand on its own feet and promise a gain on fundamental grounds. Convince yourself that what you plan to buy has a real chance of going up in price. Don't let inflationary fears stampede you into buying stocks casually or on hearsay, just because the general trend of stock prices is rising.

49 *Judge the Quality of Earnings as Well as the Quantity*

The popular practice of quoting price/earnings (P/E) ratios can lead you far afield if you are unable to judge the quality of the earnings used in your calculation. There are five major factors for you to think about in appraising earnings.

The first relates to the nature of the industry. In prosperous years, business has been so good that many have forgotten that much of business is cyclical in nature. Earnings that are realized from such industries are appraised differently in the market from earnings of more stable companies. P/E ratios can be particularly misleading where cyclical companies are involved, unless they are averaged over a period of years. At times, when earnings are low, the P/E ratio should be fairly high, anticipating a recovery. When profits are large, P/E ratios should be modest, if some profit recession is expected to follow.

Another important factor in judging earnings' quality is the profit margin. It takes some understanding to correctly evaluate this, for different industries vary widely. There are times, especially in a new and temporarily monopolistic field, where high-profit margins are sure to be reduced as competition grows. There are times when low-profit margins leave room for improvement. There are also situations where low-profit margins may persist for years because of the nature of the industry, which may be overbuilt.

A third point is the accounting. There just is no such practice as standard accounting. The earnings reported must be checked against the full earnings statement with particular reference to the footnotes. I mostly find that earnings statements reflect whether a company is putting its best foot forward or whether it is going in the other direction and making the most modest statement possible. The field for varying treatment is enormous within the framework of what a CPA will certify as a fair presentation. You must realize that the entire earnings statement and balance sheet might be fair whereas the one item of reported per-share net which is used in figuring the P/E ratio might be misleading because of management decisions to handle certain items in a way which can either overstate or understate earnings.

You should consider the direction of earnings, which is currently being given maximum attention by analysts. The current tendency is to put a premium on strong growth trend, even though one cannot be really sure that the ascending curve of the last few years will be continued into the years ahead. Nevertheless, in modern markets this is one of the first factors that many investors examine. The result has been to split the market into growth stocks with very high P/E ratios and other stocks with relatively low ratios. If a high-priced growth stock suffers a setback in earnings, the resultant market decline can be doubly sharp.

The factor of leverage is also important. This is understood by professionals but frequently overlooked by the average investor. It is a vital factor because it plays a major role in many acquisitions, which are so popular. Acquisitions are engineered in many ways and all are not alike. However, there are many recent mergers in which borrowed capital, or preferred stock capital, is largely used. Thus the resultant earnings per share on the common can be highly misleading. Their derivation must be understood to appraise earnings correctly. Leverage can be a great advantage in a bull market and a great hazard when the market turns down.

If you will learn how to judge the quality of earnings, your market record will be very much improved.

50 *Ask Yourself, "What's the Other Fellow Going to Do?"*

When you contemplate buying a stock, you have to consider how other investors will react to general news and corporate developments. You have to ask yourself, "What is the other fellow going to do?" Start off by determining whether the company in question is likely to earn more, less, or the same. This is finding out what the other fellow—in this case, the management—is headed for in terms of earnings.

Then you have to try to anticipate whether the news is going to be better or worse, or the same. This also is figuring out what the other fellow is going to do, whether it is somebody abroad, somebody in Washington, or somebody in Wall Street.

Finally, you have to think about what the other fellow is going to pay for a given situation. Is he going to pay the same, more, or less? In other words, where is the price/earnings ratio headed?

Of course it is useful to be able to read a balance sheet and determine whether a company is solvent or not, or has enough money to carry on its business. You can take a look at the direction of sales or profit margins or something of the sort. But, in the final analysis, it always comes down to the same thing: What is the other fellow going to do?

Markets, of course, are based on expectations. Sometimes these expectations come true, and sometimes they don't. But the price of a stock or the direction of the market at any given moment is a reflection of what people are expecting rather than what is happening at the precise moment that the sale takes place. So, in a way, you have to ask yourself if people are expecting more prosperity or if they are worried or confident or growing frightened or whatever. You keep guessing what the other fellow is going to do—whether he is going to buy or sell or just be out of the stock altogether. Thus, you will have an approach for thinking in the right market direction.

War, the monetary situation and Presidential actions have an enormous influence on stocks, regardless of the earnings or prospects of individual companies.

It is well to remember that if investors are selling now out of fear concerning war, possible higher taxes, or the flattening of the business curve, they will not be sellers when their expectations actually materialize. They will have already done their selling. This is why market prices are usually ahead of general news and corporate developments. It is an important factor for you to take into consideration.

51 *"Odd Lot" Investing Worth Looking Into*

An "odd lot" is any number of shares from 1 to 99 bought or sold. Dealings in odd lots have been declining from 20 to 25 percent of the total New York Stock Exchange transactions to only 7 percent in a recent period. It is thought that the major part of this loss is through diversion of investments by small buyers to mutual funds. The trend toward stock splits also tends to reduce the number of odd-lot investors because they can buy more shares at the reduced price per share, or the additional shares received for stocks already owned may turn odd lots into round lots.

The mutual fund generally costs more to buy and always more to own than an odd lot. In return for this extra cost, the buyer gets professional management of his investments. Some investors feel they also get wider diversification from mutual funds.

The growth of funds is partly due to the superior salesmanship of their distributors. The outstanding performances in recent years by some of the aggressively managed companies also increased the desirability of mutual funds for a time. Later, disappointing results caused disillusionment. On the other hand, the odd-lot firms do little or nothing to promote their wares, leaving it to the registered representatives of brokerage firms. The odd-lot commissions to registered representatives are smaller than those received from the sale of funds.

A good case can be made for wider use of odd lots by the more serious investor. He can easily get the degree of diversification he wishes. This can be accomplished not only by investing in several issues but by selecting companies which in themselves are widely diversified in their sources of income. He can also buy an odd lot of a "closed end" fund which is listed on the New York Stock Exchange.

Usually, as the investor becomes more experienced, he prefers to reduce his diversification. The mutual-fund buyer does this to a degree by selecting funds which tend to concentrate on a particular industry or type of stock.

Considerable selection is involved in buying a mutual fund. Mutual funds differ markedly in size, aim and management. Far greater selectivity is possible for you in buying odd lots. The results you secure from them will reflect your own skills—or lack of them—to a larger extent.

Another development of the reduced activity in odd lots raises the question of its effect on the general stock market. Amounts of money formerly invested by countless small buyers or sellers are now handled in large sums by professional managers. The latter are almost compelled to make their transactions where markets are broad and active, whereas the odd-lot buyer is guaranteed a purchase or sale on the next transaction if he uses a "market order." The odd-lot dealer must, by the rules, fill the order to buy or sell. Thus the odd-lot investor has a wider choice of issues to buy and sell without fear of causing the wide price swings which worry the professional fund manager.

It would seem that the premium on size and marketability is increasing. Stocks which are infrequently traded (inactive) seem to command lower market valuations. Volatility of the trading leaders is probably increasing as well. Investment managers know each other, and many follow the leader just as most of us do.

There is also the growing handful of traders who think that the published odd-lot transaction figures are a clue to market direction. They are now wondering whether the signals have been changed. The truth is that odd-lot figures never were understood, and were not as indicative as was generally believed.

Odd lots are a very important field of investment for the new and small security buyer. Like savings-bank insurance, "no-load funds," and a lot of other things not widely advertised or promoted, odd lots need to be sought out by the investor. The quest can be rewarding for those who will make the effort.

52 *A Good Cash Position Is Good for a Company*

How should you assess a company's cash position? The answer to this encompasses several points of view. One of the prime requirements of a sound investment is that the company should have an adequate amount of working capital. You certainly don't want to buy into a company that is heading into financial difficulty. You will want to know in advance if it needs funds for expansion so you can judge how raising them would affect the stock. Shrewd investors try to avoid what they term "dilution of the equity," which means having to give up a percentage of ownership in a company that has to sell stock or convertible issues to raise money.

There are many companies which hold much more than the cash needed for normal operational purposes. What is done with the excess is, to a degree, a measure of managerial acumen, and is of paramount interest to the investor.

Analysts always consider what a company earns on its invested capital and on its equity. Unproductive cash or the equivalent reduces the percentage that can be realized. There are some companies that will sit with an overly strong working capital position. At the same time, they often have an overly strong capitalization, possibly all common stock.

There are situations where failure to use a safe and reasonable amount of borrowing power is harmful to overall performance, just as the retention of more liquid capital than prudence requires can limit results. In such situations, I think that unless you can find compelling reasons in the profit record of the company, you might do well to look elsewhere for investment.

There are two major directions where management can seek means of putting extra cash to good use. One is to earmark it for acquisition or expansion. Here it is important to determine how well the cash is used. You will never benefit if excess money burns a hole in management's pocket and if it is used without intelligent promise of maximum returns.

The second way is for the company to purchase its own stock. This has long been regarded as defeatist. However, I find that this is not always the case. I have seen many instances where contraction of capitalization by a company's purchase of its own stock has been of benefit. Obviously the stock at the time of purchase should be considered by the company to be low in price. The company's purpose is to increase its earnings per share, and usually that raises the market price. There are other uses for stock bought in this way. Where management option plans exist, the necessary stock can be supplied without a dilution of equity. This stock, bought in the open market, can also be used for future acquisitions.

It might seem to you that any company in a field with a static future or with a management that cannot profitably use money on hand is a poor investment. This is not always true. The reverse kind of management—one that strains a company's resources by dissipating cash and going to the absolute limits of borrowing power—is much more dangerous.

Many stockholders may say, "Why not increase the dividend?" The obvious answer lies in the portion that goes into

Uncle Sam's pocket rather than into the stockholder's. There are a few companies paying no dividend, with plenty of cash in the bank and plenty derived from earnings, who still buy in their own stock. Their reasoning is that stockholders will benefit more by the rising price of their shares than they would from a dividend.

Before you buy or decide to hold a stock, you cannot ignore consideration of the company's cash position and capitalization. Certainly, if I had to choose between a company with too much cash and one with too little, I would take the former.

53 *Which Are Best? Blue Chip or Glamour Stocks?*

Which are the best types of securities to toss into your safe-deposit box and lock up as investments for the future? The giant, long-established blue chips? Or the new glamour favorites?

All stocks, regardless of their type, should be watched. The lock-up idea is all right only if occasionally you take a mistake out of the box and replace it with something that offers more hope.

Undoubtedly the majority of the older and more experienced investment advisers feel that the basis of a common stock portfolio should be the biggest and most established of our industrial leaders. Such companies have a favorable record going back many years. Their stocks are purchasable at seemingly lower prices in relation to their values, earning power and dividend payability. They are generally thought to have more stability.

The younger investment managers tend to disagree with this point of view entirely. They feel that giant size at times is a limiting factor. They don't believe that it guarantees the stability generally attributed to these stocks. They estimate that in some cases the industry represented has a static future. Younger managers favor what are popularly known as glamour stocks. They feel these are actually cheaper and safer and offer far more possibilities for profit.

Which view is correct? I am inclined to lean to the youthful modern viewpoint. However, there are exceptions in both groups, and it boils down to the individual situation.

The key to selection among the largest companies lies in picking the right industry and the company with the right management. Even more important than this is the right timing. Among the really giant leaders there is more to be made in looking upon their stocks as cyclical than in expecting continuous further rapid growth. The records show that leaders in size are not automatically leaders in desirability. Investment attrition is more prevalent than is generally realized.

In looking the other way for youth and future, considerably more experience is required. The rewards can be very much greater, but so are the pitfalls.

The word "glamour" can be a misleading one. This is especially true if the measure is simply the glamour of a spectacular price advance. True glamour lies in the record and the promise of tomorrow.

In selecting such stocks, the most difficult task is to recognize when the companies are past the gestation period and are really solidly growing profitwise. Those who try to buy in at the basement usually have so many failures that the net result is poor. It is better to be sure the elevator works and get aboard at the second or third floor.

It takes real professional know-how to judge such companies, particularly their ability to finance their growth without diluting their per-share earnings. It also takes experience and a great deal of actual field work and industry contacts to know what the possible future competition might be.

Moving from industrial prospects to stock market factors, the price of desirable stocks is sure to be high in current terms and takes expert evaluation as to the amount of premium to pay for potential profits.

A great deal of guidance can be had from studying the new selections of the most successful of the aggressive fund managers. This does not mean you should buy a stock just because it appears in the portfolios of the leading funds. Rather, it means that the issue is one to check on your own and, most important, to buy at what you consider the right time and price. Overpopularity of a stock among funds can be a bad sign.

I remember when International Business Machines, which combines size with good management and a good future, was considered very speculative—those were in the days when its name was "Computing-Tabulating-Recording Company." Many of today's speculative glamour stocks will similarly grow into the mature giant blue chips of the future.

54 *The Performance Ratio Becomes a New Guideline*

The wide divergence in individual stock action is spurring almost all classes of security buyers to discover ways of buying or switching into the particular issues that promise to go up the fastest and the farthest.

"Performance" is a key word in stock selection. Every day you hear it used more and more, or read it over and over. "Performance" means the best possible current market action. To an increasing number of investors and traders—institutional and private—it is overshadowing the old-fashioned fundamentals that should be the determining factors.

There is nothing new about trying to seek out the stocks that are doing the best. What is new is the growing number of people who are trying to do it, and the great help they get from the computer.

Years ago, a limited number of "tape readers" tried to seek out, with varying success, the best-acting stocks by observing frequency of trade and volume figures. Now you can have it done for you by the computer. You can buy the computer's findings from several sources.

The essence of the method is to distinguish the degree to which individual stocks rank in relation to the main body of stocks and to each other. It is their performance ratio that is calculated. The results are indicated in various ways, but it all amounts to the same thing. For example, the market moves up 1 percent on the averages. The computer shows which stocks moved up the same amount and which moved more, or less, and to what degree. The same thing is done if the market action is level, or moves down.

There is some basic value to this form of assessment, if used in combination with other factors, and by those whose experience and expertise gives them the know-how.

There are many pitfalls. The popularity of the method, as in the case of the popularity of charts, works against consistent success in its use. Here again, the old saying that marketwise "what everybody knows is not worth knowing" applies. Thus, the more widespread the use of these figures becomes, the less their value. Years ago, with but a small handful of professional traders aware of computer applications to the selection of stocks, it was a way of discovering informed, superior buying or selling. Today, with so many watching the price/earnings ratio figures and acting on them, there is a dangerous feedback. Once a stock starts to show up well, it attracts followers who accelerate the trend and improve the P/E ratio, that is, increase the number of times the earnings investors are willing to pay for the stock. This, in turn, is noticed and attracts even more investors to the stock.

The psychology is not unlike that of the motion-picture-theater manager who holds patrons outside even though he has vacant seats inside, so that people are attracted to the line at the box office, which then becomes even longer. It works in reverse as well. If a stock acts badly, the trend and P/E ratio figures disclose the fact quickly and to a large audience. The result is that investors abandon the issue, and the figures get even worse.

One area where individual opinion counts heavily is in the use or interpretation of the indexes or trendlines. This revolves mostly around how long or how far a trend is required to persist to promise its worthwhile continuation and enhancement, thus making it seem worthwhile to act on it. The ideal would be to buy a stock when it acts at its worst in relation to the general market but is just on the verge of improvement. Then you hold it until it advances to the most superior type of action but is just exhausting its move.

For all practical purposes, this is a theoretical situation which one practically never spots in actual practice. What most adherents of the trend and ratio methods do is to wait until they feel a change is real and is going to persist. The idea is if you buy it too soon it may be a false indication. If you buy it too late the move may be almost over.

The ramifications are endless. A trend or a ratio can reverse itself at any point. Each trader has his own system as to whether and when he closes out his commitment either at a loss or a profit. The possibilites of being whipsawed are many. Nevertheless, the use of trendlines has worked reasonably well for many investors, and such use has gained in popularity. Undoubtedly the point will be reached where trendline investing will defeat itself because it will attract too many adherents acting simultaneously. I think it is a useful tool for the experienced and the professionals. In time, those who think this is the new answer to easy market profits will find they have been naïve indeed.

55 *How to Get the Most Out of Your Broker*

At times of high market volatility many stockholders call their brokers one or more times a day. Sometimes the phone calls represent an appropriate watchfulness over the high flyers; at other times the callers only waste the broker's time.

Many years ago, when I was going over a set of architectural plans with Frank Lloyd Wright which he had brought to me for approval, I was required to signify my acceptance by initialing each sheet. After I did this, he did the same, but added the note, "the ideal client—so far." Mr. Wright knew from long experience that clients can go a long way to make or break an architectural inspiration. The great architect acknowledged that a client could get his best work —or something less—by his attitudes. The same thing is even more true in the difficult art of advising on investments. I am sure there isn't anyone on Wall Street giving investment opinions—whether he is with an investment counseling firm, a bank or a brokerage house—who doesn't find that the results he achieves for clients vary with the attitudes of the clients. One client will have confidence, another will be fearful. One will offer suggestions, another will never offer any advice. Each of these demeanors will influence the account manager.

You can most likely get the most out of your advisers if you give the subject some thought. You have to start with the realization that forecasting the stock market is very far from being an exact science. The only "value" that means anything is the price you have to pay or the price you will receive at the time you put in an order. Your adviser has some historical facts of the stock's past, and some purely hypothetical estimates of its probable future. He has to compare these with other securities in the market and with the market climate in general. Yet a large part of evaluation is psychological, not mathematical. Your adviser's conclusions are affected not only by the quality of his judgment but also by the nature of his experiences.

With the fundamentals of investment advising so complex, it is most important that you do not add to your broker's problems by your own attitudes. It is my experience that the great majority of investors have the same objectives. They want the best balance that can possibly be achieved between profit, income and risk.

The universal tendency is to express aims in far more specific terms. Many investors will stress that they want to wait until something very special comes along. This sounds as if it might be helpful, but actually such an attitude frequently damages the performance of an account. Opportunity after opportunity is missed because it is not "special" enough, according to the client.

If you are dealing with responsible people, it is a mistake to say you can't afford to lose. Everybody has to risk loss of one kind or another. If you are fearful of stock market losses, then make a division of your funds. Put whatever portion you wish in the type of liquid, short-term fixed-dollar obligations that give you peace of mind, and leave the remainder unshackled for use in the stock market.

Try to pick the best adviser you can. Try to get one who has helped friends or relatives make investments, and check their experiences with him. Once you've decided on an adviser or broker, then follow his recommendations.

If an investment turns out wrong, take it like a sport and don't let him know your concern. It is important that he feel free to advise you on investment principles. The more he is influenced by your personal considerations, the less profitable his results are likely to be.

There is only one way to handle an adviser who fails to satisfy you—replace him. If he has done a poor job on his own, he will only do worse if he has to deal with criticism. He doesn't want it that way, and neither do you. He wants to do his very best, and he cannot do so if he is under a great deal of pressure.

Another factor is the frequency with which you contact

him. The best way is to talk it over early in the relationship and reach an agreement. Usually it will be for him to keep you posted at predetermined intervals. In addition, you might decide to have him post you even if there is nothing to be done in your account. The frequency of such contact will depend on the type of account and its size. A quarterly report from your broker is fairly standard. However, there are accounts that justify consultation monthly or even weekly. Here and there a short-term trading account might call for a number of phone calls a day.

It will put dollars into your pocket when you do your best to be an "ideal client" and not add to your investment adviser's market problems. Diverting him to cope with a "prima donna" client is always costly—to the client!

My experience suggests that if you select your broker or adviser carefully you will be giving your man his head almost completely in bull markets. However, in a bear market some pressure from you to sell appears to be almost mandatory. No one likes to take losses. It is many times more difficult for a conscientious person to take losses for other people. Consequently, sentiment often rules over judgment and you may be kept long of stocks on the hope that they will come back.

Sometimes the individual handling your account may want to sell, and be willing to do so, but be blocked. If he is working for a firm that holds a large number of these shares for their collective clients, and should the picture deteriorate, you run the risk of being frozen because a market has to be found for all the stock they control; on the other hand, if you give an order to sell, it must be filled.

It is the exception to find an account manager who will greatly vary your equity-cash ratio. Account managers tend to be 100 percent invested. If they become bearish they may cut to 90 percent. It takes a highly unusual person to cut in a meaningful way or sell out altogether. This is something you have to do for yourself. My advice is always to pay some attention to your investments and to exercise some degree of supervision over them, especially in boom times and in bear markets.

56 *Handling of Your Investments by Professional Managers*

In the past few years there has been a great increase in the number of investors who have delegated the handling of their savings to others. They have bought funds or employed investment management through banks or professional investment counselors. This has come about largely because of the publicity given to some very high percentage increases in capital achieved by a few mutual funds. They expect the managers of their savings to do likewise.

In doing this investors fail to understand the risks involved. They fail to realize how very few can really achieve the unreasonably high objectives they have set. They fail to understand that the man who accomplishes such objectives in a given year is the least likely to repeat his unusual achievement the following year. They tend to pressure their own management to achieve visible results too quickly. This greatly contributes to a high volume of trading.

The record shows that the best equities, bought and held and conservatively supervised, will do more to help preserve the market value and purchasing power of savings than other popular forms of investment such as bonds and savings and loan, etc. However, one must have reasonable goals and patience.

It is only the few gifted with a flair for investing who can consistently excel in investing their own funds. It is even more difficult to try to do it for others. Financial genius is rare and is not easy to find or to hire. Wall Street can treat you well if you don't ask the impossible. Don't expect it to be easy to obtain the very best investment counsel, any more than you might expect to have Stokowski conduct your high-school band, but try hard to get the best you can.

57 *"Hedged Funds" Are for Experts, Not Average Investors*

A little-known method of participating in the stock market is through the so-called "hedged fund." Most participants are exceedingly wealthy and sophisticated in Wall Street affairs to a professional degree. They are usually millionaires with at least a quarter of a million dollars in the fund. Participation is limited to very few people.

The first hedged fund was organized in 1949. Because the funds are privately owned, much information about them has to be conjecture, but they are believed to have done considerably better than the averages in most advancing and declining markets until the severe bear market of 1968–70. A hedged fund is a form of partnership. The fund managers believe that neither they nor anyone can really foretell the trend of the stock market. On the one hand, they know that leverage is a great help in their attempts to do considerably better than the average fund. On the other hand, they want to avoid the higher risks that go with leverage. Thus, they "hedge" by being both long and short at the same time. The aim of the fund managers is to make superior stock selection pay off at a very high rate.

Their key to exceptional profits is, first, in the selection of their stocks. The managers buy stocks they think will go up, and at the same time sell short stocks which they feel are overvalued and therefore vulnerable. They hope this policy will insulate them from the inevitable errors in judging market trends.

To secure leverage the fund managers operate on margin. To achieve superior stock selection they first depend on their own supposedly astute judgment. This is supplemented by most careful choice not only of brokerage firms but of personnel within the firms which service them. The managers can command the best service because their own high professional status and the amount of business they do make them desirable clients. They are fast decision makers, and they can grasp what is told to them quickly and accurately.

How do the hedged funds' managers get paid? Their compensation usually depends on the success of the fund and may run as high as 20 percent of the profits. Generally managers participate in the hedged funds with their own capital. Almost invariably they agree to have no other interests and investments outside the fund. The managers are thus true partners with their participants.

It is likely that as more information gets about on hedged funds their number will grow and the admission price decrease. If this comes about and the newer ones are publicly rather than privately offered, the investor should be most careful. I think the priceless ingredient of a hedged fund is its management. In anything but the most capable hands, such procedures as being long and short at the same time, borrowing to operate on margin and placing more than ordinary dependence on brokers' assistance can lead the investor into more than average difficulties.

Hedged funds generally took a beating in 1969–70, and this has raised some questions about their effectiveness. The big bear was especially rough on the "go-go" and hedged fund managers.

58 *Which Stock Is Best for You?*

The temptation to take ill-afforded risks in a volatile market causes some brokers to caution small investors to "buy the best." However, the question is, best for whom?

Most stock brokers ask a new client where his investment objectives lie. In capital gains? Income? Safety? Often the client replies he wants all three. It is extremely rare for any of us to be smart enough or predict accurately enough to get this ideal combination.

The "best" stocks are usually those with the most quality and the most stability. There's no doubt that these issues are the best for the average investor. Their past record shows substantial appreciation in price. Income was usually low when purchased, but dividends have tended to increase over the years.

Nobody knows what the next few years hold in store. Between 1949 and 1968 the market trend has generally been up. Therefore, if you are an investor whose memory goes back only to that date, do not assume that this is either a "normal" or "average" expectation. The declines in 1969 and 1970 were a rude awakening.

If you are looking for liberal income, the best stocks are those that return the highest rates consistent with dividend safety. There are a few—but you will probably sacrifice growth. But you should be very careful that a high income yield is not a prelude to a dividend cut and a consequent price decline.

If you can afford to speculate, look for the greatest possible percentage gain. This is difficult to find, and most of the time it involves correspondingly high risk. Your point of view should be that if the market is going up you want to own the stocks that are rising the most. If the market is going down you will find little solace in owning top-quality stocks that decline only less than the average. At that point you should rather have cash or be short.

The rewards of intelligent speculation can be great. The spread between buying at the low and selling at the high for any given year, or for longer periods, can be considerable. Three industries which have done much better than average in the past are those that have been helped by color television, photography and office copying. As an example, let us examine highs and lows of some of these stocks for the year 1965. In color TV, Zenith, which is a relatively conservative stock, showed about a 90 percent appreciation from a 1965 low of about 63 to a high of about 120. A more speculative issue, Admiral, went up from about 15 to 73, or over 385 percent. The real sensation was National Video, up from $8 to $75, or over 800 percent.

In photography, Eastman Kodak went up from about 69 to 112, a gain of over 60 percent. Polaroid was about 44 at the low and near 118 at the high, well over 160 percent gain. In office copying, Xerox, the leader, went up about 100 percent from 95 to 191; SCM went from roughly 16 to 54, or 235 percent.

These examples are all in the fields where the earnings growth was greater than the nation's in general. They illustrate the principle that a stock tends to have more fluctuation as its quality declines. Some of these stocks declined precipitously later on. This is pronounced in bear markets, as is demonstrated most dramatically by the declines of Admiral and National Video since 1965.

There are other factors influencing movement. Some companies are stable because they are conservatively capitalized, perhaps wholly with common stock. Others can have high leverage, which means bonds, preferred, bank loans, and so on, ahead of a small issue of common. The latter characteristically make wider moves whether up or down. If your aim is to seek exceptional market performance in a stock, make certain you can afford the risk. Always remember that yesterday's favorite is unlikely to be tomorrow's.

59 *Tax Transactions Are a Market Factor*

Invariably, as the end of the year approaches, investors calculate what they think they might save by accepting losses for tax deductions in the current year. Conversely, the more fortunate investors must decide whether to defer his tax liability on profits by holding until January.

In most cases these moves don't really "save" taxes. The usual effect is only to defer them. Marketwise, tax transactions tend to further depress stocks near their lows and take selling pressure off stocks near their highs until early the following year.

I am inclined to be guided mainly by investment considerations. I would certainly not hesitate to sell stocks in the current year that I felt might be lower in January because of a hoped-for tax advantage. Overstaying the market might result in a price decline that would reduce or eliminate the profit.

If you own a stock at a loss it is important to decide: Have you made an investment mistake? If you have, then you should sell. If you feel otherwise, then you may wish to attempt to profit from the depressing effect of others' selling for tax reasons by adding to your position. This is "averaging." On the whole I am not in favor of the practice, but there are occasional exceptions.

In a year when many stocks are near their highs, it should pay to consider which might be sold to better advantage before, rather than after, the turn of the year. In a year when many stocks are near their lows and subject to some tax selling near year's end, they should be scrutinized for attractive buys. Always remember not to buy simply because something is down or looks "cheap," compared to former prices. The stock you should seek out is the one you think is turning for the better.

I have always been in favor of a policy of accepting a certain amount of capital gains each year rather than permitting them to accumulate. The longer-term trend of tax legislation has tended to raise taxes despite some reductions. Paper profits can go as well as come. Occasionally tax legislation has been enacted to operate retroactively. In the long run, an average position with a consistent yearly tax is likely to work to your best advantage investmentwise as well as taxwise.

In a favorable climate there are those with little investment expertise who may be swept into easy profits by the incoming market tide. Usually the gainer thinks he has found a new source of wealth, much to his eventual cost. Turning some of this kind of fortunate "paper" profit into real gain should be worth immediate payment of the tax.

There is a further angle. If you do later repurchase at higher prices you will watch your renewed commitment with more care than if you own it at a very low figure.

Concentrate your thoughts on investment principles and you may gain from others' tax transactions.

60 *Baruch's Guidelines for Investors*

Years ago the late Bernard M. Baruch, one of the wisest speculators in Wall Street, wrote his autobiography titled *Baruch, My Own Story*. Spread throughout the book are investment principles that contributed to his success, and may contribute to yours.

Baruch was skeptical about the usefulness of advice, but nevertheless he reluctantly cited several "rules" or guidelines. He felt these rules can help the investor or speculator who has the ability to muster the necessary self-discipline.

These rules are as sound today as when they were first written. He felt that they boil down to the crucial necessity of getting the facts before you act. Some time ago he wrote me, "After you have the facts, examine yourself as to whether you have prejudices or not, and then use your own judgment."

Bernard Baruch was at one time a stockbroker. He gave up this position because he felt a speculator should go his way alone. He used the term "speculator" quite often because he felt that there is no sure investment. His hope was to be right half the time. If one is right only three or four times out of ten and cuts his losses, it is possible to make a fortune.

Baruch never took it for granted that an investment would remain unchanged. There was a time when periodically he turned into cash most of his holdings and virtually retired from the market. He knew only one nonprofessional who consistently made money in stock market speculation. The reason he gave for holding onto his fortune is that many times he sold a stock while it was still rising. He did not believe in buying too many different securities. It is "better to have only a few investments which must be watched," was the way he put it.

Baruch was a man who believed that speculation is a full-time job. While he believed that you should commit all your time to it, he didn't think you should commit all your funds. One of his rules was: "Always keep a good part of your capital in a cash reserve. Never invest all your funds."

He always believed in sound economics at home. His professor once taught him that when prices go up, production increases, consumption decreases and a gradual fall in prices follows. Contrariwise, if prices get too low, production will decrease and consumption will increase until a normal balance is restored. The policies that made him rich ten years later he credited to remembering the professor's words.

Baruch wisely observed that if our general economic policies and national defense are sound, we need not worry about the market. On the other hand, if we fail to preserve our national security and credit, then nothing any of us owns can have lasting value.

He warned investors never to feel that laws can protect a man from his own errors. Money is lost in Wall Street not because the street is dishonest but because so many people persist in thinking they can make money without working for it.

He pointed out that the stock market does not determine the health of our economy; it merely reflects it. "It is the thermometer, not the fever," Baruch aptly commented.

He wrote me once that his friend Billy Rose would have made a success of anything he undertook that required application and diligence. Perhaps this is the kernel of his message on how you can improve your investment results, or, for that matter, any of your undertakings in life.

61 *Stocks That Pay and Grow*

The no-dividend, small-dividend or stock-dividend corporation is losing its appeal to many stockholders when this status continues indefinitely.

Publicly owned corporations can be divided into groups. There are those so young and financially weak that they need all they can earn to keep afloat for financing necessary expansion. They cannot and should not pay dividends of any kind. If you come across one that pays regardless— look upon it with suspicion.

Then there are companies that traditionally pay very liberal dividends. These tend to be in relatively static industries where earnings are stable but opportunities for profitable expansion are small.

In the middle ground are perhaps the most numerous of all—industries where management makes a division between profits paid out to stockholders as dividends and funds retained in the business for one purpose or another.

The real question of what to do with cash arises where management feels that investment of all profits promises to be more beneficial to stockholders than paying out a proportion in dividends. Involved here is the anticipated return that reinvestment promises and the loss in net dividend payout from company to your pocket in taxes. As an example, assume you receive $1 in cash dividends. You pay possibly 50 percent tax, and thus you have 50 cents net in your pocket to spend or reinvest.

On the other hand, your company retains the cash and successfully reinvests the dollar they would have paid you. By doing this they increase your share of its earnings by, say, 10 cents a share. Such a company would probably see its stock selling at a high multiple in the stock market. At 30 times earnings your additional 10 cents equity in earnings would, under such circumstances, add about $3 a share in market value. If you sell out and pay a full 25 percent capital-gains tax on your profit, then you would have $2.25 in your pocket instead of 50 cents. Capital-gain tax rates are rising, but the principle still holds.

Despite the potentialities of compounding profits, the cash dividend is growing more desirable to most investors. Stockholders want to receive some of their profits currently even at the cost of receiving less over the long pull. The stock of a corporation paying reasonable cash dividends will almost certainly command a better market price, over a reasonable period of time, which is important to management that may wish to finance or trade shares in a merger.

The ambition of management to use a stockholders' money to better advantage than the stockholders themselves could is not always achieved. Expected profits fail to materialize, price/earnings ratios fall below expectations.

I have often said, Never make a rule of selecting stocks

for income alone. Buy for expected gain. But collecting some current cash as you go is good.

A really successful company should earn enough to both pay and grow. There is no better example than General Motors, which tends to pay out almost 70 percent of its earnings and has grown to be one of the nation's top profit-makers.

Time runs out for all of us. Ahead lie the inheritance tax collector and the specter of being the wealthiest dead man in the graveyard. The squash racquet, surfboard, skis, etc., that a dividend may buy in youth will not appeal to you much in old age.

62 *Sometimes "Knowing Less" Will Gain You "More" in the Market*

Is there ever a time in Wall Street when knowing less may pay you off with more? There certainly is. It is when (and if) you engage in the art of "trading."

I am a little hard put for an up-to-date definition of stock "trading." To me it means exchanging your dollars for a security that shortly you hope to exchange with someone else—for more dollars. There are just two basic considerations. First (if you are a buyer) you want and need to have the stock you buy advance. Second, it should do so rather quickly.

In the long run facts always prevail in Wall Street as in everything else. They are essential to the intelligent investor. Consistent success is impossible without them—but they can be a roadblock to you if you are trying to "trade."

Most trading is done from an interpretation of the price movement of securities. Some traders look at the stock tape, some at the stock table in their daily newspaper, many at various kinds of "charts." All together they account for a sizable percentage of the transactions in the active speculative trading leaders. Traders rarely analyze or evaluate a security. Outside of price changes and volume of sales, they look only at spot news. If you want to trade you must do the same. If you look further or deeper you cannot be a successful trader. You will find stocks advancing that seem too high already, statistically speaking. You may be right eventually, but you can be very wrong for a long time. This is because stock movements almost invariably run to excess. Occasionally they seem to be running wild, only to reveal later that they were discounting some unexpectedly favorable development.

I know these principles. I have known them from direct experience for many years. I can trade successfully if I do not know anything about a trading market leader. If I do know—then even today I am likely to stumble every now and then. My trading judgment is being warped by my investment judgment, and the two have no place together.

Recently I saw a stock active and strong and giving every trading sign of going up immediately, fast and far. Unfortunately I knew a great deal about the company, its earnings, capitalization, problems and prospects. My conclusion was that the stock was overvalued. I did not buy it and missed a good profit. Successful trading has little to do with values, just as successful investing has everything to do with values. In this case knowing more blocked my potential gain.

There are investors who succeed and there are traders

who succeed. I doubt very strongly if there are many who deal in securities and mix viewpoints who get anywhere at all.

63 *Annual Reports Provide Good Investor Guidance*

Spring is the time of year when you get the most authentic, complete and up-to-date information on most of the companies in which you own stock. You should use this knowledge as a basis for a comprehensive check of your investment holdings.

For all the stocks you own that report on a calendar-year basis, there will be an annual meeting, an annual report and a proxy statement. An increasing number of companies will send you a post-meeting report highlighting the annual meeting for those who cannot attend. The financial press will report on the larger concerns or on any important controversy.

Many an investment list needs a spring housecleaning. This is one of the best times for you to see if your portfolio is in this category.

Most likely you will need professional help. You start with a careful study of your own. This will give you about as much factual information as you are likely to receive from management. Your investment adviser or broker can explain what is not clear to you. He also has a file of back annual reports of your company and those of competing ones in the same industry. These are important in shedding light on whether management tends to overstate or understate things. A comparison with the competition is essential.

Finally you will need to evaluate your conclusions from the vital standpoint of market price and trend.

If you give this study the time it deserves, and if you receive intelligent assistance, you will surely improve your investment score. I am often asked where to look in order to single out the important facts. The source varies with the industry and company. Never miss looking at the "notes to financial statements" at the bottom of the balance sheet and income account. This is sometimes in fine print, but can be more important than the headline in the press release sent to financial editors.

Sales and earnings per share are more revealing than statement totals. They expose equity dilution. Nonrecurring items and charges to surplus should be checked so that earnings from regular operations can be estimated. The balance sheet will suggest whether finances are strong enough for survival or for financing greater business. The comparison of results over the years gives a picture of growth or lack of it, stability or instability.

Annual reports and other company information for stockholders are improving. They could be further improved if the accounting profession improved its standards, although important steps have been taken recently along this line. The role of the advertising and public-relations departments should be reduced. Top management always has the final say. If they spoke only once, realistic appraisal and interpretation would be difficult. After a few years it is another story. They quickly become recognized for their degree of trustworthiness, frankness and clarity. Studying official reports with this in mind can protect you from a "snow job" and from investing because of overoptimistic management appraisals.

64 *Investing in New Products*

Is there profit for you as an investor in a new product or service? It all depends.

The mortality of new products introduced by companies formed and promoted for that purpose alone is exceedingly heavy. I am tempted to go so far as to say such companies almost never profit, but I will settle for their "rarely" profiting. I know many instances where eventually a new-product business did succeed, but before this occurred new capital had to be brought in, much time went by, and the original investors either dropped out or were forced out, or their equity was greatly diluted. Promotion costs alone to finance something with no record of earnings are generally excessive, introducing much "water" into the capitalization. This is a form of investment that involves the greatest pitfalls and highest risks to the investor.

The odds are greatly improved when such products are introduced by an established, publicly owned company of good reputation listed on the New York Stock Exchange. In such a case funds are either available or can be secured at normal costs. A portion of the probable initial operating loss can be charged off against earnings. Here we find failure as well as success but the odds for success are good. Once in a while an enormous success will result.

New products, new designs and new services appeal to

the imagination. Hence they are sometimes overemphasized by management or brokers.

This is especially true of something exotic or glamorous. The first question to ask if you are told to buy a stock because of something new is how much contribution to near-future earnings is expected. Very often you will find that it will be an item of expense rather than of profit for some years at best. And in other cases you might discover that the maximum potential for the next several years is a very small percentage of the total earnings of a big company.

There are exceptions. A new drug with a high profit margin and protected by patents can be an important earnings factor. There are companies whose products are necessarily always being changed, and here correct judgment can pay off. This would apply to automobile models, motion pictures, television programs. The replacement of an established product by an improved product of the same type can have an early impact on profits. Success here is more frequent.

As in every other investment situation, market action never exactly coincides with realization. The average stock goes up on great expectations. Very often the rise is excessive and it frequently occurs well ahead of actualities. Sometimes the whole expectation is never realized and the new product fails to take on or produce a profit.

Traders can benefit from emotional temporary moves. Investors never can.

There are profits to be made in such situations. To succeed as a trader you must be careful not to overstay your market. As an investor you must dig very deeply into the facts.

65 *Investors Should Find Their Own "Philosophy" for Success*

What kind of investment philosophy pays off the best? The answer is the kind that suits you the best.

There are many portfolio-management methods. Statistics have been compiled to show the supposed superiority of one over the other. These statistics lack two vital elements. The first is that it makes a great deal of difference what period of time is chosen for the test. One policy is favored by a straight-up market; a second by a decline; a third by see-saw conditions. The second vital element concerns the makeup of the manager of the fund. This is true even with the use of so-called "formula plans," because not one of us can stay consistently with the plan any more than we can with a New Year's resolution. I have a minimum of faith in abandoning judgment for a formula, a set theory, "dollar averaging" or any "automatic" philosophy.

There are those who believe in the completely static plan of buying and holding through thick and thin in ever-changing times. I cannot advise you to follow such a policy. If you must, the most rational way to go about it would be to keep half your funds in topflight listed closed-end funds or the best "no load" mutuals and the other half in the best savings banks or in short-term Government bonds. This may be the safest kind of investment plan for the complete tyro. If it is a matter of buying all stocks and sticking to them or keeping all fixed-dollar obligations and sticking to them, I would pick all stocks, though I don't endorse the idea. See chapters on fund selection.

A more workable approach is to stay fully invested in equities but to make changes as your conclusions dictate.

197

This is a policy directed by individual security analysis. It involves taxes and commissions not generated by the static plan. These costs are well worthwhile. A policy of this sort has been very much favored by the markets since 1949. It would have suffered greatly in the 1929 period. It is popular today because all of us tend to remember the more recent past more clearly. Many present-day investors never experienced 1929. They are learning from 1969 and 1970.

There are those who place great faith in "timing." This means having stocks when the market is going up and cash or equivalent when it is going down. Of course, if anyone really knew, this would pay off the best under any conditions.

Actually, none of us do know. In a bull market the theoretical optimum would be to own all the most volatile, best-acting stocks of the day using the largest amount of credit permitted. In a bear market you would not only have cash but would sell short. For all practical purposes, this happy state is theoretical and unobtainable. Therefore, most of us protect ourselves against inevitable errors of judgment by setting various limits to the degree we shift our account with our shifting opinion. Perhaps you might be 75 percent in stocks when you felt most optimistic and 50 percent in stocks when you felt most cautious.

If you combine a moderate effort at timing with the most careful security analysis, I feel your opportunities are the best.

66 *Investing for a Reason*

You should not make a security investment simply because you have the funds on hand.

If you want to be the one in thousands that really succeeds in your investment over the years, you must aim high, keep the risks low, and not be afraid of keeping uninvested cash. Only inexperienced investors label such funds as "idle."

Investment is difficult, and one reason is that wealth simply does not grow to support expectations. At a time when long-term high-grade bonds returned close to 8 percent, the Dow industrial type of stock paid only 4.2 percent. When you deduct taxes and make allowance for expected continued depreciation of the dollar, there is no real net income left.

Stocks return less than bonds because investors expect them to advance. Studies have shown that the average rate of return on investments in common stocks combining dividends and appreciation tends to work out around 9 percent.

One answer to successful investment is never to buy unless the opportunity seems exceptional. Buy stocks only when you have a very strong ruling reason for your purchase. One reason might be that you think the averages are down and headed for a recovery. This is a reason, but a weak one. A good reason is anticipated higher earnings or dividends or both. If these are your reasons, be sure they are not already discounted in current prices. I would also caution against very long-range forecasts or very large anticipated gains. The reasons for the improvement must be logical and attainable.

The changing market valuation of a stock moves it far more than fundamentals. You must strongly feel that the stock you plan on buying will gain in investor popularity and improve its price/earnings ratio. There are tables available that illustrate how potent changing popularity can be. Assume, for example that you bought a hot growth stock at 30 times earnings expecting an earnings growth of 20 percent per year. If, a year later, the earnings growth had been achieved but expectations of future earnings were reduced so that the price/earnings ratio had dropped to 20, then your loss, despite the earnings gain, would be substantial.

A reason for buying a stock might be related to favorable chart action. This often works out, but you must understand why you are making the purchase. If the chart action becomes unfavorable, you must take your profit or cut your loss and not look for other reasons to stay with it.

Some traders buy purely on psychological grounds. They think some concept or group will be the darling of speculators in the coming months. They expect this popularity to carry prices to excessive heights. They may know they are paying too much but feel others will pay even more. This is called the "greater fool theory." It works only if you are nimble.

There can be dozens of other reasons. Changes in management often lead to market improvement. The same is true of a promising new product, or the discovery of a body of ore or an oil or gas field in a mining or petroleum venture.

Years ago I often felt that money in a checking account paying no interest was a better investment than just owning stocks that might go down. Now you can get substantial interest while waiting for the right kind of purchase.

Many investors think of 1969 as a bear year. This is because they were fully invested and their accounts dropped with the averages. Some stocks advanced in 1969. The investor who kept liquid and only bought the very, very few that highly appealed to him did well if his judgment was good. But no matter how good his judgment might have been, he could not have done well with many issues and most of his funds committed.

It is better to buy nothing than to take a chance on doing the wrong thing in a bear market which has gathered momentum. In a surging bull market, the reverse is generally true.

67 *Hedging Against Inflation*

A major motivation of many investors in stock has been to hedge against inflation. Doing this successfully requires more than just buying and locking up equities, rather than holding cash and fixed-dollar obligations. You can also lose by owning stocks. You can lose quicker with the latter. The best inflation hedge is to be knowledgeable about a particular investment.

It is unfortunate that many investors still think of the Dow averages as indicative of the entire market. They think of the Dow stocks as the leading corporations in the country. But it is not true that the largest corporation or the oldest or the strongest is necessarily the best investment.

Corporations are like human beings. They go through periods of infancy, growth, maturity and decline. A profitable time to own them is in the growth period, though the idea needs some qualification. To make money in "growth" stocks you need to buy them just after they have emerged from infancy and before their nature is so well known that their prices have outrun expectations.

The point I want to make here is that the Dow stocks as a class are not always lock-up investments. Some are so big that further growth is difficult. Some have obsolete management. Some are top-heavy with excessive personnel. Many are just in the wrong business.

Over half the Dow industrials could have been bought in 1969 at about the same price (adjusted) as prevailed ten to fifteen years earlier. Their average yield over the years was mostly low. Allied Chemical, for example, sold at 27 fifteen years ago and sold at 27 in 1969. Its median yield over the period was 3.6 percent.

Here are some of the stocks that, going back the number of years shown, could have been bought at the same price (adjusted) in 1969. Also shown are their median yields: American Can—15 years—4.3%; Alcoa—14 years—1.9%; Anaconda—14 years—5.3%; Bethlehem Steel—14 years—5.3%; General Electric—10 years—2.8%; International Harvester—10 years—5%; International Paper—13 years—3.3%; Standard Oil of California—16 years—4.5%; Standard Oil of New Jersey—12 years—4.4%; Swift—15 years—4.2%; Texaco—16 years—3.4%; Union Carbide—15 years—3.2%; United Aircraft—13 years—4.4%; U.S. Steel—14 years—4.3%. Dupont probably qualifies for this list although it is difficult to calculate because of the General Motors distributions.

If you will estimate the taxes that had to be paid on dividends and add the losses from the decreased purchasing power of the dollar, it is very clear why locking up recognized blue chips has not been good investment policy.

Over these years all these stocks had their rallies and reactions. The mileage they covered up and down, in points, was considerable. There were times when each one of them was a good buy and times when each was a good sale.

In 1963 the Center for Research in Security Prices at the Graduate School of Business at the University of Chicago released the Fisher-Lorie study called "Rates of Return on Investments in Common Stocks." This study, covering a 35-year period, shows figures for a variety of conditions. A very good anticipated average pretax return was 9%. This included capital appreciation as well as dividends. The answer to hedging against inflation remains unchanged. Your best chance is informed, selective buying and selling.

The Arthur Wiesenberger Services have long annually published an interesting table on perfect industry selection. Back in 1916 the best group to own was the steels. In 1922 it was public-utility holding companies. In 1925 it was agricultural machinery. These groups are changing all the time, and investors must keep in step.

Earlier we listed some of the unsatisfactory results of lockups. A table of winners for the twelve years from the 1957 low to year end 1969 shows the following: The 1957 low of IBM was 29 and the year-end 1969 price, 350; Disney 5—124; Polaroid 3.75—139; Avon 3.62—169; American Research and Development 1.70—78; Xerox 0.65—105. One hundred shares of each of seventeen issues of this type would have cost $7,600 at their 1957 lows. These same shares twelve years later were worth $158,700. This is a compound annual growth rate of almost 30 percent. Listing it now is what is known as "after 3:30 P.M. trading" —in other words, after it has happened. Nobody can possibly select a list today, before it has happened, that will do as well. You will do better if you revise your thinking and your portfolio as developments suggest.

A well-planned and faithfully followed policy of regular attention is mandatory if you expect to have a successful investment program.

68 *Three Ways to Lose in the Stock Market*

When everything is said and done, there are only about three principal ways to lose money in the stock market.

1: Paying too much.

2: Not recognizing a bad balance sheet.

3: Being misled by an inaccurate earnings estimate.

I am aware that readers will come up with a variety of other ways to lose. Most of them, on examination, convert back into the basic three. For example, if you are misled or defrauded, invariably the instigator has given you (or your informant) false information on one or more of our three points. If you ever extend yourself financially and are sold out on a decline, you have undoubtedly also put yourself in this situation by making an error in one or more of the three fundamentals.

"Paying too much" is perhaps the most frequent mistake. It is certainly the most difficult to guard against. An example might be buying the bluest of blue chips, IBM, in January 1962 at 600 and seeing it decline 50 percent to 300 in five months. The IBM balance sheet was okay. The upward-earnings trend did not change. Nevertheless IBM suffered a major deflation in price. In time the stock recovered and went to a new all-time high in 1968.

One cannot tell you how to avoid paying too much in a sentence or a paragraph or an article. If fundamentals do not change (and of course they may) you will often eventually come out on top.

An important way of minimizing loss in stocks is to take your loss early while it's still small, when it seems you have made a mistake.

A weak balance sheet, as I mean it here, is buying into a company that cannot achieve the objectives you have in mind because of insufficient working capital. The result is perhaps new financing ahead and diluting your equity. It can even be worse if it is reorganization or bankruptcy.

Failure to recognize this situation can be due to several reasons. Frequently new enterprises will not generate enough cash to take care of future needs. There are cases where misstatements were made.

Revenue Properties Co. Ltd. fell from over $20 to a price of 65 cents in a matter of months. In this case, the reason was allegedly false figures. There was an offering of stock at $17 in November 1968 by 72 topflight underwriting houses who apparently were also unaware of the misrepresentation.

R. Hoe & Co., well-known maker of printing presses, went into bankruptcy in July 1969. The stock, which had sold above 50 in 1968 and 1969, declined to 2.

Earnings estimates are everywhere. Many are too high. Some are too low. The further away in time the estimated earnings, the more likely they will not work out. An estimate for the next quarter is far more likely to be reliable than one for a few years hence. In new offerings most estimates can hardly be more than pure conjecture or misplaced optimism. They are worse than useless. They are often misleading.

When I came to New York in 1922 one of the first men in Wall Street I met was Jacques Coe. He was writing market letters for J. S. Bache & Co. at their old ground-floor office at 42 Broadway. Recently I received a letter from him with some very pertinent remarks. He wrote: "What I cannot understand is how, with tight money and high rates, we can continue to have third- and fourth-rate companies go public, underwritten by small firms which have had no previous experience; and someone buys them, and they go to a premium. This I don't understand, and I wonder what's going to happen to these poor people when they wake up and find that they have to take terrific losses, provided they can find someone to whom to sell their stocks." Events since this was written have borne out Mr. Coe's fears.

In established businesses with a background, there is usually a basis for a meaningful projection. These are often just extensions of a past trend. Many come from consultations with company sources. The latter may lean to optimism. Sometimes they are overconservative. It takes a very high degree of expertise for the analyst to judge how close to reality his source is. One needs to understand psychology as much as finance. Very few optimistically buoyant, widely circulated earnings estimates are made by competent people interviewing the right sources.

Penn Central sold above 85 in 1968, mostly on optimistic earnings estimates that were expected to result from the merger of the Pennsylvania Railroad with the New York Central Railroad. Failure of these earnings to develop was the main reason for the decline in the stock to under 30 the following year, to under 6 in 1970—and finally into bankruptcy. Automatic Sprinkler (now ATO) dropped from above 70 to under 15 in 1969 and to under 7 in 1970 on disappointing earnings. Litton is another example. It sold above 120 in 1967, fell to under 40 in 1969 and to under 20 in 1970. Earnings were not up to expectations.

In some cases a decline in earnings can damage a company's image and cause its price/earnings ratio to fall right along with the drop in net.

Knowing coming earnings correctly is not of itself a certain way to profit. The essential ingredient is that your anticipation is not already discounted in the marketplace.

In considering many of the points raised here, you will have to depend on other people. In most cases, they or others in their organizations will be doing the actual field research and the actual analysis. It will be their findings and conclusions that you will have to weigh and question. This is a drawback but not an insurmountable one. You learn to rate your sources as time goes on. You will naturally question anything extravagant in the material and ideas presented to you. Some will appeal and appear logical and reasonable while others will not.

Nothing can protect you against a certain number of losses. You can hold them to the minimum by checking the risks as well as the rewards. Never act unless the ratio is well in your favor. Be doubly careful if the predictions seem extravagant. Decide when you buy how much you will risk, and cut your loss if the point is reached.

69 *Who Is Your Investment Chauffeur?*

Are you one of the increasing number of investors who delegates the management of your investments? One way to delegate is to buy funds. The other is getting your own personal investment adviser. If you follow the latter course, it will take some time and effort to find the right one. This is especially true if your investable funds are small. The minimum amount needed to have a management account with a bank or investment counselor has increased sharply in recent years. Formerly the minimum was $100,000. While there are many exceptions, there are now banks that look for a minimum of $250,000, and some investment counselors require minimums substantially higher.

This situation has increased the number of small investors who depend upon their broker for investment guidance. Brokers are hard-pressed because commission rates on small orders have not changed for twelve years, while the costs to brokerage firms of handling these orders have risen sharply.

Robert W. Haack, president of the New York Stock Exchange, was quoted on the subject in an issue of the Big Board's monthly magazine, *The Exchange*. *"The Exchange* needs and wants the small investor. It is the flow of small orders that creates liquidity and provides the basis for a continuous auction market. The growth of direct-share ownership," he was quoted as saying, "depends in great measure on the development and servicing of small orders by brokerage firms, which in turn require commissions offering adequate incentives."

Mr. Haack is talking primarily of accepting small orders. The problem of finding a properly qualified registered representative who has the time and desire to act in an investment-consulting capacity where small amounts are involved is not easy.

Investors have said to me, "How can I have confidence in an investment adviser when I have had my current investments analyzed by three experts and all three disagree?

One tells me to buy A and sell B, and the other says sell A and buy B."

I wonder how much experience of the world such investors have really had or how observant they are. I know of nothing in life about which I have found universal agreement. If you will put any problem, personal or of general interest, to this test, the answer will always be: There is no agreement.

When it comes to investment, differences likewise exist. If we could determine precisely the right thing to do at any given time, we would all be buyers with nobody to sell to us, or all sellers with nobody to buy from us. The stock you buy because you expect to double your money is being sold by another investor who very likely feels it is too high and wants to liquidate.

We also must remember that there is more than one successful way to do a thing. Some ways are safer and some are more hazardous; some are slower and some faster. These factors may mean that, at a given time, two advisers will both be good and still far apart in the direction of their advice. These differences often occur because their interests and connections are not the same. Adviser Number 1 may live in a world of growth stocks, Number 2 in a world of blue chips. They spend their time with different people, study different reports, examine a different part of the newspaper. Each of us should know how to recognize the outward signs of competency. It is a fundamental business of life.

If the man you choose is the right man, he will probably have chosen the right firm to work with. Investment-counseling firms usually allow their representatives less freedom than brokers do, and banks usually allow less again. You must decide for yourself whether you want a man who is closely supervised or a man who is given the scope to be venturesome if he chooses.

It is important to note that if a man is working for an institution he may purchase stocks for you which have also been heavily purchased for other clients of the firm so that the collective ownership position in certain stocks is very substantial. If the picture deteriorates, you run the risk of being frozen because of lack of a market which can absorb all the shares. To have your shares sold, give a definite sell order rather than leave the decision to the man or the firm, which must consider all clients who own the stock. A sell order *must* be executed. The number of stockholders in American corporations is over the 30 million mark. Unless you are among the minority who have the flair, the time, the contacts and the experience, your best way of achieving investment success is to find the right "investment chauffeur." Give him your investment goals, sufficient opportunity, and plenty of encouragement.

No one will ever assume for you the risks you might assume for yourself. But you want your man to come as close to this as is reasonable. Have him keep you fully informed but let him "drive." If he fails to satisfy you, fire him. But as long as he is at the wheel, try not to be a backseat driver except when a bear market makes it mandatory.

70 *Books to Help the Investor*

Preservation of capital requires keeping up with the literature on the subject. The best way to select those that promise to mean the most to you is to visit a good bookstore and your public library periodically and scan the new titles.

As a boy, I did not start my reading with Horatio Alger. Instead I read the financial fiction of George Randolph Chester. His "Get Rich Quick Wallingford" stories, which began appearing in the *Saturday Evening Post* in 1907, were highly entertaining. They also had enough factual background on how dishonest promoters cheat the unwary to actually save me money when I came of age. The Chester books are long out of print. The fiction of Edwin Le Fevre, especially his *Reminiscences of a Stock Operator,* written in 1924, is easily obtainable today.

Every investor should read stock market, monetary and business history. A good example is the story of the 1929 drop in the stock market by John Kenneth Galbraith called *The Great Crash*. There are several other worthwhile books. One of the newest is titled *From the Crash to the Blitz: 1929–1939* by Cabell Phillips.

You will secure great benefit from reading the life stories of successful men. I always see merit in reading about something that happened, rather than theoretical tomes of what ought to happen but rarely does. Good examples of the former are Alfred P. Sloan, Jr.'s *My Life in General Motors,* Bernard M. Baruch's *My Own Story* and Eugene Lyons' *David Sarnoff—A Biography*. One of the newest books in this field is *Think,* a biography of the Watsons and IBM. Two more recent books are directed at women investors. *A Women's Guide to Wall Street* is by N. Leonard Jarvis. I have known Len for years as a successful, experienced stockbroker and one-time president of the New York Society of Security Analysts. As one would expect, this is an excellent guide to Wall Street. I think any married woman who buys the book will find her husband as likely as she to read it word for word. *How Women Can Make Money in the Stock Market* by Colleen Moore is written by a woman for women. She has obviously learned a great deal from her stockbroker father-in-law (now deceased) and broker husband, and has expressed it in understandable terms. Claude N. Rosenberg, Jr., wrote *The Common Sense Way to Stock Market Profits* about a year ago. He quotes Voltaire as reflecting that "Common sense is not so common," which is very true. The text of his book is "uncommon" in its easy-to-understand rare good sense. One of the best portions is the almost sixty pages devoted to telling you what not to do. *Stock Market Behavior* by Harvey A. Krow condenses and brings up to date much of what investors take to be the technical approach to investing. *The Money Men of Europe* by Paul Ferris gives an insight to what is going on in the countries that carry real financial weight in Europe. With the world growing smaller every day, this is good reading for those who have the time, inclination and resources to be exceptionally well informed. Faye Henle has written a paperback, *350 New Ways to Make Your Money Grow,* which is a sort of primer on almost everything having to do with investments, insurance, wills, even social security.

Back in 1955 the late Burton Crane used to cover the Wall Street beat for *The New York Times.* I never did know how many years he did this, but it was very many. In any event, he had much practical face-to-face contact with the people who made Wall Street run in those days. He wrote several books, but my favorite is *The Sophisticated Investor,* revised and expanded a few years ago by Sylvia Crane Eisenlohr with assistance from such famous people as Oliver Gingold (deceased).

When I read a book and I come across something doubly worth remembering, I jot down the page number. I find I did this over three dozen times in the original edition of *The Sophisticated Investor,* which is something of a record for me. When I received my copy of the revised edition I checked back on some of these references to be sure that none had been "revised out." I was glad to find them still there.

Right on his first page Mr. Crane recalls that the idea that "The market will always make new highs because it always has, therefore anytime is a good time to buy" is not one of his favorite arguments. He remembers that the market as a whole took twenty-seven years to climb back to its 1929 high. I can supplement this by pointing out that none of us owns "the market" and that some individual stocks never come back.

If you take long motor trips, or if you prefer listening to reading, my own book, *The Battle for Investment Survival,* has been narrated by George Bishop on a cassette tape for Nash Voicebooks, 9255 Sunset Boulevard, Los Angeles, California 90069. It can be bought by mail at $9.95 or purchased at many retail stores. It takes ninety minutes in all to hear both sides.

Only a limited number of books are suitable for the varying requirements of different individuals. The fact that something is in print does not of itself guarantee its usefulness or even its accuracy. A great deal of care needs to be exercised in selection. Books that make extravagant promises of easy ways to make money should be regarded with suspicion. Good books are more often than not misunderstood by readers.

The literature of Wall Street is essential to you as an investor, but take it judiciously.

71 *Investment Supervision Is Necessary Every Day*

Investment supervision is necessary every day of the year. If you have failed to watch your investments in the past, then resolve to start doing it right now. There are various ways of checking your investment score. I think the most practical is to value your investments at the end of each year. If you had a net unrealized profit over cost a year ago, be sure to deduct the tax due as a contingent liability. Next, make the same type of valuation for the present year's end. Be sure to deduct any dividends or interest received. Also, deduct the taxes you owe or dividends and interest, and on net capital gains realized during the year. Finally, set up an adjusted contingency reserve for the taxes accruing on any net unrealized profits. In doing this, use your average regular income bracket for short-term gains and the going rate for long-term gains. There are some inaccuracies in this method, but in my opinion it is the most realistic and practical.

After you find out your percentage improvement or loss, you should judge it in the light of your own objectives. It is unrealistic to measure it against the change in the Dow. It is equally unrealistic to measure it against the changes in the published figures of funds that have had a windfall in new, small, unseasoned companies, in formerly low-priced issues, high-leveraged conglomerates and glamours, unless you were willing to take the risks involved and buy such stocks for yourself.

If you motor thirty miles an hour in a heavy Cadillac and always use your safety belt, your risk of injury is obviously way below that of the youngster who breaks the speed limit in a small open sports car. The same reasoning applies to investment comparisons.

After you have evaluated your performance, you will next want to set your goals for the next year. The first will be your cash-stock ratio. How much of your funds do you wish in reserve in 91-day Treasury bills and how much in equities? The decision here will reflect your opinion of the market and of the degree of risk you desire to take. What will be the makeup of your common-stock list? What percentage do you want in solid blue chips? You will have to set a percentage against every group in which you wish representation. You might or might not want to include a proportion of growth stocks, glamours, cyclicals and new issues. Some investors, who have the time and the ability or the connections, set aside a proportion of their funds for short-term trading.

The cash-stock ratio and your type of security mix will enable you to make an approximation of what you expect to make versus what you risk losing during the year.

Finally, you will need to adjust your present portfolio to your new year's framework. I would examine small positions. If they are not promising enough to increase, most likely they should be liquidated. I would check over big positions to make sure they are still current favorites of yours. I think it is always important to give special attention to those stocks that have acted the best and those that have acted the worst. It is a good idea to think of the former from a standpoint of whether you want to nail down

215

some profits. Carrying them realistically with a contingent tax liability will help you to make a true investment decision. Where stocks have been disappointing, it is wise to sell them, unless the situation still appeals to you so strongly that you are willing to buy more.

Make a resolution to follow whatever program you set for yourself and take definite steps to insure your carrying out your good intentions. Do not let things slide.

72 *Per-Share Valuations Can Be Misleading*

Investors almost universally think of market valuations in dollars per share. They speak of "Bargain Basements Inc." selling at $9 a share as being "cheap," and "Hidden Assets Inc." being "dear" at $75. "Explorers Extraordinary, Inc." is up $7 on its newly drilled oil well. This is a superficial and misleading way of looking at security valuations.

A more realistic way is to calculate total dollar valuations. The total market valuation of the equity is the per-share market price multiplied by the number of shares outstanding. If "Bargain Basements" has a common-stock capitalization of 10 million shares, its equity at $9 a share is quoted in the market at $90 million. If "Hidden Assets," selling at $75, has only 1 million shares outstanding, its equity is valued at $75 million. The $7-per-share advance for a new oil discovery might be $70,000,000 if 10 million shares were involved.

The market value of straight bonds and/or preferred stock, if the company has any, also needs to be calculated. This figure and the value of the equity added together will give a quick idea of the market's valuation of the company. The relationship between the common equity value and the value of its prior obligations will give an off-the-cuff estimate of whatever leverage is in the situation. The professional analyst will go much deeper.

The totals will be found to have real practical value. "Bargain Basements" sells for $90 million. What do you get for your money? It will be revealing to compare these totals with gross sales, income and balance-sheet totals.

I recall the great New York Central Railroad. It owned rail properties, hotels, shares of other companies like U.S. Freight, undeveloped real estate, etc., etc., with a book value of $933 million in 1953, when the late Bob Young was buying the stock at $20 per share. There were just 6,447,410 shares of common outstanding. This made the price of the equity only $128,948,200. Imagine buying the New York Central equity for that! The debt of the Central was very large, amounting to par value of $833 million. Thus, control of the equity meant use of $833 million of other people's money. The whole situation becomes clearer with totals than with only per-share figures. (New York Central stock rose substantially after Mr. Young's purchase and before post-merger troubles.)

Per-share figures can be misleading in other ways. This is especially true if a corporation has considerable prior charges ahead of the common. Taking the New York Central as it was capitalized in the year Bob Young took it over and Al Perlman began bringing it back to life, earnings per share of $2 sound like twice $1 per share, and so they are. But on an overall basis, it took $56.6 million to cover prior charges and show $1 a share, and only 10 percent more to cover prior charges and earn $2 per share. The same leverage works in reverse. A decline of $6.5 million or 11 percent in overall income would, at that time, have thrown New York Central in the red.

If $128 million seemed "cheap" for the New York Central equity in 1953, a total market valuation of $38 billion for IBM seems "dear." It may be or may not be. Only time will tell. I never advocate using any single measure to form a conclusion. Total valuation is one useful factor out of many others to help reach a broadly based opinion. The huge valuation of IBM does make one stop and "think" (as the elder Mr. Watson posted everywhere in the IBM offices) of what it takes for this valuation to double!

I knew IBM when it was called Computing-Tabulating-Recording. Its total market valuation was low and so was its growth and its price/earnings ratio. Its investment popularity was low. Just being small did not mean it was a better buy. Earnings of IBM did double per share between 1952 and 1954 and, as the company grew, the number of years to double earnings again lengthened. In IBM's case, regardless of size, a large growth rate has been maintained. I regard it more as an exception than as the rule.

Looking at total figures along with per-share and other factors is helpful; investors should do this more often than is usually the case.

73 *Investment Letter Stock*

One wrinkle in the mutual-fund field gaining in popularity concerns funds specializing in what is known in Wall Street as "investment-letter" stock. This kind of stock has been available practically since the 1933 SEC Act. It was probably first bought by General Doriot's highly successful

American Research and Development Company starting in 1946.

New closed-end mutual funds, which primarily will purchase investment-letter shares, are being merchandised to the investor. Investment-letter stocks are shares not registered with the SEC. As a consequence, their resale is restricted. Information concerning them is relatively meager.

Some stocks can only be bought privately. A letter is signed, signifying that they were bought for "investment purposes" only and not for public resale. Until they become registered (some do, some do not), they can only be resold privately to a buyer who signs the same type of agreement. There are some exceptions, but the rules are vague. Many believe that if held for over two years, this is sufficient proof that the original purpose was for investment only. This cannot always be assumed to be true. Registration can only be done by the company itself.

Investment-letter stock can consist of shares of a company with no stock in public hands. It can also consist of unregistered shares in a company that has registered stock publicly held and quoted. In the former case, the purchase price is wholly a matter of bargaining. In the latter, the investment-letter stock tends to sell at a discount. This often runs from 25 percent to 50 percent, or even more, of the going price of their publicly traded shares. The entirely private letter stocks, with no public quote, seem to be the best purchases.

New and small promotional companies save time and costs by doing their initial financing with investment-letter stock.

The attraction to the buyer varies. Sometimes it is the discount. At other times it is the hope of getting in "on the ground floor." In a successful situation there is always a substantial profit between the original speculative limited or nonmarketable stock and a public offering. Worthwhile blocks of investment-letter stock can usually be bought prior to a public offering. Public offerings may involve many small allotments and immediate large premiums. Very often, part of the investment-letter deal calls for future registration, the company's fortunes permitting.

This is a logical field for the funds. Professional fund managers should be able to analyze, price, select and follow such situations to much better advantage than the ordinary small investor. Some can be helpful in the management. The risk lies in the great pools of capital now becoming available, and the limited number of meritorious opportunities.

We saw something of this same kind of situation when the SBIC was formed by the Government to help small business. The amount of money exceeded the ability to get sound management and good buys.

As in most funds, these new investment-letter corporations are mostly initially sold net, including underwriting costs. They also involve management fees and operating expenses. They need to be closed-end. Letter stock has insufficient liquidity to provide for redemption on demand. After the initial offering, the shares sell in the open auction market.

To the extent that funds hold investment-letter stock of an issue also publicly quoted, there are many possible ways of evaluating their holdings. Each fund uses a different method that can vary from overconservatism to putting one's best foot very far forward. Where no stock is publicly quoted, the difficulties of fair valuation increase.

Determining the true relationship between real liquidating value and market quotations is next to impossible.

Changes for the better or worse of important holdings or decisions to go public are rarely known until after they happen. There is a big risk that the supercharged appetite for new issues which may prevail at a given time will normalize later.

Despite the hazards, there is a place for this kind of investment fund. The investor basically is up against the oft-repeated advice to "buy management." This is easier said than done. It is here more difficult than usual because of the newness of the concept and the lack of track records.

New promotions have a great attraction for the average investors. They don't want to be told to buy American Telephone. They want something brand-new and exotic. They want to feel they are buying in at a basement price before it is public and anybody can buy. What they fail to realize is that doing this requires many contacts and far more expertise than they possess. Also, no one can succeed on a one-shot basis. You must participate in a succession of situations and rely on a ten-strike to cancel your losses and put you on top. Otherwise it becomes purely a matter of luck rather than one of intelligent speculation.

The investment-letter funds help to fill this need.

74 *Mergers Pose Problems for Security Owners*

The merger fever, which has been growing by leaps and bounds, poses some new problems for security owners. It used to be that the sophisticated investor left the static companies to others less shrewd. Today the smart buyer goes on a hunt for possible "take-over" candidates. Overage management, overrich cash assets and abnormally low return on capital traditionally kept the aggressive investor away. Today, if a take-over is a possibility, these can be sound reasons for becoming a buyer.

The original merger was probably between the coalman and the iceman. This turned two seasonal businesses into one all-year operation. As time went on, combinations evolved for an increasing number of reasons. It made sense to take over a company in a related line where economies of operation were clearly achievable.

A high proportion of recent mergers is not so well founded. The motives of the acquiring company include overambitious management, shaky empire building through accounting legerdemain, and just plain raiding. It is true that occasionally two and two can add up to five, but only in a minority of cases.

Each merger has to be weighed on its own merits. Some mergers are giant combinations. Every day there are deals made by various-sized companies. It goes without saying that the stockholders of the acquired company almost always benefit. They can sell out at a premium. There are times when it may pay them to stay with the new situation. There are acquiring companies which have gained in earning power and market price with each acquisition. This is especially true where the situation has not grown overlarge or overcomplicated.

Investors should look at neglected situations to determine if they are possible take-over candidates. The investor who is fortunate in seeing his stocks advance sharply on merger rumors or actualities must carefully weigh their possibilities and decide whether to go along or liquidate.

75 *Turnover*

A good percentage of the increased trading in securities stems from the increased "turnover" rate. The turnover of all stocks listed on the New York Stock Exchange was recently at a rate of over 20 percent annually. This means that, on the average, about 20 percent of the outstanding shares of each company changed hands during the year. It was about 12 percent ten years ago.

The so-called "performance" funds, which have striven to achieve the greatest percentage gain in assets per year, have led in increasing the overall rate. There are some who turn over their portfolio 100 percent. In other words, they do not own a single security at the end of the year that they owned at the beginning.

As a practical matter, most investors do not give their investments the attention they deserve. Consequently, they do not make as many changes as would tend to improve their own "performance."

There is no useful guide to any "normal" ideal turnover. It should vary year to year. It should differ with different portfolios. I think it is important to make some changes periodically. I cannot visualize any investment list that was the better for being kept static.

In considering what to do, the primary factor is your opinion of the future of each of your holdings. There might be some at the bottom of your list about which you feel you made a mistake. They should be sold. There might be some at the top of your list that have apparently achieved your objective. It is a mistake not to nail down some profits. New opportunities appear from time to time. They should be examined and compared with what you already own. This may point out a way to upgrade your list's potentialities.

I have just read a sentence written by a very successful and shrewd professional, E. S. C. Coppock, of San Antonio, Texas. It goes: ". . . Amateurs sweat many an hour over *what* to buy—while the pro works at *when* to buy." I am sure Mr. Coppock works the professional way. Looking at the record, I cannot agree that the majority of pros actually put the "when" first, as Mr. Coppock believes, and as I think they should.

Perhaps the reason they do little is because determining the "when" is vastly more difficult than determining the "what." I think you should try. This means varying the proportion of your funds allocated to cash or 91-day Treasury bills versus your stock holdings. I suggest one-half stocks and one-half reserves when you are most pessimistic, or have a minimum of stocks you really like for special reasons. My maximum for most investors would be 90 percent stocks and 10 percent reserves. I always want some buying power. A successful, experienced, aggressive young speculator or trader might have no stocks at all, or actually be short, when he is bearish. He might be long on margin when bullish. There are many ratios in between.

Tax considerations affect your turnover and performance. Investors should consider the advantages of taking losses short of six months and gains after six months—but this consideration is always second to investment evaluation. I favor closing a percentage of transactions annually and paying some capital-gain tax every year so as to spread the cost, rather than building up a huge unrealized tax liability. The latter policy inevitably freezes your viewpoint.

Never forget that time marches on. The value of money changes. The availability of things you can buy varies.

Your own capacity for enjoyment changes with the years. Tax rules and rates change. Unexpected developments affect your investments. It is vital to realize this. Watch your affairs and act. Investment today is not geared to dividend or interest "income" but rather to total net changes in the value of a security account. I always counsel withdrawing a set amount, usually 6 percent of equity annually, and spending it. Spending more will hamper the growth of your capital. Not spending at all until "your ship comes in" may deny you the fruits of your savings.

76 *Yardsticks for Selecting Mutual Funds*

Mutual funds have made the financial scene in a big way. New funds with insurance-company sponsorship are coming in. Are funds for you? How do you select the fund or funds that best fit your needs?

I know of about 400 funds, ranging in size from less than a million to almost three billion dollars in asset value. Some are broadly diversified common stock funds; others include those which are balanced between stocks and bonds, growth, income, bonds and preferreds, convertibles, single industry, foreign, hedge, no-load, special situation, closed-end, and so on.

The cost of buying varies widely. Management costs differ. Some funds sell at liquidating value, some at premiums, and others at discounts.

The commission received by the salesman or broker also varies. The incentive to push those that pay the highest commission is very strong. Advertising, sales promotion and literature are also much more extensive from the funds that receive the revenue from the highest commissions.

Funds can be good investments and are suitable for many people. I think that (as in most years) equity investments will continue to prove more secure in the foreseeable future than fixed-dollar investments. Funds have advantages for those who do not have the ability, connections, time or desire to care for their own investments.

The original appeal of mutual funds and other investment companies for the investor was that after he bought the shares of the fund he could leave the investing to them. This concept has been changing. Now you have to exercise as much care in the selection and timing of the purchase of an investment company or fund as you would in buying any individual stock.

The novice investor uses "performance" as his principal yardstick in making selections. Necessarily this is based on *past* performance. The popular tendency to buy last year's big gainers is a very poor approach to the problem. Being last year's hero generates built-in handicaps against leading the league the following year.

How should you go about it? You will have to begin by doing a little research on your own. None of us really can be sure about the trend of the market. There are times, however, when prices and risks seem high, and other times when they seem low. There are times when the trend appears clearly down. You should make as much effort to buy funds favorably as you do individual stocks.

Mutual funds are sold by dealers, among whom are many New York Stock Exchange member firms. The member firms also fill buy orders in closed-end investment companies. They have the most information available. They handle a greater number of funds than other sources. There are some funds that are sold through their own sales organization which sell nothing else. No-load funds are generally bought from the individual companies themselves.

The first thing for you to do is to examine the literature on investment companies. Some reference books are very expensive but many can, of course, be seen at your brokers. The best known book on the subject is Arthur Wiesenberger's *Investment Companies* (Wiesenberger Financial Services, 5 Hanover Square, New York 10004). It is a 9 x 12 volume of about 400 pages and sells in a limited annual edition for $45. It contains virtually every type of information and discussion on investment companies. It can be examined at most libraries. Johnson's charts are very popular and are available at most brokers' offices. The Trendex Research Group in San Antonio have started a new weekly service to keep investors aware of the changing trends of performance, hopefully in time to make profitable changes, sales or purchases. The price is about $95 a year. This is a new type of relative-performance-ranking service, rating companies from 1 for the strongest down to 20 for the weakest, on an intermediate-term basis. It is aimed at sophisticated investors. It is especially valuable in maintaining proper regular supervision of the market action of your funds after you have purchased them. Investors need to learn the importance of watching their fund holdings with as great care as their ordinary shares. *Fundscope* magazine ($45 per year, 1800 Avenue of the Stars, Century City, Calif. 90067) is a popular 100-page monthly, *Reader's Digest* size, combining comment with tabulations of fund results. *The Manual of Funds* by Yale Hirsch ($1.95, Newspaper Enterprise Association, 270 Park Avenue, New York 10001) is an informative paperback. It is a very useful annual reference book, especially for the novice.

Arthur Lipper Corp., 140 Broadway, New York 10005, publishes *The Lipper Perspective Service,* which costs $5,000 per year. It includes 4-page forms on individual funds with over $100 million in assets. The service approaches each fund as if it were a stock. The tabulated information is very valuable to professionals able to interpret it. The Lipper people also supply weekly performance figures at a cost of $600 per year. *Barron's National Business and Financial Weekly* publishes Lipper's Mutual Fund Investment Performance Index by Groups with a comparison with unmanaged portfolios. *Forbes Magazine's* annual *Mutual Fund Guide* is excellent.

As you delve into the subject you will find a wide variety of funds. After you have settled on a few candidates, send for their latest annual and quarterly reports and their offering circulars. These cost you nothing and will be of great help in making a decision. Study the lists of stocks they hold and decide whether they are the kind you would be happy to own. Here are some pointers:

Management: This is the most important consideration. It is also the most difficult to measure. With a few publicized exceptions, you are not likely to know the name of the manager, his tenure or his predecessors. You have to depend on the long-time record and reputation of the management company.

Determining the kind of management you desire is not easy. It cannot be done just by buying the fund with the best recent performance record. I cannot recall any fund which has been number 1 for two calendar years in succession. I can recall funds which were number 1 in a past year that in a later year dropped very far down the list, and others that improved their position. This can occur for several reasons. Few of us who manage investments possess sufficient flexibility. We do well when the market matches our philosophy. We fail to change and we do poorly when the market changes. There are some small funds that do very well at first and grow fast. A point is reached where the ability to acquire desirable blocks or to move in and out quickly is reduced. Management changes. Investors rarely know the individual responsible for the investment decisions in a fund. They rarely know when management changes hands. They can really never know the effect of the passing years on a man's investment viewpoint.

Listen to what one topflight investment manager told me some time ago. "During 1968 I have been less flexible than I ought to have been. I have simply had difficulty in 'changing my spots.' The price risk inherent in the type of companies I favor has recently received notable publicity, and the prices of many of my most important holdings have declined precipitously. I also am caught in a situation of overstaying several of the conglomerate companies. A third factor in my current record is my reluctance to invest in several groups which are having the best performance on the tape. I own no savings and loans, no building stocks, and no cement stocks. I do not mean to imply that these industries and these securities are not attractive. It has simply been difficult for me to alter my strategy."

This is typical of problems that at varying times plague us all. Investors simply do not realize what is involved in delegating investment management. The performance figures they use as yardsticks are misleading measures. The average return the investor might expect over the years is nearer 9 percent than the "phone numbers" he sees for this fund or that over a short period. The majority of funds are only broadly confined to concentrate on growth or income. Few managements have the flexibility to change from group to group as fashions in stocks change. For example, the management that favors oil issues does well in an oil market, but is unlikely to switch to savings and loan if market leadership alters.

The figures for a period of years are more realistic. You must remember that when stocks go up steadily, fund buying is a major contributor to this advance. This is, to a degree, lifting oneself by one's own bootstraps. The downside performance in declining years is more important than the percentage gains in the good periods.

These figures alone are almost valueless without examining the reports of the funds under consideration. Look at their current and past portfolios. Look at their closed transactions. See if they own the kind of stocks, make the kind of decisions, and run the kind of risks that satisfy your desires. You must be sure their objectives are what you are seeking.

You can diversify funds just as you would individual stocks. You might want 50 percent of your equity money in a fairly standard fund, 25 percent in a growth fund, and 25 percent in some type of even more speculative special fund. Diversification costs a little more, but gives you more.

You can switch funds, just as you switch individual stocks. This also costs more, but the emphasis should always be on net investment results after expense and tax, balanced against risks assumed. There are many reasons that might make switching advisable. You might wish to buy small new young funds and switch back, when they seem to have reached less flexible proportions, into newer and still small issues. Emphasis must be placed on the investment expertise of the management over the size of the fund. Mistakes in small funds are much more damaging than in large.

Investors who manage their own portfolios often include special types of funds. Getting the best result from a 100 percent fund portfolio requires you to investigate and supervise your fund portfolio as closely as your individual stock list. You don't buy a fund and forget it if you want maximum results.

Type: It is fundamental that you select the type of fund that best fits your personal objectives. The groups available are endless. Some of the important classifications made by Arthur Lipper are "growth," "growth & income," "balanced," "income." Then there are the industry, dual, letter and many other kinds.

Size: There is a relationship in size between objective, performance and risk. It is a difficult problem to resolve. Large funds are probably safer. Medium-size funds are good all-around selections. Very small and new funds tend to involve the greatest risk, with occasionally offsetting gains.

Cost: There are varying acquisition, redemption and operating costs involved. Open-end funds can be acquired at commission rates, perhaps 1 percent. Their market prices relate to liquidating values—some at discounts and some at premiums. Management fees were formerly a set percentage but lately many depend on profitability.

I think costs are a relatively minor factor. High costs do not guarantee superior management, nor do minimum costs mean the reverse. The thing to do is to select your fund on other factors. It is wise, nevertheless, to know what you are paying.

Performance: The *Forbes Magazine Mutual Fund Survey,* published each August, correctly calls their performance ratings "consistency ratings." They are given for how well funds do in three bear markets as well as in three upswings. This is a most vital consideration. Thinking of performance in this way is meaningful when combined with other measuring factors.

If you do your homework as suggested here, you will reach a much sounder decision than just selecting at random, by hearsay or sales pressure.

E. S. C. Coppock of Trendex says, "The fact that some fund performed in excellent fashion during past years is *not* assurance that it will perform as well in the future. Many factors are involved. For example: members of the former management team may not be on the present staff; the changed size of a fund can make it less agile; changes in the popularity of various classes of stocks can upset the performance of certain funds."

A security-analyst friend of mine once told me, "I only need $50,000 more and I will have enough to retire. I will buy a mutual fund, get a check a month, and never look at the financial pages again." This is not an impossible dream. It can be part of a retirement program that includes other assets and resources. You end your capital-accumulation years. You start your capital-consumption years. For this purpose, you select one of the largest, most conservative, old-line mutual fund companies.

There is a place for mutual funds for almost everyone— if he can find the right ones.

77 *Six Salient Keys to Safe Investment*

The moment you have money at hand to invest, its value begins to change. If you buy a security, it is sure to go up or down. If you wait, you might eventually pay more, or you might get what you wanted cheaper. How do you make a safe investment? I use the following six keys:

1. *The Master Key to the Lock of Investment Safety Is Correctly Forecasting Coming Change.* I say "safety" and also mean "profit." No investment is safe unless it also shows a profit. If an investment fails to gain in price (with a few obvious exceptions), it will drop. The gain must be sufficient to offset dollar depreciation. The gain must be enough to cover taxes. A good investment is expected to return spendable money regularly. I do not mean so-called "income," which is a misnomer. Returns in the form of dividends or interest are simply added into the net profit or loss package. For current personal funds you should withdraw from your net capital a set percentage annually (or quarterly if that is more convenient to you). On the average, 6 percent a year or 1½ percent a quarter is a sensible amount.

Only if an investment improves in value as calculated here can you correctly label it safe, or know you have received a true profit.

Do not feel squeamish about possibly "spending capital." This method is more conservative than spending dividends at times when capital values are decreasing. It has a built-in safeguard because the amount withdrawn periodically varies with the value of your principal.

Most investors, who are basically engaged in other pursuits to make a living, erroneously see safety in quality. Quality is of secondary importance to trend. Those who bought long-term super-quality bonds a few years ago have lost. They failed to correctly see the change in money conditions that caused interest rates to increase.

2. *Risk Is Another of the Six Salient Keys.* And risk, to a degree, is related to quality. You should avoid companies that might run short of cash and be forced unexpectedly to put debt ahead of your common stock, or to dilute your equity.

3. *Price.* The price must not be so high that it already reflects the coming favorable changes you foresee.

4. *Time Is Important.* How long do you expect it to take before your favorable developments occur? Six months to a year and a half is a typical period. Important changes usually take time. The longer the period, the less likely you are of being correct. Three- to five-year predictions are in most cases valueless, in my experience. A 100 percent profit in one year is only 50 percent in two. If it takes five years, the annual gain on the original investment is cut to 20 percent annually.

5. *How Much Will You Invest in a Single Commitment?* I feel it should at least be substantial and important to you. A great many trivial investments will never pay off. A few carefully made ones can. Confine yourself to worthwhile positions that check out well enough for you to take the risk. The percentage of capital used will vary with your wealth and your ability and experience. If you are a beginner, you will naturally go light. As time goes on and you find success, your purchases will become greater. If you find you are not cut out for it—quit. Find someone to do your investing for you.

6. *Finally, Always Look Down as Well as Up.* Look at potential losses as well as hopeful profits. Your initial appraisal should have the odds well in your favor. But if you

are wrong, take your loss. This can be for various reasons. The news you expected may not be forthcoming. Unfavorable price action or an unfavorable change in the general market climate might make it prudent for you to close out and take an unbiased second look. If time passes and your commitment does not work out, that might be a reason to cut your loss. Five months is an especially good length of time to take an extra hard look. Losses are worth more if they are short-term.

You cannot bury your head in the ground and be a "do-nothing" and "think-nothing" and get safety. Your savings will be changing in value regardless. Only supervision, thought and action can help you in your battle for stock market profits.

78 *Tips*

Everybody dearly loves a "tip." There is something secret and special about it. You feel like you know something that the other fellow doesn't. A voluminous report printed in four colors on coated paper is supposed to be impressive, but it doesn't ring the bell like a confidential tip. Everyone knows the report took a long time to prepare. It takes an effort to extract any real points it may contain. It doesn't help that thousands of copies are available for the asking. Getting a tip can have a variety of meanings. Tips or rumors float around about supposed takeover or tender bids above the market. You hear about a broker with an important institutional following about to put out a favorable report on a particular stock. A famous fund manager is said to be buying a certain stock on the floor. A company has a new product or has discovered a new ore body or oilfield. A forthcoming earnings report will be good, a dividend is scheduled to be increased, or a stock split forthcoming. A dormant company is to be galvanized into new life with new aggressive management.

Good tips are valuable. They can be a source of profit. A really good tip can be classified inside information. You start with the trustworthiness and knowledgeability of your source. You must know your man. Is he honest? Is he in a position to secure the information he is giving you? To what extent does he benefit by telling you? Why is he telling you? What has he told you in the past and how has it turned out?

Some kinds of information can be checked on your part and other kinds cannot. You can check the market and see what is happening in the stock and what has occurred in it recently. This will give you an idea whether you are hearing something early or late in the game. Take, for example, a stock which has been dormant for months, with practically no transactions. A few sales occurred between $6 and $7 a share. Suddenly the volume of trading jumped sky-high and the stock advanced in six weeks to the $20 level. The recipient of "information" could judge at what point in a move his information was received. Obviously, you want to get a tip early for it to offer reasonable odds as to what you might profit against what you might lose.

Once again, remember what everybody knows is not worth knowing in the stock market. If you are told that XYZ manufacturing will earn $5 this year compared to only $2.50 a year ago, it is vital to know whether the $5 estimate is reliable. It is equally vital to know if it is still largely unexpected and undiscounted, pricewise. You can ask your broker the earnings estimates from several street sources. If he says $2.50 or $3, you may know something that can pay off. If he says $5, your information is probably largely valueless. The price of the stock will tell you a story as well. Has it already advanced to discount the $5? Or is it still at a $2.50 earnings level?

A good tip is gold in your pockets. Beware of a bad one, perhaps given to put your gold in the pocket of its purveyor, and watch the new SEC rules covering tips.

79 *Puts and Calls*

Are puts and calls of use to you? I think they have their value if bought and used the right way.

Most calls today are simply the right to "call"—that is to buy—a particular stock at an agreed price within a fixed period of time, usually either 90 days or six months and ten days from the purchase date. A put is just the reverse. You buy the right to sell at a fixed price within the agreed time. There is also a "straddle," which is the right either to put or to call.

These contracts are often termed "options," "privileges" or just "papers." They can be bought and sold, as well as exercised, through members of the New York Stock Exchange. All contracts written by members of the Put and Call Brokers and Dealers Association are guaranteed by New York Stock Exchange members. These are the only kind to buy.

The price you pay varies with the demand and supply and the volatility of the stock covered by the "paper." For a six-month-and-ten-days option, something like 15 percent of the price of the stock is average. A six-month call on a very active stock selling at $43, for example, would cost about $600. Calls on the old blue chips and Dow stocks cost less. A six-month call on Standard Oil of New Jersey will probably be under 10 percent.

What uses can you make of your option? There are many. A sophisticated professional can do quite a list of complex transactions. At any rate, on your first attempts, you probably will use your puts and calls to make a direct profit, or for protection as an alternative to a stop-loss order.

Let's say that a stock is selling at 43. You think it is going to 60 in six months. One hundred shares would cost you $4,300. A call on 100 shares would possibly cost only $600. If the stock does go up to 60 you can sell your call after six months. After commissions you have a profit of about $1,000, taxable as a long-term gain. Should the stock do nothing or decline, you would lose the $600 you paid for the call.

If the stock on which you have bought your call should go up more, or less, you have other courses open to you. It is sometimes possible, for example, to make several trades within six months and ten days. Information on all the possibilities may be obtained from a well-posted broker. S. D. Harnden, chairman of the Put and Call Brokers and Dealers Association, 19 Rector Street, New York, N.Y. 10006, has a simple 30-page booklet covering some of the fundamentals, which they will mail you for $1.

How can you use a put for protection? Let's suppose you buy 100 shares of stock at 43. If you buy a put at the same time for $600, you can limit your loss to 6 points (plus commission, etc.). You have paid an insurance premium for this protection, whether you use it or not. A stop-loss order costs nothing unless filled. But it may be filled at some discount from the stop price.

A put can be used instead of going short. It is just the

reverse of the use of a call. Likewise a call can be used as a short-sale protection, as an alternative to a "stop buy" order.

I think that you can benefit from the use of puts and calls. However, it is important that you get a full knowledge of how to use them. A recently published book (*Puts and Calls*) that covers all phases of the subject is by Paul Sarnoff, M.B.A., an authority on options and a lecturer in finance at the Hofstra University School of Business. Mr. Sarnoff defines what he calls the "Puts and Calls" method of investing as enabling the risk taker to know in advance how much he stands to lose (if he is wrong) or the profit he might make (if he is right).

80 *Contrary Thinking*

The really successful in the stock market, as in all lines of endeavor, are very much in the minority. It is obvious that they do something differently than the majority. Perhaps from these facts springs the largely incorrect idea that they succeed by doing the opposite. In the stock market those who endeavor to go against the crowd are generally tagged "contrarians."

There are necessarily two sides to every bargain. "Everybody" can hardly be buying stocks unless somebody sells, or vice versa. How can you tell what "everybody" is doing? Can you profit from knowing?

The idea that the crowd is always wrong is erroneous, yet many speculators try to base their operations on this premise. There is a time to go with the crowd and a time to go against it.

Bernard Baruch was a master of judging such times. In 1929 he gave many of his friends a book entitled *Extraordinary Delusions and the Madness of Crowds*. He wanted them to learn that the stock-market boom, which ended shortly thereafter, was a mania like the tulip craze or the Florida land boom. His timing was perfect. Had he given the book when the crowd began to take the bit in their teeth, his friends would have been out of a big bull market far too soon. It takes crowds to make major rises and falls. The art is to judge correctly when the momentum is really there, and when its strength is spent. Such movements always go to excess. It is an old Stock Exchange proverb that "no price is too low for a bear or too high for a bull."

Many investors look in many directions, hopefully to find the key to a trend. There are those who watch the odd-lot transactions for clues. They have their theories about the "little man" being mostly wrong. Others look at the opposite side of the coin to published data on what the big fellows and so-called "insiders" are doing. Others read market letters that tend to express contrary opinion. Some of the best known are written by Eliot Janeway, Humphrey B. Neill, William J. Baxter, Harry Schultz, Walter Heiby and Garfield Drew. In a sense, the so-called "formula plans" are designed to go contrary to the trend and, therefore, often contrary to the crowd.

The growing use of computers is fostering an excess of market "togetherness." There is currently a preponderance of important professional portfolio managers who believe in very similar principles of stock selection. These methods get programmed into a number of machines that tend to turn bullish or bearish at about the same time. The effect is to increase the intensity of the signals and alert a constantly widening participation.

Mr. Neill, who has written more on the subject than anyone else, includes in his advice on how to be contrary such essentials as "using your own head" and "trading along." He suggests closing your mind to the opinions of others, paying no attention to outside influences, disregarding reports, rumors, and what he styles "idle boardroom chatter."

Here again, we are in a gray area rather than one that is black or white. If you want to be contrary, you obviously have to know what others are doing. It is important to know if a stock or the market moves in a certain way, and whether rumor or fact may be behind the movement.

It seems that the more one studies and examines the numberless techniques of security and market forecasting, the more the true answer is a combination of experience, contacts and flair.

81 *The Big Blue Chips*

Why do the standard "blue chips" sell at much lower market valuations than the growth and glamour shares? Are the old-time corporate leaders cheap? Are there profits to be made in the "Dow" stocks? Some of the answers become evident by taking a long look back at what these stocks have done in the past. A collection of 100 charts for the period 1924–67, published by the F. W. Stephens Company of Newfoundland, New Jersey, gives an investor much to ponder.

The Dow-Jones industrial average chart begins at 100. It goes up to its 1929 high of 368.10, then drops to its 1932 low of 40.56, and steadily advances (with reactions, of course, along the way) to its early 1966 top of 1,000. Then comes the decline into the autumn of the same year followed by the 1967 rally and subsequent decline.

It seems from these averages that stocks have just kept going up and up. None of us buys "averages." Their methods of construction vary so widely that they can be most misleading. It is a different story if you examine some of the individual stocks in the Dow and other lists.

The chart of American Telephone is revealing. There have been excellent trading profits for the investor who bought and sold at various times during the years. One of the major moves was from about $30 in 1958 (adjusted for splits as are all of the prices used) to $75 in 1964. AT&T sold at $50 in 1969. It sold at $50 in both 1929 and 1930. An investor who bought and held from 1936 to 1958 saw it at $30 in both those years. The purchasing-power loss to the investor of almost 40 years ago who bought and sat tight is substantial.

IBM is not in the averages. It is a great exception because it has been a persistent growth stock, going from about $20 per share in 1955 to a high of $375 per share in 1968. Here, sitting tight paid off.

Looking over a few others, you note that Standard Oil of New Jersey was a dud for many years. In the period 1951 to 1964 it did well, but not since. Chemical stocks were reputed to have great growth potential years ago. Union Carbide, for example, advanced from $20 to $75 in the ten years 1949 to 1959. It was $45 in 1969. It was $45 in 1955. There have been big trading moves up and down in between. The man who held has missed many big moves in other stocks and has seen the purchasing power of his investment decrease. The rise in the cost of living has not sparked a rise in Union Carbide. As an inflation hedge in this period it has fallen flat.

Holders of old-time blue chips like Consolidated Edison (over 90 in 1929, 27 in 1969) and New York Central, now Penn Central (over 250 in 1929, 29 in 1969) have never seen daylight. The investor in Chicago & Northwestern (above 100 in 1929) suffered a calamity, with his equity practically gone, by 1939. During 1941 to 1943 the stock was delisted. It had its ups and downs until 1963. Then with new management it really took off, going from 10 to a 1967 high of 175½. In 1969 it took another nose dive. The buyer of Sears has prospered while the owner of Woolworth has marked time.

Thus we again are reminded, looking at these and others of the 100 charts in the book, that timing and selection, now as always, are the only keys to consistent market profits. You can look back and say, "If I held this or that, how much I would have made." The trick is to look ahead. This is what Oscar Hammerstein would have called a "puzzlement."

The standard blue chips sell for less because in many cases they offer less. It might be that their size is a handicap. Or they may be perpetuating old-time management. There are some managed for jobs, fringe benefits and pensions, rather than to realize the largest profits for today's shareowner.

There are profits to be made, nevertheless, in these giants. Some, big as they are, will get even bigger. Others will change for the better with changing management. Others may be at the low points of their cycles. Even the prosaic can become glamorous. In these days of conglomerates and mergers there need be no such thing as a "mature" corporation.

The answer is not to buy the companies that seem cheap, but those that appear to have a reason to improve. Looked at this way, many blue chips offer the chance of important gains at what often is minimum risk.

Remember, latent values are no help. Look for management that has the ability and aim to develop and realize on these values for the benefit of you today and now. We are in a time where this is happening with increasing frequency. There can be much more glamour and growth in cutting up a pie already baked and ready for eating than in going through the motions of making one.

82 *The Computer Is an Indispensable Investment Tool*

The computer is a present-day essential in information storage, retrieval and tabulation. It is becoming almost universally used for these purposes. It can print out such things as a tabulation of your portfolio arranged to show its diversification, valuation, income and almost any statistics of interest to an investor.

When you phone your broker he pushes buttons on a machine which obtains a variety of current information from a computer and displays it on a screen.

The advertisements on the daily financial pages are referring more and more to computer techniques. Among some of the current appeals are such headlines as "Computer-based Supervision for Your Portfolio," "Weekly Buys and Holds from a Digital Computer," "Computer Programming for Profits," "Computer Backed Predictions," etc. The material supplied is all procured by programming computers in various ways.

Computers are being used in the financial world in a growing variety of ways. A brokerage firm might decide to recommend the sale of all of a certain stock held by the firm and its clients. He would ask the computer to print out a complete list of holders. Stock analysts of diverse types will request varying information from their computer to reach investment decisions. A so-called "fundamentalist" will request material on earnings, working capital, price/earnings ratios and the like. A "technician" will be seeking such technical factors as "relative action," volume, "upticks and downticks," ad infinitum. Many weekly services to which investors subscribe are based on computer-tabulated material.

Computers are also used to test theories concerning market behavior. As far back as 1963 James H. Lorie, associate professor of finance and associate director of the Center for Research in Security Prices in Chicago, programmed a computer to determine the rate of return on common stocks for the 35-year period 1926–60. This study, financed by Merrill Lynch and the Ford Foundation, received widespread attention. It tended to highlight an apparent superiority of common stocks for their pretax realized rates of return compared with other investment media, such as banks, savings and loan, mortgages, corporate bonds and other sources.

The final hoped-for use of computers is to program them to come up with what amounts to a decision or a conclusion on what to buy or sell and perhaps when and at what price. Here we are still quite a distance away from anything really conclusive. It always takes the human mind to make the final decision.

Jim Lorie summed up a speech by saying, "If you know what earnings will be, you can get rich—if not, there is very little you can do." Nevertheless, investing without computerized assistance will in time resemble travel by foot as against car, train or plane. Advanced computer applications can in a few moments perform work that would take literally thousands of man hours. The amount of money spent for computer research on securities is going to continue to grow by leaps and bounds.

Up-to-date individual investment management requires access to computer material through your broker, investment counselor, bank, or by subscription to a service. But the final decision is a human one.

83 *What Is the Real Income Yield from Your Investment?*

All of us need income to support our daily needs and pleasures and to pay our taxes. Securing income from dividends and interest is not always the best way.

I am always surprised when people are impressed with compound-interest tables suggesting what they might be worth many years in the future. These tables are only valid if they starved, paid no taxes and lived that long. As they supposedly are eventually to reap the benefit of their sacrifices, it is part of the prospect to hope that their capacity for enjoyment at a ripe age is not diminished. It is blithely assumed, too, against the evidence of the past, that the dollars they finally receive will purchase as much as when they were saved.

A practical approach is to spend a selected percentage of the market value of your investments annually. Withdraw this sum, plus your taxes, from your account. The money you need is taken from your total fund, calculated after interest and dividends, profits and losses realized and un-realized, and taxes payable.

Looked at this way, the income yield of an investment becomes very properly minor to the real yield, which includes the change in value of your investment and the taxes due. The logic is irrefutable, yet many investors cannot really learn to think straight on this score. They think a company that pays a dividend is better than one that doesn't —and this is not necessarily so.

I have heard and read many arguments for and against paying dividends. Each case is different. The tax situation of the recipients of the dividend is often given more consideration than it deserves. The most important factor is the success the company's management can achieve with retained funds.

One of the very best expositions of dividend policy was once made in an address before the New York Society of Security Analysts by Oscar S. Wyatt, Jr., chairman of the board and president of Coastal States Gas Producing Company. Coastal States management has proven by its record it knows how to employ funds very profitably. In a five-year period, for example, Coastal States had a compounded earnings-growth rate of 24 percent annually. Taking net income as a percentage of stockholders' equity as of the start of each year, it had a return of 25 percent or better during the same period.

Mr. Wyatt told the analysts why he was against Coastal's paying a cash dividend at that time. He explained his point of view in these words: "Let's take a figure of $1 a share annually in cash dividends. That means $8,380,000 a year less in equity, or over $33 million less in capital funds potential. (Coastal is permitted as much as $3 of debt for each $1 of equity, subject to the various terms of its indenture.)

When you consider Coastal States' rate of return on equity you can appreciate our reluctance about distributing cash. Were we to pay out cash dividends, we would most likely have to go out and borrow money to replace it, thereby adding an extra interest charge to our operations." This covers points usually missed by those who think only that dividends are taxed to the recipient at ordinary rates while possible capital gains from selling stock are taxed at lower rates.

If you own non-dividend-paying stocks or stocks that pay you insufficient cash income for your needs, sell the required number of shares to secure the money you wish, or borrow against your stock. It should profit you far more in the long run from capital appreciation and lesser taxes paid than fooling yourself by buying supposedly high interest or dividend-income yield.

Suppose you leave $1 in dividends in a company doing as well as Coastal has done in the past. Your $1 under such circumstances would earn 25 cents in a year. If the market priced such a stock at 18 times earnings, the extra 25 cents in earnings could be worth 18 times that much to you, or about $4 in market prices.

Just be sure the company you own can use your money to advantage. If they cannot, it is better to sell the stock and to switch into a better investment than to hope to profit through a return from large and highly taxed dividends.

84 *With Profits Come Problems*

Making a commitment is many times easier than closing one. When you consider buying shares you can avoid a decision to buy altogether if the situation is in any way puzzling or not completely to your liking.

But once you own your stocks, the decision as to whether to hold or sell is quite another matter. You are forced into a yes-or-no answer, no matter how uncertain or confused you may be. It is like having your car straddling the railway track with the express coming down the line. You are on the tracks and the train is coming, so you must back up or go forward.

When speculation is at a high level that will be difficult to sustain, then the importance of correctly timing your selling becomes paramount. If you have a loss, then I think the solution is automatic. I am always in favor of limiting losses and charging them off as insurance. You should think of the price at which you plan to cut your loss when you make your purchase. This is partly to try to avoid the necessity of selling out stocks should they break widely known trend or support areas. At these points there is likely to be a considerable number of stop-loss orders and other sellers.

It is when you have a profit that the problem intensifies. It is vital to investment success to let profits run, but not melt away. Everybody hopes to hold stocks six months for more favorable tax treatment. This should be considered, but investment factors should always rule.

Near the top of the market you must be guided more by trend and action than by price. Certainly, if any of your shares stop going up, or start marking time, or start going down, consider that they are flashing a yellow light. Sometimes when stocks are very high, they will run up sensationally and turn right around and lose all their gain. Chart readers call this a "stilt" formation. This is almost always a reason for thinking about liquidation.

There will be no one day that you can label "the top." Even in a roaring bull market, individual stocks will make their highs many months apart.

As a practical matter, most of us have different guidelines for our policy in bull or bear markets. The sophisticated speculator will want to be long on nothing and short on anything in a bear market. In what he thinks is a bull market he will want to buy on credit and buy issues with the greatest leverage. On the other hand, there are investors who never feel happy unless their safe-deposit box is stuffed full of stocks. They might cut down somewhat if they think the market is dropping, but will ride through a storm with most of their shares. There are those who always keep fully invested but do a degree of switching. They vary the percentage of speculative and volatile issues as compared with the more stable-quality stocks.

In selecting stocks to sell, in most cases it will pay to go against your emotional inclinations and first sell your weakest shares. There are exceptions. Profits should be realized sometime. I think the age and extent of a rise is an important factor. I would be more inclined to sell a stock that has been a leader for two or three years than one that had just begun to move.

I do not believe in fixed formulas, but I do think that in a broad way a great deal of protection lies in decreasing your percentage invested as stocks advance into what seems to you to be the overvaluation zone. You must guard against owning more shares when the market is apparently starting down than you did when the rise began. Without disciplining

yourself you will get more courageous as stocks advance—
just when you should be getting more cautious.

I have been investing since 1920 and have learned that
there are no hard-and-fast rules about when to sell. Some of
the suggestions here will help. Probably as good a time as
any to sell is when you are mentally patting yourself on the
back for being such a successful and shrewd trader.

85 *Evaluating Market Risks for Sound Investments*

Popular ideas of the degree of risk in security investments
are largely misconceptions. Investors tend to think that
bonds are safer than stocks. They also lean to the idea that
securities which have the narrowest range between their
highs and lows are the safest. They cling very stubbornly to
the thought that stocks that have advanced the most thereby
incur the most risk.

These are all fallacies.

It is vital to appraise risks correctly. Any measure of
relative performance is meaningless without knowing relative risk. There is more than one type of risk. There is the
risk of market decline. There is the risk of decreasing earnings or dividends. There is the risk of inadequate finances.
There is the certainty of the decreasing value of money and
the increasing burden of taxation. This creates the risk that
the total of interest, dividends and capital gains (if achieved)
minus taxes will fail to keep even with the increasing costs
of living.

Bonds of medium maturities and high credit fluctuate less
than stocks but they cannot offset dollar depreciation. This

is a real loss. I know an investor with all his fortune in a single medium-grade stock. He had purchased it very cheaply when the company began business. Earnings had grown at a fast rate every year and the market price had grown even faster. In an endeavor to protect his profits he liquidated a portion of his shares and invested in high quality long-term tax-exempt bonds. Both the bond and stock market declined. A year later his stock had declined in market price more than his tax-exempt bonds. The earnings of his company kept increasing. Two years later his stock recovered from its market decline and sold at new high prices reflecting the continued growth of his company. His bonds declined further. Thus, what he thought was conservative proved in practice to be the opposite.

This illustrates the various natures of risk. If the earnings of his company had stopped growing or had decreased, his bonds would have lost him less than his stock. If interest rates had eased, his bonds would have advanced to a degree. The moral is that the least risk lies only in the security most likely to advance. If at any time you feel you know nothing that promises to show you a profit, then safety lies only in cash, or its equivalent in top-credit very short-maturity loans such as 91-day U.S. Treasury bills.

The greatest risk in stocks is the risk of market decline. It is impossible to know in advance what constitutes market overvaluation or undervaluation. Investment ideas are constantly changing. Optimism and pessimism always go to extremes. News is largely unpredictable. However, losses from overvaluation are fairly certain to be recovered in time, if the fundamental growth of owned companies continues.

The risk of decreasing earnings and dividends is highly significant. Losses here can be permanent. All stocks declined in 1929, but those that regained their earning power recovered.

The risk of a weak balance sheet is very high. Nothing can be worse than a reorganization and wiping out of all or a large part of your equity. Bad credit risks can be catastrophic. Certainly no careful or informed investor should continue ownership of stock in a company with a depreciating financial position.

Stocks that have the narrowest range invariably fluctuate little because the companies they represent are static. As in the case of bonds, static equities fail to keep up with the loss of dollar purchasing power. They offer no protection against this always present type of risk. Moreover, nothing really stands still in this world. What fails to improve generally depreciates.

Stocks that have advanced the most reflect some cause for their gains. The investor must determine whether the moving force behind their higher prices is permanent and fundamental or whether it represents pricing errors or misconceptions as to future earning power. The safest investments of all are more often than not in stocks that have gone up, are going up, and seem overpriced. The favorable market action and premium prices in such cases reflect the opportunities for high-percentage long-term gains.

Thus it is not an easy matter to evaluate true risks. Yet it must be done if you actually want your investment policy to be efficient, and as safe as you can make it. It is foolhardy to ignore the problem and bury your head in the sand. Risks can be much reduced by continuous review. Check your initial conclusions periodically and in the light of unexpected or new developments.

The best investment, and the one with the lowest risk, is

the one with most certain promise of profit. Unless an investment is also a good speculation it will not prove to be a safe investment at all.

86 *Dual Funds Offer Investors Maximum Income or Capital Gains*

The divided closed-end investment funds offer investors who want maximum income one type of security and those who want capital gains another. The leverage in their makeup tends to give the income shareholders almost twice the income they would normally receive from the ordinary fund. Likewise, the capital shareholders tend to make or lose at almost twice what would occur with the straight form of fund. These percentages change as markets rise and fall and premiums and discounts change.

The managers pay all the net income to the owners of the "income" shares. All the net gains (or losses) are credited (or charged) to the owners of the capital shares.

There are two types of dual funds. The first type includes those that are offered for cash or are traded in the market. The buyer can select the income or capital shares as he desires. The other type is floated in exchange for stock. The buyer or owner receives both income and capital shares and makes his separation at some later date that fits his objectives.

Dual funds have a definite maturity averaging around fifteen years. The income shares receive the income quarterly. The capital shares have the right to cash in only at maturity.

Investors in varying tax brackets, or with different objectives, can select the type of share that gives them more of what they want than the ordinary fund. The terms of funds vary, and prospective investors should check the differences closely.

Most important is the reputation and record of the management which selects and supervises the fund portfolio. Everything is secondary to the skill with which the investments are managed.

Dual funds vary, as to the precise terms, between the income shares and the capital shares. There are different legal restrictions and expressions of policy for each. This is extremely important, as individual shareholders will have varying views as to which funds seem to favor the income group or the capital group, as the case might be. There are also differences in the calculation of the management fee and the redemption of the income shares.

The market valuation of the income shares should be basically affected by the course of their dividends, the going rates for money and the policy of the fund managers as regards the type of stock they buy. An important factor is the degree to which management turns over the portfolio. Activity tends to favor the capital shares. Being new, dual shares will take a little seasoning so that investors can judge the performance of management, particularly with reference to the kinds of stocks they buy and the rate of turnover. Their market price will also later be influenced by the approach of their maturity date.

The income shares should prove the more stable of the two. They are in some respects preferred. They are suitable for low tax-bracket investors or for institutions that pay no tax at all.

The capital shares will be quite volatile and speculative. They are best for high tax-bracket accounts that can accept high risks for, hopefully, high gains.

The factors that make for open-market valuation of the capital shares are quite complex. For various reasons, closed-end funds tend to sell at discounts from liquidating value. In this class of stock, there is a leverage or margin situation. This means that if investors are bullish on the market and if the record of a particular fund is outstanding, it is likely to sell at a premium over its book value.

On the other hand, if the fund's management performance ranks below average in the market, or if a downtrend in stocks makes investors bearish, the discount can be substantial. The tendency is for the capital shares to advance much more than the general market and also to fall much faster if stocks seem to be headed down.

It is likely that as the larger funds secure listings on the New York Stock Exchange they will be in demand from traders who want to take a position long or short to benefit from a move in the averages.

Dual funds fill some investors' needs and will gain in popularity as their track records become more available for examination and as the principles under which they operate are more widely understood.

The income shares offer current income and a probability of increased dividends as the years go on. Under favorable circumstances this should give some measure of help in hedging against the seemingly inevitable rising cost of living. I prefer variable-income investments to fixed income, bonds, mortgages, savings and loan, or savings-bank deposits.

The most profitable participation in dual funds will be

through buying the capital shares when actively traded and listed, at times when the general market appears to be a good buy and starting a sustained uptrend.

87 *Good Management Is a Sound Investment*

One of today's popular pastimes for a dissident minority, as well as for publicity-seeking stockholders, is to raise an outcry against what they label "exorbitant compensation" for top corporate management.

How should this affect your investment decisions? Should you go along and support such efforts?

I think this is entirely the wrong way to look at it. Good management is cheap at any price. Poor management is always an extravagance, no matter how low-paid.

When you make an investment in a company, you are putting your money into someone else's hands. You should be concerned with their capabilities.

I remember the multiplicity of small independent automobile manufacturers in the early twenties and before. There were Chandler, Stutz, Mercer, Pope Hartford, Hupmobile, Maxwell Chalmers and many others. Maxwell Chalmers was fortunate to get Walter Chrysler. He made a fortune out of Maxwell, turning it into the Chrysler Corporation. The Maxwell stockholders did very well by paying for his genius. The others with less capable direction fell by the wayside.

There are many public sources of record of corporate compensation. University people, management consultants and others have tabulated these figures by industry in relation to the gross business of the company involved. The predominant factor should be the relationship between pay and results.

A really successful enterprise might be launched and guided by one dominating personality. There is no real permanency in such a situation unless the company's compensation plans are designed to attract a strong second-echelon team and to build with youth beneath that. As an investor you want to be sure that your corporation's compensation policies succeed in such endeavors.

Today our income-tax rates are such that old-fashioned individual savings are growing more difficult. Under modern political philosophies, both labor and management need provisions for the future in options, pensions and other similar plans.

The steadily increasing "fringe benefits" demanded by organized labor are a factor that needs investor attention. Excessive costs can reduce or eliminate profit margins. They can cut sales by forcing a company to price its products out of the market. The death of the New York *Herald Tribune* is a perfect example of such a company.

The price of executive manpower comes to a much lower total. The danger here is in having the wrong man at the helm. Each publicly owned corporation is in competition with other companies, as well as with privately owned businesses, to attract and hold the best executive manpower.

In most listed corporations the total of top-management salaries, fringe benefits, and equity dilution through stock options is a very low percentage of net income. The mistakes of corporate officers hired purely on a low-price basis can greatly reduce net income or even eliminate net earnings entirely.

If you are dissatisfied, I see little practical gain in attempting to reduce excessive top-executive pay. If you see a chance for outside interests to gain control by tender, market purchase or acquisition, then stick it out. Otherwise it is wiser to sell your shares and buy into a company whose management and prospects you like better.

When you look at your proxy to see what your management earned for themselves, turn to the earnings statement and see what they earned for you.

88 *Time Is Money*

If you were a professional man and were able to increase your hourly gross from $24 to $25 an hour, what would it mean in a year? If you worked 48 weeks a year and 40 hours in a week it would mean an additional $1,920 annually. Few professional men work only 40 hours a week. If you worked 50 hours, which is more like it, you would gain $2,400. And if you could manage to increase your hourly return by $5, you would increase your gross income by $12,000. This is pointed out in a story in *Medical Economics,* a publication available only to the medical profession.

I am writing for everyone and not for just professional men. It has long been my contention that our personal time is worth at least as much to us as our paid working time. With the demands of our work, sleeping, dressing, etc., what time we have left to do with as we please is worth a great deal to everyone.

I don't think we give enough thought on how to conserve time for our own pleasure. Here are two propositions:

Anyone who wastes your spare time is robbing you at a

dollar cost at least equal to what you earn. It doesn't make any difference what your hourly earnings are. If they are low, your free time is just as valuable to you as a big earner's is to him—perhaps more so. If you earn $5 an hour, and a barber charges you $2.50 for a haircut, the real cost to you is the $2.50, plus how much of your time he consumes. If you do not have to wait, and he cuts quickly and efficiently, the real cost may be $2.50 for the barber and $1.50 of your time or $4 in all. But if he makes you wait and does the job slowly, it might cost you $7.50, assuming you are in his shop a full hour. Think about this in relation to anything that can steal your time.

The second proposition is that anyone who makes you do something yourself that they could do for you is making you pay more than the advertised price. A trip to the supermarket on a Saturday costs time plus, perhaps, transportation. Are the savings more or less than ordering on the phone from the small corner grocery, which charges a bit more, but delivers?

The answer to these two propositions is very personal. Mathematically it varies with different rates of earnings, taxes, and what product or service you are buying. Then, there are folks who like to do some of these chores—in which case no calculation applies.

I am very conscious of the value of my time. I want to be the one who determines what pleases me the most to do with it. Years ago, before the advent of the railway dining car, the Sante Fe long-distance trains stopped for meals at the famous Harvey Houses operated by the railway. Each one had a sign, "Let us do the rushing—you take it easy," or something to that effect. It was a top-notch service idea. If you go into a restaurant for a quick bite and they are so understaffed that they delay you unnecessarily, they are stealing your time and your money. Your meal costs you more than the menu price. The walk in the park you wanted to take is shortened. The time you wanted to read your paper has been wasted for you.

Curiously enough, the inefficient restaurant man has lost as well. He pays by-the-square-foot rental for his space. If he delays his patrons, he can serve fewer of them, and his revenue decreases. He has made his restaurant smaller, as it were. All he has to sell is so many meals per hour. By doing it slowly, he serves fewer meals.

If we all thought more about making the most of our discretionary time, we would gain personally and collectively. The time-wasters would be gradually squeezed out. There is no successful business that is not ever watchful of the most efficient time utilization.

It can work just as well for you for your leisure hours. These words have not helped you to make money in the stock market, but, like I say, time itself is money.

89 *Things to Consider When Buying Convertible Preferred Stocks*

"Convertible preferreds" have become popular and have been issued in large amounts since 1966. Convertible preferreds are stocks that rank ahead of common as to claims on assets and dividends. They are also convertible into common at the owner's option. The precise terms vary widely with different issues.

From the standpoint of corporations out to expand through acquisition and merger they have some compelling advantages. They allow the acquiring corporation to buy

another company and make a favorable per-share earnings
report to their own shareowners because the convertible
feature reduces the number of shares which the acquiring
company has to issue in exchange for the other company's
stock. This might mean increasing the per-share net or preventing it from decreasing.

The accounting angles deserve a great deal of scrutiny.
In order to get a true picture of a situation the investor in
the common stock of a company with convertible preferred
outstanding should view earnings as being spread over the
outstanding common stock plus the shares that would be
issued on full conversion. Fortunately, earnings on a fully
diluted basis are now shown in company reports.

Convertible preferreds can be attractive buys for the investor. Each individual issue must be individually evaluated.
I feel the only issues to consider are those which are listed
and actively marketable.

Next, consider the industry and the company. It is vital
that you like the outlook for both. There is no point in ever
buying a convertible preferred unless you like the common
stock of the company in question. The fact that it is a preferred issue and ranks ahead of the common is secondary.
Never consider buying simply because you have that kind of
"protection." Always buy into a company where you expect growth or recovery. This applies to bonds as well.

Finally come the price and the terms. These are all important. A convertible preferred is only relatively "safe"
if it sells near its investment value as determined by its dividend and money rates. Convertible preferreds that sell very
high because their conversion privileges are already of value
and are the determining factor in their market prices are
to a great extent as vulnerable as common stocks.

In between are the issues that sell at investment value

plus a reasonable premium for the "call" they have on the purchase of common. Such a situation, combined with the probability of an early and worthwhile rise in the common, is the ideal situation for purchase. This occurs relatively rarely and it takes an expert to single it out.

If you own a common stock and your company issues convertible preferred ahead of your claim, thus causing potential dilution of your equity, satisfy yourself that you think the deal is of advantage.

If you are considering buying convertible preferreds in the market, consider the points above. Do not overrate the "protection" in the appellation "preferred." Instead, concentrate on evaluation of the terms, price and future.

90 *Earnings Mirage*

It is revealing to look back at previous earnings forecasts and add up the score in the light of subsequent actual results. A useful source for such information is *Standard and Poor's Earnings Forecaster,* published weekly. Much can be learned about the precarious nature and unreliability of such predictions by taking a hard look at the earnings forecasts made at the close of 1968 for the full year 1969. Naturally, estimates changed as quarterly figures were released, but an investor who pinned his hopes on some of these annual forecasts was very much disappointed with the outcome. As unsatisfactory 1969 earnings were made public, they caused some extremely sharp market moves— mostly down.

As an example of how very far from the actualities some of these forecasts turned out to be, note Penn Central.

Analysts doing "field research" late in 1968 publicized 1969 estimates of $4.25 to $5.50 a share for Penn Central. The actual figures turn out to be earnings of just 16 cents a share. There were Chrysler estimates of from $5 per share to $8. The final figure was $1.87.

These two were especially wide of the mark. Likewise some analysts were talking of $3 a share earnings for MGM in 1969. The actual figure turned out to be a loss of over $6 a share. Time, Inc., earned $2.45 a share compared to estimates as high as $4.50. There were disappointments in many directions, including companies like American Smelting, Armco Steel, Certain-Teed and TWA.

A few declines in individual stocks occurred as some companies publicly announced changes in their method of reporting. The actual results were the same—they were merely reported more realistically to stockholders. One such example was Career Academy, which announced a retroactive change in accounting methods that reduced prior earnings by 50 percent. The stock declined over 50 percent.

Substantial market declines occurred in Astrodata, Memorex, Control Data, and others on disappointing earnings results. Astrodata dropped from 32 to 18 and later to 11. Memorex was down 24 points between sales.

Investors should learn from these figures how difficult it really is to forecast earnings correctly a year in advance. Yet some analysts and corporate officers attempt to forecast three to five years ahead.

It is almost as difficult to be right in a year of rising earnings as in one of falling earnings. In 1965, a year before the major TV networks went into all-color, I found corporate officers giving me projected profits that were sharply under the final results achieved.

A further hazard for the investor is that in too many cases

the bottom line fails to report the actual operating profits for the period covered. The quality of earnings varies, depending on the degree of leverage in a corporation's capital structure. You need to look at the footnotes of the statements for the year and for previous years to make up your own estimate of what really happened. In some cases you will find nonrecurring capital gains. In cases where mergers have occurred, there may be many accounting loopholes. Often where management changes occur or where companies experience a bad year, they take excessive write-offs that will be written back up again as "profits" in a future year.

Ronello B. Lewis, well-known financial counselor to management, in his book *Management Control Techniques for Improving Profits* comments on recognizing these accounting practices for what they are. He concludes: "Investors are to blame when they willingly purchase the shares of such companies without even noting the annual report or the footnotes in which some of the 'pseudo' elements are revealed."

The accounting-principles board of the American Institute of Certified Public Accountants issues a publication, "Opinions," for the purpose of correcting these misleading statements. The SEC and the NYSE also endeavor to correct misleading statements but the corrections come slowly and late. Some corporate managements have excellent forecasting records. Some have just the opposite. We know this, because much of what they expect is put into writing. Just keep a file and look back a year or so or check with your broker or investment counselor. It is worth the effort to check history.

The price actions of stocks are often warning signals. If the figures publicized suggest higher prices and if instead you see a sluggish or weak market, be doubly careful. We also know this because of the big blocks of stock liquidated after the release of disappointing figures. Control Data once lost practically half its market value in six weeks when earnings expectations were scaled down. On the other hand, big blocks of a company's stock are often bought at higher prices after unexpectedly good figures come out. The important thing to realize is that wide price movements, up or down, accompanied by high volume, usually indicate that earnings are, or shortly will be, more favorable or more disappointing than generally expected.

The price/earnings ratio has come to be a popular method of stock appraisal. Before you accept it, think over the unreliability of both factors. We have shown here how little dependence can be placed on the earnings portion of the ratio. The multiplier used, whether it be 10, 20, 50 or whatever, is even more unreliable. There are theorists and mathematicians who will tell you what the multiplier ought to be; but in the market it rarely is. The multiplier is more likely to be the product of investor psychology, and its swings are as wide as the difference between the mini- and the maxi-skirt.

Earnings are the dominant influence on the actions of individual stocks. As Ron Lewis says, "Pseudo-profits are a disgrace. And their existence is a weakness in our free enterprise system."

As for the investor, forewarned is forearmed!

91 *Don't Count on Luck*

Does luck play a part in stock market success? Occasionally. Webster defines luck as "a favorable or advantageous event happening by mere chance." It occurs unexpectedly. It is never the result of effort or merit. Sometimes it is good and sometimes bad. There are those who believe in a "run" of luck. This exists at times. It is never predictable. You cannot know when your luck will run out. The investor who consistently does well with his investments rarely succeeds because of luck. If you have been lucky, the important thing is to recognize your luck for what it really is. Never inflate your ego and credit your windfall to an ability you do not possess. In the long run the result will be disastrous. Emotion should play no part in investment decisions. In reality, it always does. Your aim should be to keep it to the minimum.

It seems inevitable that when an investor has a series of profitable transactions, "lucky" or otherwise, his courage and opinion of his own abilities increase. His tendency is to assume greater risks. If he follows such a policy, a relatively small percentage drop in a maximum position can wipe out the total of a series of smaller previous gains. Whenever I have found reason to feel extraordinarily satisfied with my market achievements, it usually turns out later on that this would have been a good time to consider a change in policy. If it was a huge unrealized profit, it more often than not was a spot to turn the paper gain into cash. If the market fell out of bed when I was rich in cash and low in equities, then perhaps it was time to buy! Obviously there can be no possible fundamental background to such occurrences. It is also equally impossible to prove that they happen every time. There is no way of my knowing how typical my experiences have been. I rode through the 1929–32 depression making money each year. I thought I was surely entitled to feel my abilities had been proven for life. Little did I realize in 1930, when Ortega y Gasset wrote *The Revolt of the Masses,* that in the years to follow social revolution would increase the hazards of investing to a far greater extent than depression.

Over the many years that I have observed investor behavior, there does seem to be some psychological mechanism that triggers mass action at the precisely wrong moment. People own stocks. The market drops and drops. They find reason after reason to hang on. Then inevitably they lose faith and sell impulsively at the bottom. The financial writers call this a "climax." Investors with a less emotional way of thinking step in and buy what the loser sells. It also happens on the way up. Investors with money to invest wait. They see stocks get away from them and they do nothing. Then all of a sudden their pent-up emotions explode and they buy. Knowledge, experience and flair (not luck) are the cornerstones of investor success. Investment decisions must be dictated by investment opportunity and not by the rosy glow of personal financial hopes. Emotions should be subordinated to realistic thinking as much as is humanly possible. Cold analysis, not self-flattery, is what brings in the dollars. What passes for "luck" can often, like genius, be defined as an infinite capacity for taking pains. The consistently successful investor works to achieve his success, however "lucky" he may appear to others. Most of all, he contemplates the element of *change* in seeking a unique investment opportunity. Change is the life of speculation; it is the life of investment; it is the life of making money. Look for change. Too many people focus on what they call "growth and glamour." There is profit wherever down is followed by up. Such change can be due to cycles, to replacing bad management with good, to a change in fashion, and to other innumerable influences.

92 *Buy for a Move and for a Reason*

An important move in a stock—a big, worthwhile move —is really concentrated. It isn't slow and gradual. The reasons may build up over a period of years and not be reflected. Then, all of a sudden, they are not only reflected but are overreflected, and the stock shoots up like a rocket. Afterwards the stock will probably go into a decline or into another consolidation period. This kind of action causes investors considerable loss. Some see the situation correctly but get tired waiting for an important move and sell out. Later on, when an important move materializes, others, seeing the stock go up sharper than usual, instead of thinking this is the beginning of something, reason that the stock is now overpriced and due for a reaction. They then may sell or go short and be surprised at the persistence of the move.

Many moves, and big ones at that, have been seen on half-truths and overenthusiasm. Such moves, for instance, have been seen in the vending-machine business. Automatic Canteen advanced quietly during the period from about 1952 to 1958, with earnings coming up steadily. Then it exploded and the stock went from 10 to over 50. Earnings were 77 cents a share when the stock was 10 in 1958. They went to 91 cents in 1959, then back to 77 cents in 1960. In 1961 they were 75 cents and subsequently went lower. In 1962 the stock came back to 10, where it started. Buyers of this and other vending-machine stocks who bought to resell, with the idea that the public would be carried away and pay too much for them, did very well. Those who bought because they thought the vending-machine business was going to grow and grow and grow and grow became sadly disillusioned. When looking at lists of America's fastest-growing companies, it is well to take a double look and try to figure out if their excellent records can be continued.

Another stock that went up purely on expectations never realized was Technicolor. It was $10 a share in 1960. Two or three months later it zoomed to $40, then fell back again to $10 within a year. What happened? The company had new management and brought out a new projector. It was expected to be a success but wasn't. It was difficult to tell, at a time when the stock was around 25 and rising sharply, that it was moving up on hope rather than actualities, but in time this proved to be the case. You often hear the expression, "Don't argue with the tape." I am one of the believers in this saying, but be sure you know what it means. In this case, around 25, the tape was saying that there were more people who would be buyers at higher prices who believed in the success of this new magazine projector. It didn't say that the earnings were going to be up or that the projector was going to be an immediate success. It said that it wasn't, when prices skidded on the way down.

These illustrations should ram the point home that you can't generalize. It is essential to buy for a move and for a reason. Furthermore, every effort should be made to get the timing right. Just being in a variety of stocks with the general idea that the trend is going to be up will usually result in a mediocre performance. Almost surely, for each stock that goes up there is one that goes down and one that marks time, and the net result is not impressive.

I don't agree with those who think, "The time to buy stocks is when you have the money." Far too many newer and younger investors think the thing to do is to buy stocks and lock them up, figuring that if you buy growth stocks you can be sure that regardless of happenings and fluctuations, the market price will catch up and show you a profit. I think this is fallacious. You must do your best to be right on the market. You are not going to be 100 percent right, but you shouldn't be 100 percent wrong either, and an effort of this kind from a practical standpoint is going to pay off. The dangers of buying stocks and locking them up are many. There are some stocks that never come back after a severe drop, or that take a lifetime to come back. Remember, too, that nothing is ever said, in theoretical calculations of marvelous gains that occurred in the price of certain stocks about the people who buy stocks intending to lock them up, and then at some future time—and it is usually the wrong time—come to feel that the idea they had was wrong, and they get out just when they should be gritting their teeth and staying in. Selection and timing have to go together. This, to my mind, is the most serious and careful kind of investment.

Just as some people think that investment is something good and speculation is something bad, others think locking up a stock is good, and trying to buy it at the right time and price, and trying to sell it at the right time and price, is "playing the market." *I say that there isn't a good investment that isn't at the same time a good speculation, and, furthermore, there are many speculations that are much safer than many supposed investments.* The same thing might be said about many conservative accounts that pay some attention to correct timing and to the correct size of their positions. They are far more conservative, far safer, and far more intelligently handled than the account of the man who locks up his stocks and thinks he is handling his funds in the most conservative manner possible.

The world, and especially the investment world, revolves on change. The blue-chip stocks of today often had poor ratings years ago while many blue chips of years past are sometimes poorly rated now. Even the Dow-Jones average would be at a different figure if some of the stocks which have been dropped from the average were still there. (It is interesting to note that these averages were started a year or two prior to 1900, using about a dozen stocks that were selected for their quality, size and generally high standing. Only two are left in today's Dow 30 industrials, namely American Tobacco—with a name change to American Brands—and General Electric. One stock in the average was known as "Distilling and Cattle Feeding.") Looking at the changes over the years in the portfolio of a well-managed investment trust a while back, I found that there was only one stock among the ten largest holdings which was in the list of the ten largest holdings a decade earlier. The management explains that they dispose of mature issues which have run their course and replace them with "comers."

Don't let anyone sell you on the idea that an easy road to successful investment or speculation is simply buying something and staying with it.

93 *Human Foibles Play a Major Role in Shaping Trends*

Human foibles play such a major part in shaping economic, financial and political trends that the best research and analysis often leads us astray. It is sometimes the unusual and little noticed indicators that alert us more. All the movements of men are motivated by their minds. The human mind is more emotional than factual in its decisions, so it follows that an understanding and recognition of mass psychology is the dominant factor in making many correct decisions. This is doubly true when dealing with something as sensitive and as easily moved as the stock market.

Let's take a look at past history to prove a point. Quite a few really smart men were alarmed and bearish in 1927. Their conclusions were based on fundamentals. They were wrong for the last leg of a tremendous business and stock market boom because they did not take the inevitable excesses that lay ahead into their calculations.

I sold every stock I had in 1927, on fundamentals, long before the top was reached. Stocks kept going up, proving me wrong, or so I thought—so after a time I bought them back. I said, "Everybody's doing it," so of course so did I. I tossed fundamentals out of the window. I stopped trying to be an analyst and tried to become a psychologist. People make prices. It is people one needs to study. Behind the prices are profits, and profits are shaped by people. They save too much, or not enough; borrow more than they should or (believe it or not) sometimes almost not at all; go on buyers' strikes, or pay any old price no matter how high.

I am familiar with those who believe in being contrary.

This is only half the story. The full story is that you must go with the crowd while the crowd is in power. Being contrary at such times is like fighting the tides. The only time being contrary pays is if you can judge when the crowd's power is spent.

Let me tell you about the climate of the market when it was unwise to own stock. These recollections are not in chronological order. I did not keep a diary. They are true nevertheless. In 1929 the popular "price/earnings ratios" were a hazard—because pretty soon there were no earnings. The expression "the bigger they are the harder they fall" was very apt. The leverage men who went up on the double came down just as fast, or faster.

Mob psychology is catching; beware of it. I found myself one of the sheep. One of the most popular groups of the day was the over-leveraged, pyramided utility holding companies. Cities Service was a leading one. On a hot tip from a bank I bought Cities Service. I was saved when I woke up an hour or so later and realized how I had caught the fever. Cities went from $68 to $1 or $2. Pride goeth before a fall. When you feel like patting yourself on the back for doing so well, remember this, and remember the law of averages. Also remember that just as night follows day, and winter follows summer, so in the stock market up follows down and vice versa, except that there is no consistent pattern.

The most compelling stop light was the realization that saturation had been reached. One "hot" issue that came along was rationed to the extent that investors who wanted even thousands of shares were given odd lots. I was turned down trying to get a meaningful block for a large, well-known and influential client. Just after this offering I received a support order to keep the stock from going below its offering. If ever there was a sure sign of indigestion this was it. A stock that was a cinch for a fantastic premium needed support!

I know of no statistical measure as revealing as the following. Back in 1921 E. F. Hutton & Company's loans fluctuated in a narrow range. When they approached the upper level it seemed a good time to be cautious. The great bull market took these loans to many times their traditional heights. At first one fought the market. Then as they went higher one gave up and joined the crowd. There was no ascertainable height of these loans that one could tell beforehand was the real danger signal.

The reverse was true on the way down. I was in Munich on the bottom day of the first leg of the decline in late October 1929. The firm's loans were down $100,000,000. Stocks were way down from the top. Both later proved to be very far from the bottom. Our loans were paid off and we had unused capital in the bank before the end. There was no yardstick any banker, broker, investor or economist could possibly have used to make the right decisions.

The key words are "excess" and "mob psychology." One must realize everything is always carried to excess. The problem is that the degree varies every time. This is where psychology might help.

There is something of "keeping up with the Joneses" when an investor joins an enthusiastic crowd participating in popular market upswings. We see it in the competition for near-term performance. I put it this way because a good performance for a short period of time could turn out to be a very poor performance over a year or two or three. "Keeping up with the Joneses" sometimes causes investors to do things they otherwise would not do.

During those times Mike Meehan, the famous speculator and floor specialist in the high-flying RCA stock of 1929, opened the first office on a steamer—the North German Lloyd luxury express liner *Bremen*. I sailed on her for Europe in early October 1929. I think it was the maiden voyage of the sea-going board room. At least, so far no firm has opened an office on a jet.

I was not immune to the optimism of this period. I laid the groundwork for a stock market country club: membership fee, $100,000; $50,000 to build the club; $50,000 to go into the club's stock market fund. I was to have power of attorney to run it. We expected it to earn all dues and expenses and pay back the capital. The club was to include all the usual country-club facilities with no chits to sign. In September I approached two of the big speculators of that day who were worth certainly over $100,000,000 each. They said yes to my proposition as though buying a flower from a poor woman on a street corner. I returned from Europe, as it happened, on November 14th, the low day of 1929, and the club deal went out the window immediately.

In the second or third week of September, trading in and out for a client using an equity of about $750,000, I realized short-term gains of $242,000. In just one week. In November this client told me I was losing my grip because we made nothing in a week. It is like thinking that some of the high-performance percentages of recent years could be maintained. The Government, the savings banks, building and loan, insurance companies, realty mortgage brokers and the like would have to close shop if the funds were always able to average 30 percent and 40 percent and 50 percent and more per annum. Of course, this will not happen.

1929 was a merger-and-acquisition time. And a romance time. Birdseye Frozen Foods is everyday fare nowadays, but in 1929 it was all promise for the future. General Foods and Goldman Sachs bought Birdseye for some $25,000,000. A year or so later the GS half was sold to GF for $1,250,-000. After many years and untold dollars, frozen foods and Birdseye became a profitable business.

Fine brokerage offices were other straws in the wind. We built a showplace in Palm Beach. The interior wood was all weatherbeaten and genuine, collected along the Atlantic Coast. We had a patio, a fountain, palm trees, of course, a real fireplace, and two or three cars to lend just in case a client needed some transportation. I think the mayor of Palm Beach was our manager. It did not turn out to be a good market weathervane. Stocks went down and volume of trading dried up. One of the unusual and little used indicators of stock market trends is brokerage-house profits. In a broad way, stocks are a buy when brokers are in the red and a sale when brokers are making more than they ever believed possible. The trouble with this indicator is the same trouble we find with all indicators. It's a question of how hot is hot, and how cold is cold?

94 *Speculation or Investment? A Challenge for the Ambitious*

If you want to accumulate capital—speculate, don't invest. As I have mentioned earlier, and repeat now for emphasis, there is no good investment which is not at the same time a good speculation.

"Investing" means trying to put your savings in a safe place and getting some income from them. Let's face it—neither corporate bonds nor stocks, if bought primarily for safety and income, are really safe.

The lack of safety in bond investments lies in the almost certain fact that the dollars which are received at maturity will not buy the same values as the dollars which were originally invested. Occasionally they will buy more, but most of the time they will buy less. In recent years the cost of living has been advancing faster than the after-tax take-home income paid by securities. In effect, investors have been getting "minus income." Borrowers have had the use of money for better than free.

In the case of stocks bought for safety and income the real determinant of whether they meet investment objectives has been the change upward or downward in the price of the stock rather than in the dividends received. The dividend rate has had an indirect value of great importance, but only as it affects the price of the stock.

"Investing," therefore, is more theoretical than real. Investors are speculators without fully realizing their status.

THE SPECULATOR SEEKS CAPITAL GROWTH

"Speculating" means trying to put your savings where they will increase in value. Any income received is incidental. No one can say how long it will take to double one's money when speculating. That depends on the ability of the speculator and the economic conditions prevailing over the period of the speculation. The speculator has many advantages over the investor. The greatest advantage is that he strives for gain and seeks at the same time to minimize risk. He is, in effect, watching the road and watching the traffic signals. The investor tends to be lulled into a false sense of security and often neither points his car in the right direction nor watches its progress until it is too late.

The investor pays varying rates of income tax on his interest and dividends that could run so high as to be confiscatory, depending on one's tax bracket. The speculator often does not owe any tax until he sells, and in many countries does not pay any tax at all. The United States, because of the need for revenue and the realities of the political situation, taxes the profits of the speculator at varying rates up to a rising maximum of 25 percent and up on so-called "long-term capital gains." This is really more a form of capital confiscation than a tax. It persists because it is collected from a minority of voters. The majority is not well enough versed in Adam Smith to understand how it works indirectly against them as well. Despite this discrimination against it, speculation offers more potential take-home profits than investing. The annual price spread between the high and low of prominent stocks is many times the annual dividends paid. It is amazing, too, how even our very best equities can move over a wide range. It is not necessary to buy high-risk low-priced "cat-and-dog" shares to realize high percentage gains from speculation. For example, in almost every period of market improvement one can find a good blue chip that will double in price in a year or two. Standard Oil of New Jersey doubled from its low of 1950 to its high of 1951. Ford Motor doubled from 1958 to 1959.

The successful speculator advances by leaps and bounds: $10,000 becomes $20,000; $20,000 becomes $40,000; $40,000 becomes $80,000; $80,000 becomes $160,000. The rate of gain for the winner far exceeds anything even remotely possible in the way of compound interest.

EVERY YOUNG MAN A SPECULATOR

Youth deserves to speculate. The young owe it to themselves. Certainly those who are just starting out in business should be ambitious enough to test their own abilities while they are young and exploring the business world. Obviously not all are going to succeed. It is time enough to admit natural limitations after having given natural qualifications a chance to function. Security and pensions should have no place in the thinking of young people until they have made a try at reaching for the moon and until they have some practical measure of the length of their reach.

Unfortunately the term "speculate" has incorrectly been associated with gambling and recklessness. Gambling means betting on an outcome over which the gambler has no control or foreknowledge. Speculation means taking a calculated risk on an intelligent estimate of future possibilities. Practically every great success in this world of a national as well as a corporate and personal nature has come from intelligent and successful speculation.

95 *Growth Stocks*

Growth and glamour have become important words in the investor's thinking. In fact, there have been periods when almost any other causes of market fluctuations have been disregarded. Nobody can deny that growth is desirable. However, it is absolutely vital that when we look at growth we look at what might be termed undiscounted growth in earnings. Except for the in-and-out trader, who doesn't care if he pays too much provided somebody else takes it off his hands for more, growth stocks have to be approached with caution. It is folly, for instance, to pay more for growth than it is worth when achieved. It is also well to remember that every growth stock at some point reaches maturity. There are many formulas for valuing growth stocks but, in my view, most rest on the fallacy that the rate of growth in the past will continue into the future.

There are various types of potential growth stocks. The average investor will find it virtually impossible to buy into tiny companies at their inception. The degree of necessary investigation is high; the possibilities for loss, great. This sort of thing is successfully done by companies such as American Research & Development and, privately, by the Rockefellers, the Whitneys and others. It always involves an enormous amount of research, a tremendous number of rejections, many failures, a long wait, and, finally, ultimate success through a few tremendous gains that make the whole thing worthwhile.

The most popular growth stocks with the average investing public are those that have already grown. Here there is grave danger of paying too much and getting in too late and too high.

There are compilations of the leading growth stocks that have shown consistent growth for five years in a row. It is worth noting that often the law of diminishing returns just begins to operate shortly after listing is achieved. While here and there a growth industry or stock just keeps on growing, more often than not their most rapid growth has occurred before general recognition rather than after.

The most practical area in which to look for growth stocks is somewhere in between. They have to be past the promotional stage and not yet at the popular glamour stage. To find these is easier said than done. It is very much like designing automobile styles for a market three years ahead of time.

96 *The Elephant in the Living Room*

Is a good investment or a good speculation difficult to discover? Are the ruling reasons for purchasing a stock so intricate and so varied that only a few can ferret them out? The answer is no. While there are growth situations that are not immediately recognizable, there are also situations so obvious that a friend of mine calls them "the elephant in the living room."

Believe it or not, a company can have a good record, the stock can sell at a higher income yield than one might expect from looking at the record, its P/E ratio can be low, and it can stay this way year after year with nobody seemingly aware of it. Undoubtedly during this period people do take a look and, because it is so obvious, think something must be wrong somewhere, that "someone knows where the body is buried." But then one day something changes. Perhaps an investment trust buys a block and this influences other people to look at it when the record is published, or maybe a broker puts out a letter recommending it, or a smart investor buys some shares and tells a friend of his, moving the stock a little. He tells another friend, and the first thing you know its movement attracts other analysts who take a look. They find the record good. They buy some.

The truth is that one must never approach anything in relation to the stock market with any preconceived hard-and-fast notions. The important thing to keep in mind before taking a position in a stock, even in an obviously favorable situation, is to have some ruling reason for feeling that the status of the company and the price of its stock will change for the better.

97 *Dividend Delusions*

One of the widespread fallacies embraced by investors is that dividends are "income." At long last the falsity of this notion is beginning to be generally understood. Webster defines a dividend as "a share of anything that is divided." In corporation finance, this means that management elects to pay stockholders a proportion of cash earnings or, in some cases, surplus. They are fully taxable. The value of the stockholders' equity is reduced by the capital withdrawn from the company and this is reflected in the market by deducting the amount of the dividend on the day the stock sells "ex."

Many misguided investors think that spending what is left of dividends after paying taxes is "living off income." They think that selling a few shares of their stock and living off that is "living off capital." They are living off capital in both cases! Living off liquidated stock dividends or by selling a few shares of stock can result in spending less real capital than the cash-dividend way. Most stockholders know that taxes are lower on capital gains than on dividends, although the spread is narrowing. What they rarely consider is that selling off a few shares or selling off a stock dividend does not always result in a taxable gain. It sometimes results in a loss. Many investors pay taxes on cash dividends in a period when the value of their stocks is shrinking. The tax regulations are complex, with varying rates applying to different individual situations. The following example illustrates one of many individual situations. This investor has $10,000 in a stock selling at $100 and paying a $6 annual cash dividend. He is in the 50 percent tax bracket. His dividend is $600, less his $300 tax, leaving him $300 net. Consider another investor in the 50 percent bracket owning a stock paying $1.50 in cash. His dividend is $150 which, less his $75 tax, leaves $75. If we assume he sells a few shares to augment this by $450, his tax situation could be one of several possibilities. If he held his stock long term (which he would need to do to collect a full year's dividend) and had a capital gain, his tax might run half that of dividends. Ignoring surtaxes and rounding out figures, if his stock had appreciated to $112 he might sell 4 shares for $448. His taxable profit would be $48. Taxable at 25 percent, the net tax would be only $12. If his stock had remained at $100, he would have no tax. If it had declined, he would have a tax credit.

It is time that investors understand the true (and illusionary) nature of dividends. Once they understand, corporation policy can be changed for the better. Institutional investors can then buy non-dividend-paying shares without being criticized. Most people expect a regular spendable cash return from their investments. Corporate needs for cash are changing all that. Many pay cash dividends and then offer stock holders "rights" to put their money back into their company. (Incidentally, "rights" is a badly descriptive term for what often amounts to an elective assessment.) A small but growing number of corporations have an "automatic dividend reinvestment plan." You sign up to have your cash dividends automatically reinvested in the stock of the corporation that declared them. You also need to dig down into your pocket to pay the tax on the dividends you cannot spend!

Management that pays cash dividends when the company has need of the money generally does so only because, despite awareness of the bad mathematics involved, they feel that investor attitudes will cause their cash-dividend-paying stock to sell at a higher market value. This may have been true years ago but it is fast losing its relevance. Sophisticated investors have learned to avoid high cash-dividend-paying shares. Recent figures reveal dividend income from stocks almost 3½ percentage points less than the interest income obtainable from high-grade bonds. Fifteen years ago stocks paid more than bonds. The spread is widening.

The record over a meaningful period of years shows that high-income stocks as a group act less favorably in the market than those that pay less. Would you rather own an IBM with an income yield of 1½ percent or a U.S. Steel returning almost 8 percent? IBM appreciated in market value over ten times its 1955 price by 1970, while U.S. Steel sold at the same price level at the end of this period as it had fifteen years earlier.

I think the time will soon come when recognition of dividend fallacies will no longer be understood only by experienced and professional investors, but will gradually become a matter of general knowledge.

98 *Short Selling Results Have Been Drab Even in a Bear Market*

The recent history of short selling has been drab indeed, even for the professionals and even with market conditions supposedly made to order for the bears. In 1969, for instance, almost all the hedge funds, privately owned by wealthy capitalists and run by top professionals, shorted the wrong stocks at the wrong times in a very weak market. With the market going down almost every day, the short interest on the New York and American Exchanges fell to a three-year low. Not only did the odd-lot short seller chicken out, but exchange member and specialist short sellers went into hiding as well.

If you examine the list of what groups and what individual stocks were weakest in the bear market of 1969, you tend to find that the published short interests of the weak sisters were among the smallest. Thus, while the idea of selling short when stocks are going down is appealing, it rarely works. I think most investors will do very well if they can reduce their long position rather than go the whole way and go short.

Most investors are so consistently bullish that the idea of liquidating even a small portion of their holdings is completely against their nature. If they do think of going short, the tendency is to pick something that has advanced more than average. Sometimes these are stocks with very small capitalizations. Other times they are stocks with a strong reason for advancing. It is difficult for the average investor to think of a company like Du Pont, for example, as a good short. It proved to be an excellent one in 1969, going down from 175 in the fall of 1968 to below 100 a year later.

The most successful short sales are made by those who know bad news is coming before other people learn of it—anticipating lower earnings or dividends, for example. This kind of news is hard to come by since company officials rarely, if ever, predict bad news. The few short sellers who do succeed look at a variety of factors. Unfavorable relative action is one. Breaking trend lines and support points is another. Failures on rallies can be significant. It is helpful if the general trend is down. You must sell on the way down and never try to guess a top. I emphasize that your primary objective if you sell short should be to secure a profit for yourself out of a bear trend. Never short a stock making new highs. You have a chance of profiting from selling stocks making new lows, but relatively little chance among those making new highs.

If you do sell a stock short, there is one rule that must never be violated. Enter an open stop-loss buy order at the same time. If you have sold short a stock where such an order is not acceptable because of exchange rules, you have probably sold the wrong stock. If you want to stay short anyway, watch it and put in your own buy order if your loss reaches a predetermined amount. Ten percent is a good rule of thumb.

There is a minimum of literature on the subject of short selling. Elizabeth Fowler's book on how to make money in a bear market is titled *90 Days to Fortune*. Harry D. Schultz's book *Bear Markets* is subtitled *How to Survive and Make Money in Them*. Other discussions of the subject include a small book called *Technique of Short Selling* by Mark Weaver. Some observations on how to act in a bear market are contained in *A Strategy of Daily Stock Market Timing for Maximum Profit,* by Joseph E. Granville.

The practical rules about going short are simple. You tell your broker of your intentions. He will tell you whether or not the shares you want to sell can be borrowed. He can also explain the costs and hazards. You have to pay any dividends that might be declared while you are short. Profits, if any, are all short term taxwise, regardless of the length of time it takes to establish them. Your order can only be filled when the next sale is higher than the last sale. This is the "uptick" rule.

You can neither buy nor sell "the market." The trick is selecting the time and price and stock. If you go short, you must remember that you are fighting the long-pull uptrend in equity prices. Most of the time the basic forces are favorable for the owners of stock. We are all working and trying our best to improve things. We don't always succeed but in the long run we make progress. The popular dislike of fiscal realism supports the long-term bull trend. Inflation is forever! It covers up our overborrowing, our overspending and our financial errors, so that politicians and public alike find hiding the cost more palatable.

Very, very few succeed at selling short, and I don't advise you to try it. Most of us are not psychologically oriented to gain from disaster. It is very much like rooting for the visiting team.

99 *Importance of the Time Factor*

Nothing is more important in life and nothing is more important in investments than time—yet time seems to be glossed over in so many things and by so many people.

Union labor figures every aspect of its time. There is not only regular time but overtime, portal-to-portal time, and coffee-break time.

The best lawyers mostly use a sort of "time or importance" method of charging. If the time involved totes up to the larger fee, they use that. If charging by the importance of the case adds up to the most, time is relegated to second place. Lawyers rarely figure fractions of an hour.

When we move into personal life, most of us tend to forget time. The lawyer who charges $250 an hour, or any fraction thereof, drives down to the discount store or supermarket to pick up some $10 item for $9. Perhaps he uses an hour doing it (and uses his car as well) as against a moment's phoning for the item (at the apparently higher cost), and he thinks he saves money.

Remington Rand once advertised the high cost of executive thumb-twiddling. Here is the table they offered:

Annual Salary	Annual Twiddling Cost*
$10,000	$500
15,000	750
20,000	1,000
25,000	1,250

* at 3 minutes per hour

There is room for a great deal more thought on the cost of waiting for undermanned telephone switchboards to answer, insufficient elevator service, an inadequate number of clerks in stores or waiters in restaurants, and all that sort of thing. The price you pay for something, be it a service or a product, is only part of the price. The other part is the amount of time it takes. Places that keep you waiting are more expensive than places with adequate staffs and prompt service.

When it comes to investing, time is of the essence in more ways than one. *When* we get our money is every bit as important as *what* money we get.

How often have we heard someone say, "I doubled my money." This to me is a completely meaningless phrase. If he doubled it in a year, he was doing very well. But if it took him 12 years to do it, his annual rate is just 6 percent. There is obviously a vast difference between the two situations.

One often hears the statement "Stocks always come back." This is another meaningless remark. In the first place, all stocks don't always come back. Forgetting that for the moment, and considering those that do, many take

289

ten or twenty years. What happens to the unfortunate owner in the meantime? He may need the money. He may die. His position may be such that when he gets it its value to him is very much reduced. When you talk of money and investment, time is of the essence.

This time element seems to have much to do with the action of stocks. It seems to be in the nature of things for a stock to concentrate its movement in a relatively short space of time. This sometimes leads misguided traders to sell it short or sell it out early in its movement without consideration of the background.

For example, I recall that perhaps back in 1946 Hilton Hotels was first listed on the New York Stock Exchange. Something like ten years went by, more or less, with Hilton ending the period at practically the same price where it began. What had happened in those years? Conrad Hilton and his associates had worked day and night building up the Hilton chain. What's more, underlying property values were changing in Hilton's favor. However, marketwise, all they saw was a sidewise movement.

Finally, the Hilton stock started to move. Anyone who looked at it over the period of time of its advance might very well have thought it was going too fast or too far. What was really happening was the adding of ten years' growth, in this case after the fact. Digressing for the moment from the time theme, here was a case where the growth occurred first and the price discounting came after. This was an ideal situation because you didn't hope or anticipate or estimate that the value would be there. You knew it was there.

Knowing when such a movement is going to occur is one of the toughest problems of the investor. There are generally quite a lot of situations in the stock market that can fairly be considered "cheap." The trick is knowing when they are going to change in market value to nearer a "fair price" or even to an overvalued level.

It is vitally important also to know whether gains are compounded or not. Most sensational gains must be compounded. Compare the following two tables.

UNCOMPOUNDED AND COMPOUNDED CAPITAL GAINS, CONTRASTED

1 UNCOMPOUNDED YEARLY GAINS—net value after taxes, assuming the maximum 25% capital-gains tax (Shows what happens at various rates of gain if annually you pay your tax, spend your gain and income, and reinvest only the original amount)

	Rate of Gain			
	100%	50%	25%	10%
Start	$1,000	$1,000	$1,000	$1,000
End Yr 1	1,750	1,375	1,187.50	1,075
End Yr 2	2,500	1,750	1,325.00	1,150
End Yr 3	3,250	2,125	1,562.50	1,225
End Yr 4	4,000	2,500	1,750.00	1,300
End Yr 5	4,750	2,875	1,937.50	1,375
End Yr 6	5,500	3,250	2,125.00	1,450
End Yr 7	6,250	3,625	2,312.50	1,525
End Yr 8	7,000	4,000	2,500.00	1,600
End Yr 9	7,750	4,375	2,687.50	1,675
End Yr 10	8,500	4,750	2,875.00	1,750

The above table shows how little your fund grows, if annually you pay your tax and spend your gain and income, reinvesting only the original amount.

The table on page 292 shows the far more rapid growth of reinvesting gains and income after tax. More often the gain rate is even greater because an investment that is appreciating rapidly is kept for several years. This delays the payment of a tax, hence more of your funds are working.

2 COMPOUNDED CAPITAL GAINS assuming a maximum 25% capital gains tax

	Rate of Gain			
	100%	50%	25%	10%
Start	$1,000	$1,000	$1,000	$1,000
End Yr 1	1,750	1,375	1,118	1,075
End Yr 2	3,063	1,891	1,411	1,156
End Yr 3	5,360	2,601	1,676	1,234
End Yr 4	9,380	3,577	1,990	1,336
End Yr 5	16,415	4,919	2,364	1,437
End Yr 6	28,726	6,764	2,807	1,545
End Yr 7	50,271	9,301	3,334	1,661
End Yr 8	87,974	12,789	3,960	1,786
End Yr 9	153,955	17,649	4,703	1,920
End Yr 10	269,421	24,268	5,585	2,064

100 *Extreme Overvaluation and Undervaluation*

There is the story of an account executive in the West who used to tell his clients, "Buy what you know is good, not what you think will be good." This is one of those dogmatic statements that are right sometimes and wrong at other times. Such a comment also depends upon how people interpret it. As a matter of fact, it isn't far off from saying "Buy low and sell high," which certainly isn't wrong if you know what's "low" or what's "high" and if it doesn't take too much time between the low and the high. Similarly, we don't always know what is good, and we don't always know what is going to be good.

I know, for instance, that if I looked back into the archives of 1929 I would find that New York Central was one of the things that people then "knew" was good. It was selling over 260; it was earning $16+ per share and paying an $8 dividend. Three years later, however, it showed a deficit of over $3.50 a share, passed the dividend, and the price dropped to 10. After that it went into a trading range, but thirty years later, in 1962, it again sold at 10.

What was good in 1929? Well, one of the stocks I remember that was good was Coca-Cola. It was selling around 175 or so and in 1930 it sold higher than it did in 1929. It also earned more and paid more. After that it went into a reaction, but by 1935, way ahead of the rest of the market of course, it had topped its 1929–30 high. By 1929 Coca-Cola had attained some stature but it was still considered very speculative and people talked about its low book value and one thing and another, and I am quite sure it wasn't considered a widows' and orphans' stock at all, such as New York Central, for instance.

Another stock that was good was Columbia Pictures. I remember that stock in 1929 sold over 50. It had a sharp decline with everything else into 1932, but by 1935 it was above its 1929 high, many, many years ahead of the averages and years ahead of some sound investment stocks. If you told a widow to buy Columbia Pictures in 1929 you would have been severely criticized. Certainly she would have had a rough ride down to the bottoms of 1932, but the value was there and it told in the long run.

Of course, the really good stocks under such circumstances were the golds. Dome Mines sold around $10 at the top in 1929 and it never did have the tremendously drastic break that other stocks did, although it broke badly enough. It went down to maybe 6, but by 1931 it was above 10 and by 1934 it was above 40. McIntyre Porcupine was higher in 1931 than it was in 1929 and vastly higher in 1934, when Roosevelt was elected and the gold price started going up.

If you study the old records of stocks and what they did in the period on both sides of 1929, you come across several recurring patterns. You have a very limited group like the golds, which held very well and immediately went higher. You had a few special stocks which were able by the 1935–37 period to top their 1929 highs. Then you had others which have never come back. They went down and they have just stayed down. Then, too, you have the so-called averages, which took twenty years to come back. There is a lesson of sorts in this and that is that while for all practical purposes all stocks go down together and all stocks go up together, the percentages on each move are very different and nothing is so important as having the right issues. Thus, if the averages should decline, just for purposes of the discussion here, by 25 percent, there will be some stocks that might only decline 12 or 15 percent and others that will decline 50 percent and some more than that. Then, if the averages should rally from their bottom by 25 percent, some will rally 50 percent and some 25 percent with the averages and some 5 percent or not at all, or actually go down.

There are other lessons in looking over old records. They just show over and over again that the stock market is subject to extreme overvaluation and to extreme undervaluation. Thus, the short seller can be very right on his fundamentals and lose a great deal of money, and likewise a buyer can know everything there is to know about a company and find the stock goes down, down and down.

Another lesson in these old figures is that a real yardstick for measuring stocks is the unknown future. Looking back over the financial history of the New York Central, you see a record of earnings, say for the five years preceding 1929, of $12 a share, $14, $13 and $16; a record of dividends of $7, raised to $7.50, then to $8. It was not only an investment stock in those terms but a growth stock as well—a steady, quiet uptrend. When the stock sold at 160, on the way down from over 260, down 100 points, one might soothe himself and say, "Well, look, this isn't overvalued, just selling at ten times earnings, the $8 dividend gives a good yield." A few years later, when it was selling at 10, it was paying no dividend and showing a deficit. I doubt if anybody in the railroad or in the investment fraternity, or anyone else ever predicted this in these terms. And yet, somehow, the stock market was saying that something was wrong and somehow some people must have had a feeling that the tide was going out, although they probably didn't know how far it really would recede, or that it wouldn't come back in again.

Stirring up old memories, I flip over the pages of some of these old statistics and I come across a company called Novadel Agene. In 1929 this stock sold at 30. I am sure if anyone said, "Put your money in Novadel Agene but stay away from New York Central and stay away from Consolidated Gas (now Consolidated Edison), and stay away from Western Union," they would have been thought to be very speculative indeed. Yet, in 1930 Novadel Agene sold at 45 and by 1935 Novadel Agene was selling at 120. How could anybody know that Novadel Agene was going to be good? How could anybody know that New York Central and Consolidated Gas and Western Union and many others which were then thought to be good were not going to be good. I think the lesson is very clear that the stock market is subject to extremes and shaped by the future rather than the past.

101 *Beware of Popular Methods of Evaluating Stocks*

If a stock seems especially weak, the chances are the news ticker will print a conversation with the company's management. Such a press interview might read: "Such and such an issue is off 7 points to 96¾ after having traded as low as 94 on a turnover of more than 115,000 shares. A spokesman said the company knows of no internal reasons to explain the slide in the price of its stock."

There is always an explanation for market movements. The possible reasons are too numerous to list. Often in weak markets many stocks simply adjust to reality. A corporation spokesman is not likely to comment on his company's market valuation by stating publicly that his shares are only declining from an absurd overvaluation.

I believe that thinking in total valuation, as well as per-share price, is helpful if you are trying to value a stock. A while back, the shares of a very well-managed corporation advanced substantially on an oil discovery. A friend told me he thought the stock was a buy at 130 or thereabouts. I asked him, "Do you think their oil is worth a billion dollars?" He said he had never given it a thought that way. I replied that at recent prices the market was valuing the property at near a half billion, *i.e.*, 4,000,000 odd shares multiplied by $130 a share. Anyone who would risk buying a stock that had sold 100 points lower the year before would certainly hope to at least double his money. Hence the discovery would have to generate enough income to make the stock worth $260. The buyer had to consider the additional capital needed for the facilities and transport, etc. The $130 area subsequently turned out to be the top for this stock. When these shares started back to reality, what comment could any official make as they dropped under 100? There almost certainly was no "internal reason." It was simply an overdue market correction.

There are speculators who practice what they term the "greater fool" theory. They buy an issue gaining in popularity and price regardless of value. Their only consideration is that they can find a buyer or "greater fool" at a higher price. In my opinion such "speculators" are far from being "fools." I do not doubt that many have more in the bank and are in a higher income-tax bracket than a host of certified financial analysts. The stock mentioned previously advanced in about a year from 30 to 130. I do not know its real value. Since selling at 130 it has fallen back under 20. You might wonder if a trader who bought on the way up at possibly excessive prices, but going with the trend, and sold at a profit is the greater or lesser fool than many analysts. The real fool was that investor who, guided by what he thought were fundamental or technical factors, bought and held the stock on the way down.

Popular methods of evaluating stocks are ever changing. On the whole I think the "in" issues of the times are usually grossly overvalued. Investors lose a great deal of money by too readily accepting the popular methods of valuing stocks. We have all seen fantastic evaluations placed on certain stocks which became fads, with great expectations, only to see their prices plummet later on as they went out of favor. The successful investor must constantly bear in mind that these changing yardsticks affect stock prices to a much greater extent than changing fundamentals.

There are those that adopt various statistical formulas for valuing securities. One of the very best discussions on the subject was given in lecture form by Arnold Bernhard at the

Bernard M. Baruch School of Business in the fall of 1958. Mr. Bernhard, of course, is the well-known originator of the Value Line Investment Survey. He discussed both factual and fallacious generalizations about stock evaluation. One of his observations deflates some of the misuse made of the price/earnings ratio. To quote: "Imagine, for example, that you and I became partners and bought a small drugstore on our block. Let us say that we paid $50,000 for the furniture and fixtures and the stock in trade. In the first year of operation we lost $2,000. Would you say that in that year the value of our business was less than zero because we reported a small deficit? Of course not. You would reason that the asset value and the going-concern value entitled the partnership to a value, although there were no earnings in the one year.

"If, in the second year, due to, let us say, an influenza epidemic, which found us supplied with a great deal of vaccine and our competitors short, we earned a profit of $40,-000, would you reason that, because we earned a profit of $40,000 in the second year, our business was worth $400,-000 or ten times the earnings? Probably not."

He further observed that it may come as a shock to a thinking man to be told that billions of dollars of trades on the stock market are executed without reference to any definable standard of value. Mr. Bernhard went on to say that he was sure some standards were in use, though not defined, and possibly were applied "by ear." I will add to this by saying that what investors "hear" is simply the popular yardstick of the day. It was irrelevant yesterday, and it will be irrelevant tomorrow. This is why I keep stressing the overpowering influence of the psychological factors in determining market trends and prices as opposed to the fundamental. The appraisal of mental attitudes outweighs statistical valuation.

Whereas most market valuations of popular issues are on the high side, privately held companies are usually treated on a far more realistic basis. For one thing, book values properly count for much more than in the open market. The difference between a realistic private valuation and a public one should not really be so very great. The publicly held stock has some added real values such as liquidity and collateral value. There is a value of sorts in the fact that the stock moves, and an astute investor can profit from this. In many cases the company's credit is improved and financing is easier and less expensive. So are merger and acquisition prospects. Comparison with the public price involves a consideration that there is often a degree of privilege in being allowed to buy the private shares.

The investor must pay going prices in order to own any stocks at all. The important fact is for him to know whether they are overvalued. If he is buying stocks that are advancing (and why buy any others?), he must realize what he is doing and resolve to sell when the trend turns down. Contrary to most investors' ideas, many stocks return a profit to their holders only if bought and sold, and not held indefinitely through many ups and downs. For example, the buyer of Chrysler in 1963 at 25 gained little from holding onto the stock through the company's sensational gain in profits that reached a peak in 1969. In 1970, the stock dropped back to its 1963 price of 25. The real gainer was the investor who took advantage of the rise from 25 to above, 70, buying and selling. This need to buy and sell is especially true of stocks in cyclical industries such as the motor business. It is occasionally less true in consumer or really long-term consistent-growth companies. Even here the factors of recurrent over- and undervaluation, new competition, and other developments often upset the apple cart. For every IBM there are thousands of stocks that go up and down and over a period of time get nowhere.

You should take periodic inventory of your investments. Annualize the return. Check the historical price path and dividend record. Make your projections for the future. From this, decide if you are locking up stocks that should be liquidated. Most investors should probably be less hesitant to buy stocks whose earnings are temporarily depressed, and should also be less prone to hold onto high-priced shares that seem in a declining price trend. The downtrend of the stock can be far more significant than the weak premise of supposed "values."

102 *Portfolio Pruning Is Rewarding*

I think pruning an investment list is as important to an investor as pruning a tree is to an arborist. Of course, pruning a list is the reverse of diversifying it. Intelligent pruning can be very rewarding.

I remember years ago when an investor friend of mine hired a mining engineer to give him advice on mining stocks. Once a month we had lunch with him; he would tell us which mines he had visited during the last month and give us the results of his studies and the information he had obtained from other mining men that he had met at the Mining Club, and so forth and so on. But he always used to end up by telling us what he liked, and it would generally be anywhere from twelve to eighteen different mining stocks.

Now, of course, he didn't run very much risk there, because of those twelve to eighteen stocks, most would probably work out in an average way. Maybe he made a mistake on one or two and maybe he made a brilliant pick on one or two, and the whole thing would average out. But actually, if we bought his twelve to eighteen mining stocks we could probably have done just as well by picking them out of a manual or out of the quotation sheet of the newspaper as we could by talking to this man who had all the contacts in the business and all the knowledge. So we just had to break him down, and it certainly was a hard job. But we would get him to knock out this stock and that stock and the other stock, and talk this way and that way. Finally we distilled his list down to the one stock in the whole batch that he really thought had the greatest possibility. I can certainly say that time and experience proved this was worthwhile.

Every stock you own has possibilities of going down. You have to keep working on them. Take them up one by one. Don't just keep something because you happen to have it. Try to see which one has the greatest possibilities of going up, or weigh the possibilities of its going up versus the possibilities of its going down. In this kind of pruning, by the way, you have to be the leader. Other people don't like to take that responsibility, and with good reason. As a matter of fact, you have to goad them into pruning off this and pruning off that. Depending upon your broker, depending upon how good a goader you are, the list will be cut down a great deal or a little or hardly at all. After the fruit tree has had its deadwood pruned away, the fruit that is left will be improved; so will the stocks that are left on the live list.

103 *Pseudoprofits*

There are many ways of keeping books.

Companies provide a detailed set of figures for the tax department. These figures may take a different form in the reports prepared for management, and they may be presented in a still different fashion to stockholders. Of course, this is entirely legitimate. The reports used internally reflect what management thinks is happening. Sometimes, however, results vary so much and are affected by so many internal and external conditions that a separate set of reports, clarified and simplified for stockholders, gives a more accurate rather than a less accurate picture.

Often we find that management attempts to put its best foot forward or attempts to be overconservative, and this seems to be human nature at work. There is nothing too bad about this if it is consistent, but what is misleading to investors is when management switches its accounting thoughts backward and forward from overstatement to understatement. This may result in an accurate statement over a period of time but it may not reflect when the profits were earned. The ways of overstating or understating profits earned in a given period are intricate, and the true facts are often within the books of the corporation rather than in the published annual or quarterly reports. Because of this, it is next to impossible for investors to find all these switches in accounting procedure except for the big ones which might be pointed out by the auditors in the footnotes to their certification. It can be assumed that if the auditors take exception to something, there are likely to be other things that appear in the company's books, but not in the annual report, to which they also take exceptions. Always remember that the auditor's certification only pertains to the audited statement; he does not certify the accuracy of the chief executive's letter.

There are some people who think that conservatism is always good, but conservatism can be as misleading as overstatement. This is particularly true when a new management comes in and writes everything off, which is supposed to be very conservative. By so doing, they start with a clean slate and because of this maneuver the initial earnings will most likely put the new management in a favorable light. Later on the conservative approach may be abandoned in an effort to shore up a mediocre earnings performance.

Thus, despite the purpose of everyone concerned, you have to have your tongue in cheek when it comes to looking at published statements. Things can be written up; things can be written down. Expenses can be prepaid; they can be delayed. Maintenance, repairs, etc., can be deferred; they can be accelerated. The same is true of advertising. Windfall profits can be added in or separated. The same is true of windfall losses. Subsidiary earnings can be consolidated or unconsolidated, depending upon what the management wants to show. The point of all this is the need for consistency. When earnings are reported first this way and then that way, this should be regarded as a danger signal for investors.

"Managing earnings," a phrase that has lately come into overfrequent use, is bad for the corporation that indulges in the practice, bad for its shareowners, and bad for the entire investment community.

104 *The Trend in Security Taxation*

The Tax Reform Act of 1969 began a new trend in the taxing of income in the United States. The act outlines the tax rates and rules on a gradually changing basis between 1970 and 1973. It is not my province to give instructions on how to fill out your tax return. This should be done with a qualified CPA and tax adviser. My purpose is to discuss tax philosophy as related to investments and to suggest some areas for consideration.

One of the original aims of the 1969 act was to assure that every person with an income above a certain amount paid some tax. This meant a tax on so-called "tax-exempt" bonds. This aim was sidetracked by political pressure from the cities and states. The probability exists that in the future this subject will be reopened and tax exemption will cease or be decreased. As a matter of fact, the Treasury is currently taking a new look at tax-exempt municipal securities. Federal Government bonds were at one time wholly tax-exempt. This privilege expired in 1945.

Buyers of tax-exempt bonds, except for very near maturities, should take this threat into consideration. Personally, I don't like to purchase tax-exempts because they lack inflation-hedge qualities and they are vulnerable to unfavorable interest rate changes.

The new act divides income into two classifications. The first is termed "earned." The writers of the bill assumed that only income derived from personal services is "earned." This so-called "earned income" is given favorable treatment. It gets an eventual tax ceiling of 50 percent.

The effect on business policies of this lower rate will be widespread. Corporate management or working stockholders of privately owned businesses have long striven for the largest equity ownership through stock options and purchase plans or otherwise. Now the highest current cash pay will become the most protected type of income. This change will stimulate many repercussions. For one thing, major corporations will be able to hold their younger and more ambitious staff members by offering them higher cash salaries. The attraction of establishing their own ventures or joining young new concerns will be reduced. The latter used to offer possibilities of capital gain at a 25 percent tax ceiling, but the law now gives less favorable treatment to such gains.

The second label applied to income is "unearned." This classification includes dividends, interest, and capital gains —in short any income or profit not a direct cash payment for services but earned as a result of the use of capital. These rates escalate. Publicity has centered on the tax-reduction features of the bill. However, from the standpoint of the investor, the changes in capital-gain taxation are unfavorable.

The new tax bill strengthens several of my principles for sound investment policy. I fear taxes will continue to be increased over the coming years, as in the past. This reinforces the policy of realizing at least some profits annually and paying tax on them. The importance of the time element in capital gains is increased. The percentage of worthwhile gain must not only be in excess of dollar depreciation but of increasing taxation as well. A stock that advances 20 percent in a year and then starts to mark time has only advanced 10 percent annualized if it is in a rut for the second year.

The power to tax is supposedly not the power to destroy or to redistribute savings and capital. Unfortunately, politicians use it this way and also to achieve various social changes. The good of the whole nation would be served by repeal of capital-gain taxation. When linked with inflation it amounts to confiscation. Politics being what it is, fair taxation and a 100 percent stable dollar are both extremely unlikely. Possible improvement would be to postpone payment of the tax until securities were liquidated into cash. Exchanges would be permitted without a tax. They are permitted now in certain real-estate transactions and in a few merger situations involving the exchange of securities.

There are those who believe that it will take five years until all the regulations and rulings called for in this act are actually determined. In addition, new amendments are practically certain. Despite its punitive features, the new act has not closed all the loopholes or "soaked the rich" to the extent desired by its writers.

The odds favor an early companion piece of legislation on gift and estate taxes. The basic idea would be to tax unrealized capital gains at death. This, of course, would be just another reason why gains should be taken year by year and not allowed to build up. It is cheaper now to transfer property during life than after death. There are ways through trusts that allow a tax to be skipped for a generation. In considering current investment and tax policy, I would not count on these provisions for long.

Individual capital-gain tax provisions for 1969 remained unchanged so that the alternative maximum long-term capital-gain rates were at the rate of 25 percent plus 10 percent surtax, or 27½ percent.

Starting in 1970, the rates and provisions escalated the tax. The 25 percent alternative long-term capital-gain tax applies to those taxpayers who are over the 50 percent regular tax bracket to the extent of the first $50,000 of long-term gain. Everything over that is taxed at new rates. For 1970 the rate (including the surtax) is about 30.25 percent. In 1971 the maximum rate becomes 32.50 percent.

In 1972 and future years, until changed by some later tax bill, the rate advances to one half the current maximum ordinary tax rate of 70 percent, which is 35 percent. The absolute maximum on capital gains can be higher, depending on the influence of so-called new "tax preferences." These can only be calculated in each individual case, depending on the actual sources, amounts and type of income.

The tax preference idea is brand-new and, like all devices for increasing taxes, will undoubtedly be expanded as the years go by. As it stands now, a tax preference includes most types of income that pay less than "ordinary" rates, as well as many types of specific deductions. The "tax preference" is an added 10 percent tax under varying conditions when "preferential" items are in excess of $30,000 of ordinary income added to your ordinary income-tax liability. Security investors will note that the 50 percent long-term capital gain is a "preference," as is certain interest paid to carry investments when they total more than some types of interest earned.

The new law reduces the amount of long-term capital loss that can be used to offset ordinary income. There is also a new loss carry-over rule unfavorable to the investor.

The new regulations for the first time permit income averaging for long-term capital gains.

The bill has many other provisions too involved to detail here but important for the investor to understand. There are changes affecting corporation capital-gain treatment. Banks are required to report capital transactions differently than in the past, in a manner that should tend to put pressure on certain types of "tax-exempt" bonds. Treatment of gifts of securities is altered. Allowable deduction of interest paid is reduced. New provisions affect foundations with security income. Effective dates vary.

The Battle for Investment Survival (Simon and Schuster) in its chapters "Investment and Taxation," "Do Tax Losses Mean Savings?" and "Don't Let Tax Questions Cloud Investment Decisions" discusses further angles of the interaction of inflation, investment and taxation.

To sum up, your best policy will almost certainly be to place investment principles first. Take your profits and pay your taxes as you go.

105 *Investing Is Such a Human Business*

Keeping score cannot help you much as a guide in Wall Street. The champions of the last move may be in the cellar on the next. Why is this so? It is because investing is such a human business. If it were a question of formula or rules, then all who knew the formula would do equally well. Instead, it seems that a dozen competent investment managers sifting the identical facts end up with different conclusions.

The human power of decisiveness is not a constant thing. It is always changing. The same mind reacts differently from year to year as it grows older. Each experience alters its future point of view. It can be too venturesome after a successful transaction. It can be overcautious after a disastrous one.

All of us grow up with a kind of investment philosophy of our own. It is, in fact, a kind of bias. An ingrained daring. A prejudice. A slant this way or that. Let investment conditions happen to fit our view and we will do well. Let them change without our changing and we will do badly. The flexible mind that can adapt quickly is rare.

Thus, when we start to appraise investment results these are the first factors we have to keep in mind. For example, in a given period, you note that one investment company apparently outran the competition. A close look shows that the management favored assets in the ground and especially oil. Their investments in petroleum stock were double the average of other funds. During the same time, oils did best in the stock market. When a decline comes in oils, the chances are this management will not have liquidated. Then their investment performance will drop below average.

Every great genius has his productive periods—his time of life when he wrote his best book, or painted his best picture, composed his best music, designed his best building. Above-average outstanding investing is a similar matter of flare or genius. Men who make a great "killing" in the market rarely make two. Where group management is concerned, one rarely knows who is responsible and for how long will continue in responsibility.

Then there is the question of risk. This is not always easy to weigh. An investor splits his account between two managers. Let us say one ends a year's trial with a seemingly better result. This would seem at first glance to be clear-cut—the equity in one account has grown faster than in the other. But one must look at the risks. The seemingly superior result may have been obtained by running an all-out-of-proportion risk. If continued, it could very well bring the leading account back under the second-place fund.

Of course, some broad estimate of ability can always be had. Continued persistent failure can only mean incompetence. Refusal to be judged is something to be avoided. This is where a fund management overdiversifies or confines itself to such standard investments that it is quite evident that it will not risk an unusual position for above-average gain for fear of possible above-average loss.

In selecting an architect for a house, one naturally looks at what different men have designed and built, and chooses the man whose works seem closest to the style he, the client, wants.

As a practical matter we are forced to do the same in choosing an investment manager or policy to implement our own desires. We select the one that seems to fit closest to our requirements and we hope for the best.

106 *Psychology and Style*

Textbooks and school curricula seem to skip the most fundamental of investment subjects—psychology and style. There seems to be a feeling in academic circles that the thing to do is teach students what value you should place on a stock—or what price the stock should command in the marketplace. In the practical world it is absolutely immaterial to know at what price stocks should sell. The important thing is at what price they *are* selling and will sell. A large part of the answer here revolves around psychology and style.

A security analyst with a New York Stock Exchange member firm some years ago set up a tabulation of the Dow stocks on the basis of statistical values but kept the names of individual stocks coded. Needless to say, the indicated value—that is the price these shares should be selling for according to textbook theory—turned out to be far different from their current selling price.

Over the years, almost every type of business has at some time or other stimulated the imagination and its securities have become fashionable and popular. This vogue has added many points to real value which, of course, in time have been lost as the usually fickle public has found a new favorite. Over the years we have had war booms, growth booms and inflation booms. We have had booms based on new inventions in airplanes, electronics, radio and television, aluminum, automation, space technology, or what have you.

Marketwise, the effect always seems to be about the same, namely, a considerable overdiscounting of the situation. This is followed by disillusion. Finally, in a few isolated cases, permanent earning power develops, and this is recognized by recovery in the shares of the few companies that really make the scene.

The most important factor of investment and economic psychology is that market prices reflect the expectation. The realization may or may not come. If it comes, it has probably been discounted. If it doesn't come at all, prices naturally are readjusted as people realize that their hopes or fears are baseless.

107 *Fallacies, Myths, Misconceptions, Legends: True and False Ideas About the Stock Market*

(1) *Stocks recover if held long enough.* It is certainly fallacious to think that stocks recover if held long enough, yet this is one of the most popular ideas held by people. The record books are full of examples of stocks of invest-

ment grade that have never come back. Some of them have vanished entirely.

It should be realized that even when stocks do come back, that's of little use to the original investor when it takes them 20 or 30 years to do so. During that period his life, needs and desires have changed. The value of money has changed. In the meantime, other opportunities have slipped by. So it is much better to admit a loss, if you can spot it, while it is still moderate—say 10 percent. But even if it really gets away from you, usually it is better to take a substantial loss and start off anew than it is to be tied hopelessly into something that you wouldn't buy if you had the cash.

(2) *Short-term trading is speculating.* By short-term trading, I mean from hour to hour or day to day, and occasionally week to week, but really short-term. I am not thinking in tax terms of less than six months; I am thinking in terms of very brief trading.

It has always been my experience that it is easier to tell what lies just ahead than it is to tell what lies a long distance ahead. Strictly speaking, short-term trading is speculative, but so is all intelligent investing. What the people who use this term really mean is that short-term trading is gambling—but it is decidedly not gambling if done by traders who know what they are about. It is easier to tell what the weather is going to be an hour from now or a day from now than what it will be a month from now, and it is easier to tell what the market is going to be too.

(3) *Money is safe.* This has been discussed so much that it is hardly worth listing among fallacious beliefs. Money is only good for what it will buy. The purchasing power over the ages has been steadily decreasing. It certainly isn't safe.

(4) *Buy low and sell high.* Well, this is a beautiful idea

if you can do it. The truth is no one knows what "low" is
and no one knows what "high" is.

Right after 1929 many people thought stocks were very
low and selling at bargain prices. They never dreamed they
would go as low as they eventually did in 1932. But, by
the same token, once stocks started to go up after 1932,
many people said, "I won't be caught again; I won't buy
them unless they are real cheap." Of course, they have never
been at those low prices since. They never got real cheap. I
have seen people sell stocks that they thought were high,
based on what they had seen previously, and they have
gone higher and higher. Then reasons developed that they
didn't look high at all any more. So the buy low–sell high
idea is one of those lovely things that would be fine if we
knew how to do it. Bernard Baruch put it this way: "Don't
try to buy at the bottom and sell at the top. This can't be
done—except by liars."

(5) *You will never get poor taking a profit*. This is an
old saw that people trot out, and, of course, it doesn't work.
In fact, the thing that you see about most accounts that is
wrong is that it is human to take a profit and let your losses
run, whereas if you were going to lay down some kind of
rule it would be better not to take a profit but always take
the loss. I don't believe in any rules or formulas. I have
said that numerous times. But the fallacy of letting your
profits run and cutting your losses is better than that of
never getting poor taking a profit. People who say they
never get poor taking a profit are the ones that mean take a
profit as soon as you see it, so the profits are bound to be
small. You can be very sure that when they have a loss they
don't take it but wait, hoping for an eventual profit. You
can be equally sure that the losses total up to far, far more
than the small profits registered, so that investors subscrib-

ing to this philosophy will assuredly get poor taking a profit.

(6) *The stock market is a barometer of business.* The barometer registers the atmospheric pressure at all times. It is accurate in registering this pressure, and by reading it you can often determine what the weather is going to be, or forecast it. But the stock market at any given time does not exactly measure the business volume or the degree of prosperity or profits. What it measures at any given moment is the expectation of investors. Business may be good and the market may be going down, and therefore the expectation of investors is that business is going to suffer. Or it could be the other way around. Business is down and the market is going up, so the expectation of investors is that business is going to get better.

Over the long term, of course, the market and business do come into parity now and then. However, those who have taken a weak market as a sure sign of coming bad business, or a strong market as a sure sign of coming good business have been disappointed many times.

(7) *Never sell America short.* In a broad, inclusive sense, this is accurate enough. Up to now, America has had its setbacks, but has always come up on top. From that point of view, I find no quarrel with the phrase. The trouble is how it is applied. Of the people who use it, most use it incorrectly in applying it to some segment of a given situation —maybe their personal business or a particular stock they have, or some industry. A certain industry can be in a decline, can be moving into difficulties, could even be going into bankruptcy. And to hang on blindly and say "Never sell America short" is silly, because America can go right on growing and prospering while this particular item passes out of the picture, and indeed can be a good short. So be sure, when you see this phrase, to think of it in relation to

our economy and our well-being as a nation, and not as an argument to stay in a situation that you ought to abandon.

(8) *Real estate is a safer investment than stocks and bonds.* This of course is a mixed-up statement to begin with. We might rewrite it and say that real-estate equities are safer than stocks and real-estate mortgages are safer than industrial corporate bonds. I think this phrase has its origin among people who say, "Well, I can see a piece of real estate; stock is just a piece of paper." Of course someone can look at a piece of real estate without the judgment to know the value or the direction in which this piece of real estate is moving—and another have an excellent grasp of the scope of the industry represented by the "piece of paper." Broadly speaking, real estate isn't safer than securities and securities aren't safer than real estate. Nor is one a sounder investment than the other. The truth of the matter is that it all depends upon who is doing the investing.

I think real estate has many advantages mostly given by law. You can borrow more on real estate, and at the present writing the tax situation is better regarding real estate than stocks. On the other hand, it is much more difficult for people to be right on real estate. It is a slow and costly thing to liquidate. You've got to be more of an expert. I never said it was easy to invest successfully in securities. But I think it is less of a battle than to invest successfully in real estate.

(9) *Never pay more than 15 times earnings for a stock.* This, by the way, used to be "never pay more than 10 times earnings." This is one of the most ridiculous and inapplicable fallacies ever repeated. There is no standard price/earnings ratio for a stock. As a matter of fact, the very earnings on which the ratio is based can be expressed in so many ways and still be within the limits of acceptable accounting that you can't even begin with the earnings. Aside

from that, the price/earnings ratio of stocks in general is an emotional thing. This ratio has varied a great deal for all stocks, or for the Dow averages, or the Standard and Poor's index or any other broad measures of the market that you want to consider. If you were to take this level blindly and then apply individual issues against it, those with a price/earnings ratio above the average might very well work out better than those below. I don't say every one above would work out; I don't say every one below wouldn't. But I think that, on the average, the issues with the higher price/earnings ratios would indicate that within their general picture things were better than those with the lower price/earnings ratio. Exceptions are always excluded.

(10) *Only the rich can make money in the stock market.* Many of the rich, of course, were poor, before they saw the stock market. The stock market made them rich. There is a half-truth in this fallacy. I think it is fair to say that to some degree the rich ought to be able to do better in the stock market than the poor. The chances are, for example, that they have more time for it. The chances are that they can hire better people to help them. The chances are that they can risk more. The chances are that they have more time to spend on their education.

A lot depends, of course, on where they got their money. If they made it themselves they are more likely to know what to do with it than if they inherited it. Some rich people inherit money and get poor very quickly. One can say this about the poor too: the poor man has the drive to get rich, and the rich man is likely to be soft. Money isn't so valuable to him.

(11) *Preferred stocks are the only safe investment.* The word "preferred" in everyday life always means something that is better. But in investment parlance preferred stocks

are not better than common stocks. They are preferred as to dividends in the case of trouble and they are preferred as to assets in case of liquidation or reorganization, but actually it is better to buy a common stock that you think is going to stay out of trouble and improve—and if it gets into trouble sell it—than to buy a preferred stock and stand on your legal rights. On preferred stocks of the straight, ordinary kind your income is limited but your loss is unlimited.

The only kinds of preferred stocks that I think are attractive are those in trouble but coming out of it. They can often be bought at a large discount, sometimes with arrears, or when they have the advantage of a conversion privilege. Preferred stocks are not usually a better investment than common stocks, as some people incorrectly believe.

(12) *Sell a stock when the good news is out; and* (13) *buy a stock when the bad news is known.* Well, these two go together.

The truth of the matter is that news is only discounted once. It can be discounted ahead of time; it can be discounted at the time; it can be discounted after the time. In the latter case, that is when it is wholly unexpected. So this old axiom to sell or buy when the news is out only refers to a piece of news that is discounted ahead of time. What's more, sometimes a piece of good news is going to be followed by more good news, or a piece of bad news is going to be followed by more bad news. So, as in every investment action, a great deal of discretion has to be used. Of course, if we could say, "Sell when the good news is all out and when it is fully discounted," that would be true, particularly if you felt that there was a turn for the worse coming along in the near future.

(14) *Stock splits advance prices.* People generally think that stock splits advance prices. Usually if people hear about

a stock split, a stock goes up in anticipation of what is considered good news, and if the stock split is a surprise, then the stock may go up after the news is out. But the general idea that just because a stock is split it is worth more is not, I think, a correct one. It is the trend that counts. If a stock is split and the company keeps on prospering and the stock has split not because it is high-priced but because the company is doing better and earnings and dividends are rising, the stock is going to go up. But if the stock goes up and is overvalued and the stock is split simply because it is high, then there is trouble ahead.

(15) *Never buy a stock that returns less income than a bond.* The stock-bond ratio theory used to be that because the dividend on stocks tended to be less safe than the dividend on bonds, which were a prior charge on earnings, one should get more income than one should get from the bonds. This is quite logical. But the fact is that there is more than the dividend in a stock. There is the possibility of appreciation and there is the equity ownership which gives you some protection at times against inflation. I think it is a bad rule. Once again, the only rule, the only formula, is good judgment.

(16) *Bonds are an investment; stocks are a speculation.* I suppose most people regard an investment as a place to put their money and get back the same dollar value, keep it safe, and get some income return. I have said many times that this is a fallacy and that unless an investment is a good speculation it isn't the safe investment that people think it is in the first place.

Now, what do people think a speculation is? Most people think a speculation is simply something that is more risky than an investment. This isn't really true. A speculation actually involves peering into the future to try to see what is coming and to buy something that will become safer than when you buy it; that will pay more income than when you buy it; that will sell for more than when you buy it. Certainly these are the elements of a good speculation.

This type of action is much more often achieved in a stock than a bond. The very best-grade bonds seldom go up; as a rule they can only go down. The only bonds that are sound investments and at the same time sound speculations are bonds which have been in trouble and are coming up—in other words, bonds that are selling on a stock basis rather than on a bond basis.

108 *The Pebble in the Pond*

"Pebble in the pond" investing is a recognized source of profits to knowledgeable and sophisticated investors. There is almost always a ruling reason why one profits in the securities market. To the uninitiated, it is most often the hope of a higher dividend. Elemental as this expectation may be it is none the less valid. However, it is only one of a myriad of things that tend to influence share prices.

Drop a pebble in a pond. The resulting concentric waves fan out ever wider in diameter. Have a new or privately owned corporation "go public" and the effect is the same. It gradually comes to the notice of a constantly widening circle of investors. The inevitable result is a constantly increasing valuation of its earning power. Please, do not jump to the false conclusion that anything new will advance. In practice, successful purchase of new issues is something that normally requires skill and experience. There are usually more pitfalls in new issues than in any other part of the market. This is because the appellation "new issue" covers an enormous range of issues big and small, obscure and well known, promotions and sound financings. These are offered by an equally large number of sellers from the smallest to the biggest and the worst to the best. What I am talking about is the meritorious new issue, correctly priced and well sponsored. Occasionally the same principle applies to a dormant "old" issue that meritoriously begins to be known to a wider audience.

First, consider a brand-new issue. Perhaps a new corporation is formed to engage in some new enterprise. At the start, it is considered too hazardous for the investing 'public. There is no record of earnings and assets to attract them. A small group of men are brought together privately. They supply the initial capital. This is "getting in on the ground floor." After a time there are indications of success and a small public financing is arranged. The appeal remains limited. The price of this issue continues necessarily low but, if the enterprise is succeeding, not as low as at the start. Now the new shares are quoted "over-the-counter." Trading is so small that prices are not yet published in the newspapers. Maybe one or two dealers "make the market." If this is one of the few new companies destined for big things, the growth of earnings and, much later, dividends keeps pace with the growth of stockholders. In time the prices of the shares are quoted in the papers. Later they are listed on the American Stock Exchange or on a regional exchange, then perhaps listed on the New York Stock Exchange. Each step involves a wider exposure to investors and an increasing valuation. A dollar of earning power in a company owned by a few is worth far less than the same dollar in a company owned by many. With each broadening of the market comes an increased flow of financial information. The financial journals and the advisory services write more and more about the company. The shares begin to appear in institutional portfolios.

Finally comes the day when "everybody" knows about it. The price/earnings ratio, that popular measure of market valuation, is astronomical. The power of the pebble has been exhausted. The last ripple has occurred.

The water is smooth.

Our knowledgeable investor is no longer an owner.

He has sold out and taken his profit.

The waves from the pebble in the pond can be just as effective in forgotten and neglected old listed issues which are given new sponsorship. I recall a privately owned stock that went public. It was in an industry rather difficult to appraise by comparison. The initial price did not seem low to me, however. Earnings were in an uptrend. I felt I would see a moderate profit as a widening circle of investors became familiar with it. Actually it advanced far past my expectations. It started over-the-counter, but its rapidly rising market appraisal (price/earnings ratio) lifted it long before it grew to a New York Stock Exchange listing.

A real pebble in the pond.

109 *Goals and Aims*

Given intelligence and understanding, the higher the investor's aim the more likely he is to succeed. The qualification comes from the necessity of relating risks to aims. I have often said that if you aim to double your money and only half succeed you are much better off than if you try to get 6 percent and only realize 3 percent. On the other hand, if your aim is to double your money and run a risk of losing it all in the process, that is not at all what I mean. An old Chinese dictum tells it like it usually is: "Aiming at the large would get you in the middle; aiming at the middle would get you the small."

The average aim of the average person who makes an investment is to keep the dollar value safe and get some regular income. It is only human to hope for a profit. There is also a hope that if the invested funds are needed earlier than expected they can be realized without too much loss.

A second, and more sophisticated aim, is to attempt to keep the purchasing power of your investment, and keep it net after taxes. Here, too, some regular income is usually desired but is given less emphasis. On the other hand, investors with this objective tend to be more than ordinarily conscious of day-to-day liquidating value. The true speculator wants to make a killing of large proportions.

In my opinion, all of these aims are difficult to attain. Not many people realistically succeed in their investments.

It has been my experience that those investors who aim the highest do best. They may try for a killing and only end up protecting the purchasing power of their capital. Others may try for protection and barely succeed in keeping their dollar value intact. It seems that those who try for the least and usually think they are safest in doing so end up in the red.

It may be that the governing factor is not the direction of their aim at all but the level of their intelligence and understanding. The very fact that they are able to point in the right direction is perhaps an indication of a superior ability to get where they want to go.

To succeed, investors must classify themselves realistically and set realistic goals and aims. Let's face it—there are many whose capabilities, resources, available time, risk-taking ability and other factors do not fit them for anything more than the safest possible approach. In this world of uncertainties this calls for a hedge against inflation and deflation and investment error. This can best be accomplished by investing funds as they become available, half in short-term United States Government bonds and half in the best investment trusts, and mutual funds.

This is the simplest, easiest and most effective formula for average investing. It will never make anyone rich but it will certainly give the minimum of heartaches and require the minimum of attention. Peace of mind is a rare state and completely unappreciated by most of us. From an investment point of view, this formula will yield the maximum peace of mind. Sitting on the porch in a rocking chair will not enable anyone to scale the highest mountain but it will protect him from a fall trying to reach the peak.

110 *The Battle for Investment Success*

Has investing capital for security, income or profit become more difficult?

It certainly has. But there can and always must be winners in the battle for investment success. A winner is the lone wolf, who despite increasing handicaps finds a key to doing better than the average. The first thing for the lone wolf to do is to assess the difficulties facing today's investors.

(1) The continuing decrease in the value of money is one of the major difficulties. It once was true that in a period of stable money or in a period of deflation cash was

a haven from declining stock values. Cash either held its purchasing power or increased its purchasing power of things or services in general. This is no longer true. Stocks can go down and money can buy less, both at the same time.

(2) The tax factor has been increasingly working against investors for years. It is not just the simple matter of the tax rates one has to pay. It is also the character of the regulations. Thus, years ago, losses in the stock market were deductible in any amount from any kind of income or profits. For many years now, the loss limit has been cut back to a maximum of $1,000 deductibility in a single year from dividend, interest, salary or any kind of so-called "ordinary" income.

(3) The political influence has made markets less liquid than they used to be. Borrowing restrictions have been set up.

(4) The earning power of corporations, which in the final analysis lies behind the value of securities, has been impaired.

(5) War creates hazards beyond the investor's control. Basically, war and revolution are the greatest of all investment hazards.

(6) The seeming increase in general investment knowledge has been an influence. If everybody were so highly educated investmentwise that they knew the precise value of a security, there would be no market much of the time. If the situation were static—and, of course, situations are never static—then the educated buyer and the educated seller would both have precisely the same price in mind and a transaction would be possible. However, once the situation started to change, if both the seller and buyer were of the same opinion, there would be no buyer if the outlook was unfavorable and no seller if the outlook was good.

In more practical terms, investment education should result in decreased fluctuations. Bargain seekers should know values and prevent extreme undervaluation by their purchases. Others who know values should be sellers before stocks reach unreasonable heights.

However, despite much more widespread investment knowledge, no tendencies in this direction have really developed.

A very successful speculator I know maintains that the current price of any stock is bound to be wrong. This is because he knows it is either going up or down.

The markets in the last decade only proved again that, while we may have progressed a long way in investigating securities, we are still far from real competence. Losses have been suffered not only by first investors and odd-lot buyers, but also by professionals, institutions and large investors.

The best professional analysts exchange ideas and unconsciously convince one another. This information trickles down through all levels of the investing community.

My opinion is that investment decisions are human and psychological and are not determined by mathematical appraisal. Mistakes may be brought about by too much togetherness.

111 *Deflation and Inflation: Their Implications for the Investor*

Deflation, as used in the economic sense, refers to a gain in the purchasing power of the value of money. In a more popular sense it is regarded as a type of adversity or liquidation, and something to be avoided or checked. Since we live in a world of long-term contracts, what we all really should want is neither deflation nor inflation, but stability. The difficulty comes from the task of agreeing where to stabilize.

The conservative wants to stabilize at the point in his memory that constituted "the good old days." This, of course, would require a terrifying amount of deflation. A sound dollar, that popular phrase, can mean many things. Again, what is really most desirable is, in fact, a stable dollar. To some a sound dollar means going back to what its purchasing power was when we last went off the gold standard. To accomplish this now would not only mean deflation but visible bankruptcy.

I use the term "visible bankruptcy" because there is little difference in repudiating debts through the invisible bankruptcy of inflation and the visible bankruptcy of settling for so many cents on the dollar. We can illustrate this by recalling that Government bonds sold at a discount during the postwar period following the First World War. You got less money back in dollars if you had to liquidate before maturity, but the dollars received were hard ones and had real purchasing power. After the Second World War, Government bonds sold at par but the purchasing power of the dollars received was vastly lower. The soldier who had the money to buy an automobile at the start of 1941 but who instead went off to war and put his money into U.S. war bonds found when he came back that his dollars were repaid in full—but all he got in the way of an automobile was a fraction of one.

Thus, people being what they are, it can be taken for granted that deflation mostly takes place against our collective wills. Once it is underway, we do all we can to check it.

The feeling in modern times is that the great deflations of the past can now be controlled and need not occur in the future. This is yet to be proved.

The investor can protect himself against deflation to a much greater extent than he can against inflation. In fact, it is more correct to say that if he has foresight and stamina he can protect his assets wholly against deflation but never fully against inflation. The principal reason this is true is that deflation protection is never taxed. If you manage to keep the same amount of dollars and they keep buying more, your income and capital gains are nil from the standpoint of the Government, even though your real worth may be growing by leaps and bounds. Deflation is the summertime of the hoarder, the man who has his funds in short-term bonds, safe banks, insurance and mortgages of quality, and impeccable credit rating. It is the summertime of the consumer who, with plenty of cash and no tax problems, finds bargains offered at every hand.

The end of deflation and the start of inflation is the period when great fortunes are born. This is the time when securities can be picked up for a song. The loss of income involved in preparing for and hedging against deflation is trivial compared to the great profits that can be secured. The cumulative effect of eliminating from stock market prices the psychological overvaluation and capitalization of boom earnings and dividends on the one hand, and substituting, on the other, psychological devaluation brought on by pessimism, low earnings or actual deficits, and low dividends or no dividends reduces stock prices geometrically. The best stocks have been known to lose from half to nine tenths of their market value in times of extreme stress. In the 1929 period it took just three years. The income sacrificed by not owning shares during this time and hoarding cash could not possibly amount to more than 15 percent before taxes.

Deflation, if permitted, tends to separate the sheep from the goats. It builds character and industry among the best elements of a population. It strengthens the nation because no nation was ever conquered while its muscles were hard.

If nature has anything to do with economic cycles, the reoccurrence of deflation is as normal as the reoccurrence of winter or night. All three have their resting and reviving influences. The best cure for a faltering boom, excess inventory, overlarge installment and other loans, low productivity and other such evils, is time and a period of correction.

Nevertheless, deflation is like the bear. He'd better stay inarticulate and in hiding. One would think that such a time would be a veritable paradise for the bears. In practice, however, this has not worked out. Bears are always in a minority and are never a real match for the bulls. The latter are practically universal. Bears tend to sell the wrong stocks too early, and, just as likely as not, cover in a panic around the top, thus adding to temporary overvaluation instead of checking it.

Very few bears ever make any money and keep it.

INFLATION

Inflation, as used in the economic sense, refers to a loss of purchasing power in the value of money. This can be brought about in a variety of ways. Anything that increases costs and decreases useful production is inflationary. Likewise, anything that increases the supply of money directly or indirectly is inflationary.

The momentary causes of inflation have had generous

publicity. On the other hand, some of the other causes have not. A short work week, for example, if not offset by increased production through automation or by some other means, is definitely as inflationary in its way as would be the creation of a certain amount of paper money which dilutes the value of the currency. The willingness of the German people, for instance, to work hard, long and productively after a war period strengthened the German currency, while the indolence of another population depreciated that nation's currency.

The dangers of inflation have been widely publicized and reported but more or less disregarded. In this country, at least, inflation is thought by many to be a spur to prosperity. The average American probably owes more on his home, automobile, and modern appliances than other people— such as his insurance company—owe him. Thus he is satisfied and discounts as unrealistic and untrue what he hears or reads about inflation's ultimate costs. There are even a minority of economists who think inflation is the best way to cancel out debt and stimulate consumption and production.

Inflation and its opposite, deflation, are certainly the ruling investment influences. Bull markets, or at least apparent bull markets, feed on inflation, and bear markets on deflation. The most important factor to appraise in planning an investment program is whether prices in general are going up or down. Inflation creates the illusion of gain. Paper profits within corporation reports and paper profits in the stock market are easy to come by. They are both illusionary. We live in a world of long-time contracts, and inflation as well as deflation are constantly altering their intended effect to the disadvantage of one party or the other. It is demonstrated over and over again that the average men-

329

tality cannot embrace this fact and keeps coming back to thinking that a dollar is a dollar after all, despite incontrovertible evidence to the contrary.

Partly in order to pay for the cost of government, but very largely as a social measure, taxation is used to bar people from profiting from inflation and, in many cases, to add to inflation's tendency toward confiscation. For example, a person might own a piece of property and sell it at a profit that solely reflected a decrease in the purchasing power of the dollar. For the purpose of this example, no real gain occurred. Yet a portion of his proceeds is confiscated under the guise of a capital-gains tax on a gain never actually realized. The proceeds from his sale, less his tax, will not buy the equivalent of what he originally owned.

As another example, a corporation might report supposed earnings in an inflationary period. These earnings would be after maximum allowable depreciation to replace the depreciation suffered. The result is taxation on profits unearned and the reporting of overstated net earnings.

Inflation has its roots in our inability as a people to face facts. It can only take root where a nation lacks the moral fiber to live within its means and pay off its debts—internal, external and individual—in the same coin in which they were contracted. It is always fostered by wars and preparation for wars, because production for destruction is waste and must be matched by austerity in other directions to maintain real solvency.

It should be recognized that inflation need not be all-inclusive. We have had monetary inflation and labor inflation in the United States at the same time that we have had gluts of raw materials, tending to greatly depress prices of the particular products involved. This in turn has led to political boondoggling such as stockpiling, subsidies and bonuses for destruction, to try to bring the price of deflated commodities into line with an otherwise inflated economy.

Deflation can be countered by the careful and knowing, but inflation never can be completely countered. Over a period of time, investments in common stocks have been an excellent hedge against inflation, even though they may not appear to be so during a few short periods when inflation seems most rampant. Stocks often thrive better in the ensuing climate of more stable prices.

It is currently popular in governmental circles to talk of "permissible inflation" of 4 percent or some such figure. This is a dangerous trend. No amount of inflation is really fairly "permissible." The idea may become popularly "acceptable" for a time. In the long run it can only lead to costly escalation.

112 *Warrants and Convertibles: Volatile and Dazzling Performers*

Everybody wants a "piece of the action." A promise to get your investment back with interest in dollars is not enough. Investors want something extra in the way of profits. As time goes on we are likely to see a further swing from fixed-dollar obligations. This might include Government financing linked to the cost of living or some other index. It can lead to new concepts in corporation finance such as variable coupons.

There are many variations of warrants and convertible features which can be attached to bonds or preferred stock. It is fallacious to think they are "free." It is also fallacious to think you are buying the best of all worlds that combines safety and appreciation. You buy a package and pay so much for the bond and so much for the so-called "sweetener." The bond portion changes in price for one set of reasons, and the privilege portion for another.

The principles involved in valuing the privilege portion, whether in the form of a conversion or warrants, are closely related. Warrants have a market of their own. The conversion privilege of a convertible security, on the other hand, is part of the total price of the security. Investors in the latter should always appraise the investment as well as the conversion values. These can only be approximated. You can estimate the straight bond value at any given time. A change in interest rates or change in the credit or earnings outlook would alter this figure. The conversion value is expressed as a market premium over straight bond value. This changes with changes in the price of the stock into which the bond can be converted.

In valuing a warrant, the price divides into the tangible value of the warrant and the premium commanded by the warrant privilege. The mathematics involved are complicated. Most readers will need professional help from whatever source they use for investment counsel. Substantial investors can afford to spend perhaps $100 a year for an advisory service. These services take time and a degree of expertise to use profitably. (A good one is published by Arnold Bernhard, 5 East 44th Street, New York, New York 10017.) When you buy convertible securities you normally pay for the conversion privilege by accepting a lower rate of interest than you would otherwise receive. Warrants are generally issued as part of a package and are either immediately detachable or are exercisable after a varying period. Like an option or call, they are a way of using other people's money to create high leverage.

The accounting angles deserve a great deal of scrutiny. In order to get a true picture of a situation, the investor in the common stock of a company with convertible securities or warrants outstanding should note that earnings are given both before and after conversion or exercise. The latter figure is necessarily smaller and more realistic. Corporations try to delay conversion because interest on bonds is tax-deductible while dividends on stock are not. The corporation receives no additional funds on conversion. On the other hand, when warrants are exercised, the investor needs to purchase the stock and the company's treasury is enhanced.

In recent years, convertible securities and warrants have been used by corporations to expand through acquisition and merger. They allow the acquiring corporation to buy another company and make an immediate favorable per-share earnings report to their shareowners. This might mean increasing the current per-share net or preventing it from decreasing, at the cost of possibly lower per-share net later.

A basic principle of sound investment is what professionals call the "risk-reward" ratio. This means that you should consider what you think you might lose compared to what you think you might make. Obviously you want a favorable ratio. After you reach a conclusion on the value of the underlying stock of a company in which you are considering buying convertibles or warrants, a mathematical projection can be estimated reflecting the leverage in the privilege. This is expressed in terms which compare the percentage rise or fall of the stock with the percentage rise or fall of the convertible security or warrant. I am looking at one at random now which would rise 70 percent if the common of the company rose 50 percent but would only fall 25 percent if the common dropped 50 percent. The volatility would be even greater if bought on margin. Such calculations are tabulated by advisory services, such as the one mentioned above.

In considering the purchase of warrants or the desirability of a conversion privilege, the vital factor is the attractiveness of the stock behind it. Unless the stock is priced right and headed in the right direction, you will probably make an unwise purchase. It is preferable to pay more for an option on a stock that is going up to getting a seeming "bargain" on a privilege to buy shares that are not sound purchases on their own. Before considering the purchase of a convertible security or warrant, analyze the company and the prospects. If you would not purchase the stock directly, you should not purchase the privilege to ultimately buy it indirectly.

Warrants and convertible securities are found traditionally in the portfolios of sophisticated investors. They require more knowledge and care than buying stocks. The idea is to buy convertible securities at a price close to their intrinsic market value as interest-paying securities, with as long and as attractive a conversion privilege as possible. Convertibles are valued by sophisticated investors not so much for the possibilities for dazzling appreciation as they are for their defensive qualities in uncertain markets. The dual personality of convertibles gives the investor a chance to "have his cake and eat it, too."

Common-stock warrants are glamorous but dangerous swingers. If bought right, they can create unbelievably wide swings in price and can deliver tremendous percentage gains. They are most attractive during the initial stages of a bull market. Sometimes warrants may advance two, three, or four times faster than the common stock of the same corporation. They are dangerous, too, since they can go down just as fast. Warrants provide a unique and inexpensive way of speculating on the future of a company in which you have great confidence. When you are right, you are very, very right!

113 *How Much Risk Can You Stand?*

One's own personal makeup influences how much risk he can run. We all have our worrying points and our sleeping points. I say that anyone who carries any stocks that worry him or interfere with his peaceful sleep had better sell at once.

It is bad enough to worry about your own investments. But when you worry about other people's it is many times worse. They may be your family, or your friends, or, if you are in business, your clients. You cannot make a "killing" without risks. And to assume these risks for others is extremely worrisome to any conscientious person.

Between the ages of twenty-one and thirty as a stockbroker I was young enough to shoulder heavy responsibilities for a very few clients who were naïve enough to trust me with really dangerous market ventures. It happened that we came out all right. The clients made money. I had no disasters. I developed no ulcers or high blood pressure. Maybe I was smart; maybe I was lucky. But looking back, I know I was the fool who ventured where angels feared to tread in making dangerous high-risk investments for others. Of course, I know better now—or maybe I am just older. At any rate, I now advise investors to use great care in granting powers of attorney and even then to pay some attention and exercise some degree of supervision, especially in boom times and in bear markets.

It is amazing what people expect. The number of strangers who say, "invest all my money in the stock you like best," are uncountable. I often wonder what reason impels them. Do they really think an honest, knowledgeable person would take that risk? Or do they perhaps feel that if you are on the inside in Wall Street it is a pushover to make money? They have lots to learn.

Then there are others who have no idea what a successful businessman's time is worth. They come in and want all your time and full attention to their account to the exclusion of all else—for next to nothing. If you are a broker they expect this attention in return for the commissions you earn for buying and selling.

Another thing—nobody, but nobody, should be expected to tell you precisely when to buy, hold and sell. This is not the function of a service or an investment counselor, nor can it be read in a broker's market letter. No one is going to be able to tell you with sufficient accuracy when to buy, hold or sell. The services, the investment counselors, and the market-letter writers cannot tell you because they don't know. They can and do give you useful information and points of view that should bring you closer to correct timing.

The speculator who is a proven success in his own right doesn't really know either. What he does ordinarily possess is the rare art of understanding how to utilize and cash in on his own knowledge as well as the information gleaned from others. He has the intuition and judgment which tell him when to plunge and when to stand on the sidelines; when to be brave and when to retreat; when to pyramid, when to average, when to cut losses, when to be patient and when to be impatient; when to be in the market and when to be out; when to trust his judgment to the full and when to take it easy.

It's very hard to explain, but market forecasting is very far from a science and in no sense an exact one. An engineer can be taught stresses and strains. Given an engineering problem, he should come up with the correct answer. But this is not so with market analysts. Given all the available facts, much is still left in the realm of the unknown. The available facts themselves are usually only partially obtainable. Individuals do not have the same access to so-called "inside" information. Of course, "inside" information is very rare today. The New York Stock Exchange and the Securities and Exchange Commission both work hard to give everyone equal access to all information. The difference must come from the judgment an individual uses. There will always be "inside," *i.e.,* advance, information, but it is tougher to get and enjoyed by a constantly decreasing number of people.

But even possessing all the information to be had leaves many intangibles. What will the future bring? The world revolves and spins on through space with something new and unexpected under the sun every moment. And what will be the psychological reaction of the security-owning, buying and selling public? The price, or the price trend, of securities as a group, or any individual security, is never fixed by any bureau of standards yardstick carefully filed away in Washington. It is actually a composite vagary of many human minds swayed by fear, greed, confidence, truth, fact, rumor, knowledge, ignorance, life, death, the weather, personal financial influences, and so on, endlessly. It is not solely a matter of price/earnings ratios, yields or book values.

To give an example—a stock is bought mathematically

"cheap," but investors become fearful of the future and they sell, maybe blindly, maybe not, but they sell, and prices drop. The drop may affect the credit position of others who sell to meet their loans. The hysteria may even go so far as to affect the personal expenditures of a sufficient number of individuals so as to make for a downward readjustment in the business of the corporation represented in a stock once thought mathematically cheap. And then, even mathematically, it appears cheap no longer, and a loss results.

In 1929, in the first three quarters of the year, many of the corporate earnings achieved in the nine months and estimated for the full year were reasonable enough even with the stock prices then prevailing. U.S. Steel, for example, sold above 200, but it earned $21.19 a share. Later, in 1931, after it was down to 36, the earnings came out not at the 1929 rate, but at a loss.

This is why poor and unexpected price action needs doubly careful checking.

114 *Would You Like to Try for a Million?*

In case you are interested, here are the mathematics of making a million dollars. The investment expectancy must be a minimum of 100 percent on your investment, or doubling your money at each attempt. Trying for long-term capital gains is the only possibility of turning capital already saved into a million dollars. The essential element is that of time, not only because you desire the million before you grow too old, but also because you want it while the getting is still possible. The millionaire-making climate has been going mighty fast from fine to good to fair to poor.

It is safer, if slower, to attempt it in steps rather than in a one-shot killing. One-shot killings are rarer than the wildcat discovery of a new giant oil field. The mathematics are easy to set down; the realization is almost insurmountable. One of the drawbacks in this sort of calculation is that after each successful step the total net proceeds must be reinvested. Thus the risks of a costly loss that can set one way back is constantly growing. On the other hand, the man who invests $10,000, takes his profit and reinvests only his original stakes will never become a millionaire. He may do very well, however. And he will sleep a lot sounder. If you have the stomach for it, the following chart shows how it can be done:

Capital	100% Appreciation	Total Before Taxes	25% Capital Gain Taxes	Net Gain After Taxes	Net Capital Position
$ 10,000	$ 10,000	$ 20,000	$ 2,500	$ 7,500	$ 17,500
17,500	17,500	35,000	4,375	13,125	30,625
30,625	30,625	61,250	7,656	22,969	53,594
53,594	53,594	107,188	13,396	40,198	93,792
93,792	93,792	187,584	23,448	70,344	164,136
164,136	164,136	328,272	41,034	123,102	287,238
287,238	287,238	574,476	71,814	215,424	502,662
502,662	502,662	1,005,324	125,665	376,997	879,659
879,659	879,659	1,759,318	219,915	659,744	1,539,403
TOTAL	$2,039,206		$509,803	$1,529,403	

This, of course, looks better on paper than it would be in practice. In the first place, it is difficult for someone who takes a relatively modest $10,000 initial position to take a relatively huge quarter-of-a-million-dollar position a few years later. But I have known it to be done. In fact, it *must* be done to achieve the high aims.

Investing "on margin" can greatly shorten the length of time required to build capital, and, of course, it increases the risk. If you borrow money at going interest loan rates and use it intelligently to earn large percentage gains, you are going to magnify your results. You are also increasing your risks, but the entire theme of making a million dollars presumes willingness and ability to assume risk, plus getting the most out of it and knowing when to cut and run.

Another indirect way of investing on margin or magnifying your possible gains (or losses) is through the purchase of high-leverage stocks. Leverage can be of two kinds— financial and business.

Financial leverage means that the outstanding common shares of a company are small in relation to prior issues, be they bonds, preferred stocks or loans.

Business leverage means that the cost of a product or service is relatively fixed, and once across a break-even sales level, net earnings as a consequence can advance rapidly. To put it another way, business leverage occurs where a sizable increase in a profit margin per article sold increases sharply once fixed overhead or tool-and-die expense has been covered.

Low-priced shares tend to advance more percentagewise than higher-priced issues, and this is still another of the many factors necessary to take into account in planning a large percentage capital-gain program.

I would say from experience that it is very rare for anyone to make these really huge profits without a period of great danger and exposure. Setbacks can be crippling or even wipe one out. The type of entrepreneur who will embark and succeed in this sort of thing is usually by nature over-optimistic and the last person likely to be cautious. Even where his timing is wrong in one instance, he may manage to ride through a stormy period and come back strong. In short, you "can't keep a good man down," or, for that matter, "push a bad one up."

I remember many anxious days in the growth of General

Foods, Chrysler, Coca-Cola and other great successes. Perhaps the preceding table will serve to make many people realize that they are not cut out for this sort of thing. Maybe they will be more satisfied with their current lot. If the valley is comfortable, why climb to the mountaintop?

The success of the whole plan, and the length of time it takes to achieve it, depends first on the timing of each transaction. Starting in 1932, 1938, or 1946 would have worked out most favorably. A start in 1929, 1937, or in 1969, would have meant delay if the investor knew what he was about and disaster if he didn't.

Since 1920 I have been in constant touch with security markets concerning almost every facet of investment and speculation. From practice and observation I have seen more than one millionaire made. This has impressed me with the importance of timing. It is a most difficult accomplishment and the most valuable. It pays handsomely to be venturesome in a roaring bull market. It can be suicide to be out on a limb in a bear market or during a business panic.

A good situation is much easier to spot than to time correctly. Those who are cut out to win usually do. If at first they don't succeed, they try again. That is one of the qualities in their makeup. Those not cut out for this sort of thing, the faint of heart who worry a lot, might well adopt as their motto, "If at first you don't succeed, quit. There's no use being a damn fool about it!"

115 *The Loeb "Non-formula" for Stock Market Profits*

The dictionary says a formula is a rule for doing something and adds, "especially used by those who do not know the reason on which it is based." Others think of a formula as a system. I do not believe anyone should do anything blindly—certainly not invest in the stock market. As for systems, in my fifty-odd-years of experience I have never found a stock market system that worked. Given a formula or system, I have yet to see more than a few of them faithfully followed.

It should be clear by now that in my investment experience and philosophy there is no one formula that applies to all people and all things. I am lising below the basic principles and methods that my experience has shown are the most applicable and the most rewarding. Sometimes the rewards can be handsome and sometimes the rewards represent avoiding or minimizing losses that would otherwise have been sustained. A penny saved is definitely a penny earned. It may be more, as no tax is involved.

Here, then, are the precepts which I think increase the chances of success in your battle for stock market profits. It seems a fitting way to end this book.

(1) Know yourself. If you have limitations, put half your savings in government bonds and half your savings in the leading listed investment trusts as your funds become available.

(2) If you feel you are in the "learn it yourself" class, start gradually. No amount of shadow trading on paper without actual transactions will mean anything. Paper play is devoid of human emotions of fear, greed and impatience,

and is meaningless. The one way to learn is to use real dollars and open an account with a broker. Keep the number of your transactions small and keep the total amounts invested small. Keep a good backlog of uninvested cash to use to recoup if you lose or to use as you develop proficiency. Personally, I advocate learning on a one-stock-at-a-time basis. You are forced to a decision as to whether to keep it, take a loss, take a profit, or switch. You will learn by hard experience the lesson of cutting short your losses. You will learn to let your profits run. You will learn, in keeping a stock that is not moving, what it costs to have money tied up in a static situation while other opportunities pass you by. You will learn what to consider when the problem of comparing one issue with another stares you in the face.

(3) If you consider yourself in the do-it-yourself class, then the importance of the principles outlined in this book will be most valuable. Intelligence, understanding, flair, time, means and contacts are among the attributes required. Their value will be enhanced if you invest within the framework of the following three cardinal points:

(a) *Take losses quickly*. There is no rule for success that compares with this one for universal applicability. Losses should always be limited in scope and usually in point of time. This is the one rule that might be printed on every page for every type of investor for any goal or aim. It is the nearest to the dictionary meaning of a formula, meaning a rule to follow blindly. There is no way to know when you are wrong, but if the market goes down and your losses begin, this is a fairly accurate sign that maybe there is some error in your judgment.

Taking losses goes against the strongest of the human instincts you need to conquer if you expect to profit more than the average. As a practical matter, there are various ways of taking losses. For the small commitment an automatic stop-loss order entered "good until canceled" with your broker at the time of purchase is the best. It can be for the traditional three points or for 10 percent of the cost, or related to previous trading patterns showing typical swings in the stock and its volatility. There are spots under so-called chart-resistance levels or trend lines that are calculated exactly the same by thousands of "chart readers." At such places an accumulation of stop-loss orders on the specialist's book can make for a very poor execution. The execution of a large number of sell orders at one time can also make for a false signal or shakeout. In my opinion a stop-loss order should never be lowered or canceled. It might in some cases be increased as a stock advances and so become more of a profit-preserving stop order than an actual loss cutter.

In the case of very large commitments, such elementary procedures are not practical. Here more judgment must be used and less automatic procedure. However, the judgment must be coupled with a very firm and irrevocable resolve to keep hewing to the line and really cutting the loss. One should think of the time, place and extent of one's retreat at the time a position is initiated. Large commitments are best cut in steps or by degrees. The practical way is to cut a predetermined percentage each time there is an unfavorable market or news disappointment. These disappointments could take various forms. They might be corporate in character, or general, or primarily in market-price action. The fact is that no one knows when a small cloud no bigger than a man's hand may herald a great storm.

Large commitments are often associated with insider operations or insider information. Very often this information seems good while the market is bad. Very often the information is mildly unfavorable but is put off as being temporary. It is just this sort of thing that step by step sometimes leads the biggest people into the biggest trouble. Thus, it is all the more important to retreat and save your assets for another try when you have a false sense of security because of your closeness to a picture. Closeness often leads to blindness. Losses should be regarded as insurance premiums. They are worth many times what they cost.

I know there are examples of men who rode through thick and thin to come out on top in the end, but I would place them in a very small minority. I would not care to have gone through their troubles and worries. Just at the point where perhaps things took a turn for the better, their financial position was at its worst, so that they could not make a new purchase with previously husbanded resources. I know there are those who point out the danger of being whipsawed or losing a position. The danger exists, but it is must less than the danger of being locked in or wiped out.

(b) *Don't overdiversify.* While diversification or the spreading of risk among many securities is a proper device for the inept and inexperienced, it can only lead to average results. The profits will be no more than the average and the losses will be no more. Diversification is of value to the type of investor for whom the 50–50 split of Government bonds and investment trusts and funds was suggested earlier.

For the sophisticated investor with high aims, diversification is deadly. No one, nor any group, can select a widely diversified list of securities that will substantially exceed the average. No individual can take the time to select and supervise a large number of varied securities. The group might have the time, but if its conclusions were valid its efforts would only result in distilling its findings down to their real essence.

The real venturer—the brilliant, daring entrepreneur who ends up in our multimillionaire class—probably buys one security. He puts all his eggs in one basket and not only watches the basket but probably helps to carry it to its destination as well. However, from a practical standpoint there are very few individuals gaited to this extreme way of doing things. Hence, our "do it yourself" man may possibly diversify four to ten ways. He may diversify as to time as well, in that he probably will not begin his four purchases simultaneously. In the nature of things he will not learn of four equally good situations all at the same time. He may find as he goes along that if he does make four commitments he will see the opportunity of contraction and concentration. In other words, one transaction may prove disappointing and another especially promising. Hence, funds may be shifted from the least desirable to the most. Having a position in, say, four stocks gives one a chance for shifting and it offers a higher degree of protection against error than a one-shot operation.

Where advisers are involved, a single security position is practically an impossibility, since the responsibilities involved in making concentrated investment of someone else's money are difficult to assume and rarely appreciated or paid for. The ten-way diversification works for those who are less sure, and it works for those who are investing for others. Actually, it is no different than four-way diversification.

What really happens is that because no one really knows ten outstanding opportunities, the account is split into categories. Six fairly standard favorite fifty blue-chip rubber-stamp issues are selected. The last four represent the real meat of the account. The effect really is to lock 60 percent of the funds into an average position and actually use only

40 percent for important appreciation. Such an account has its points for the partly timid and partly adventurous.

(c) *Keep a cash reserve.* More losses are caused by overinvestment than any other single factor I know outside of downright ignorance and cupidity. The aim of intelligent investment is to risk a little and get a lot. To put it another way, ten points of profit on 100 shares of stock is much sounder than one point of profit on 1,000 shares. Overinvestment, furthermore, causes undue worry and gives the emotional factors in our makeup increased dominance over the intellectual. Money is made with the head, not with our glands. Overinvestment makes one-way streets out of investment accounts. When an emergency arises one can only sit or sell, instead of being able to buy or sell.

Someone is sure to ask at this point, What about a formula for the man who wants to make the mostest out of the leastest? This man can be many kinds of a duck. From the standpoint of employment of cash, he will certainly not only want to employ it all, but in addition borrow all the traffic will allow. He could be a young man of small resources who feels he can run the risk and knows enough about it to try and make it big. He can be a man already big with experience, with success under his belt, who wants to become a Goliath. Occasionally, unfortunately, he can be a desperate man who needs money badly and falsely thinks this is the way to get it.

To the first, I say, cut your losses, and you need a lot of luck. The second knows the risk he is running and knows what he is doing and is willing to play the game. The third is pathetic and should never make the try.

Good luck in your battle for stock market profits. You have a lot going for you!

The Battle for Stock Market Profits

These Reference and Review pages are included as a convenience to readers who may want to give more thought to particular sections in this book.

READER'S REFERENCE AND REVIEW

Page	Subject	Comment

READER'S REFERENCE AND REVIEW

Page	Subject	Comment

READER'S REFERENCE AND REVIEW

Page	Subject	Comment

READER'S REFERENCE AND REVIEW

Page	Subject	Comment

About the Author

GERALD M. LOEB has fought the battle for stock market profits successfully and consistently over many years and over many ups and downs. He has advised investors for half a century. At present he is Senior Consultant of E. F. Hutton & Company. Mr. Loeb is an astute Wall Street practitioner and counselor for "doing the right thing with money." And the right thing in the stock market, he says, "is to forget dividends but look to capital gains and the preservation of the purchasing power of your dollars."

Many readers of these words have no doubt profited from Mr. Loeb's first book, *The Battle for Investment Survival*. His market interpretations are also featured in newspapers, magazines, radio, and television. Mr. Loeb's most noted attributes are an abundance of energy and a quick-triggered mind for evaluating stocks. He keeps in touch with corporation presidents and key executives who are in a position to shed light on new business and financial developments. He, is a prober and a student of investor psychology who diligently takes the daily pulse of changing situations.

Mr. Loeb points out that in this world of changing money values it is risky for anyone who has savings *not* to invest some capital in stocks. His book makes it clear that knowledge, experience, and flair are the cornerstones of investor success, and that, before you invest, a close analysis of a company's balance sheet may often improve your investment score.